freedom
in
Molina

Gerard Smith, s.j.

LOYOLA UNIVERSITY PRESS
Chicago   60657

CONTENTS

What one sees will obviously depend largely upon one's point of view. Less obviously, but as truly, the appreciation of another person's philosophy depends upon the ability to see things in the light in which he saw them, to see them from his viewpoint. The subsequent appreciation of that philosophy will at least have the advantage of being en connaissance de cause.

In virtue of this principle the writer has been under the necessity, in order to bring out distinctly the philosophical implications of the Molinist concept of liberty, of seeing Molina's thought in the light of Molina's faith. Further, Molina's concept of liberty was not only hammered out of the fires of his own faith. It grew too from its opposition to thought which issued from other faiths. From the viewpoints of these other faiths too, it has been thought necessary to examine Molina's concept of liberty.

Such is the reason, then, why a philosophical approach to the examination of Molinist liberty must be made somewhat from the viewpoint of religious faith.

There are many kinds of religious faith, of course. The bearing which they have upon the problem which confronts us may be brought out by using as a point of reference the faith to which Molina himself constantly referred, the faith of Catholics.

The following are constant assertions of Catholic dogma: The salvation of man is the work of God and man--gratia Dei mecum. Salvation comprises three elements: grace, the super-natural act, glory. The first causes the second, which causes the third. To grace man has absolutely no right; he can do nothing to get it. By the good usage of grace man performs the super-natural act, and by the merits of his supernatural acts he se-cures glory. Thus God begins the work of salvation without man, continues it with him, achieves it because of man. On the other hand, man is free; that is, he is under neither coercion nor necessity in the performance of his imputable acts.

How reconcile the divine with the human element of salvation? Concretely: how does grace influence free will? how does God foresee the usage which man will make of grace? how does God lead the free will of man infallibly by his grace to his pro-vidential ends?

The answers to these questions will depend upon one's concept of the relation between its antecedents, divine and human, and free choice. And in this concept will be implied, or expressed, a theory of liberty. Pelagianism exalted liberty at the expense of grace. Semi-pelagianism did not give to grace all its due. Essentially unnecessary for, or merely facilitating, supernatural acts, grace in these systems implied a liberty to do good. Luther and Calvin held that, because God efficaciously determined choice, choice was necessitated; but since violence cannot conceivably be brought to bear upon the will, that choice was always un-coerced. Thus liberty was freedom from coercion, not from necessity. Midway between the Reformers and Pelagianism lie other contesting theories. St. Thomas Aquinas held that God indeed effected choice, but that the choice so effected was free from necessity by reason of the omnipotence of divine causality, which can effect the free as well as the necessary and the ac-cidental. And as liberty grew out of its divine cause, so anal-ogously does it grow out of its human cause, the human intellect. The human intellect determines the human will which determines the intellect; the accomplishment of free acts is due to a man's will, their specification to his intellect. The principle under-lying this position is the existence of free natures whose being and activity are competently caused by God. Dominic Banes[1] held that God predeterminately decrees free acts; that is, God from all eternity has determined that, say, Peter in such and such circumstances will act in such and such a way; and Peter will act in such and such a way because he will receive at the right moment an irresistible grace, or natural divine concourse, which will determine him to act in no way but the predetermined one. The act of Peter will be free because it was so predetermined. The liberty of choice in both St. Thomas and Banes is thus professedly free from both coercion and necessity: divine antecedents effect the mode of freedom; human antecedents, suo modo, do the same. Luis de Molina held that God knows future free choice because God knows, antecedently to his decree that there be a free choice, what that free choice will hypothetically be; secondly, God causes free choice inasmuch as he effects the circumstances under which that choice will be which was foreseen to have been futurible. In Molina's system, then, no divine antecedents of choice of their own intrinsic efficacity effect choice: the reason is that the divine antecedents of future choice always involve a block of futurible being, what-would-be in the hypothesis of God's election of what will be; and this block of being absorbs the necessity and leaves untouched the efficacity of the divine antecedents. Nor will Molina admit any determinism of the intellectual antecedents of free choice. These exist merely because there will be such a choice; free choice will not be because of them. Thus, if one considers grace unnecessary for salvation, liberty means the freedom to do good--Pelagianism; if one considers that grace necessitates salvation, liberty means at least freedom from coercion--Lutheranism or Calvinism; if one considers that grace is necessary for, but does not necessitate salvation, liberty will mean freedom from coercision and necessity. In the last position one may further hold either that God effects the free act, which is consequently immune from coercion and necessity, and that also on the side of its human causal antecedents some account of the freedom of choice can be rendered; or that the free act is such because such it would be upon the hypothesis that God willed it, and such it is, from the viewpoint of its human antecedents, only because man wills it. St. Thomas, Banes, and Molina all agree that free choice is immune from coercion and necessity. They differ in that St. Thomas and Banes, with differing emphases, hold the first position, while Molina holds the second.

It is to bring out distinctly the Molinist theory of liberty implied or expressed in Molina's concept of the relation of its antecedents, divine and human, with free choice that this thesis is written. The writer here holds no brief for or against any position. His purpose here is solely, in the light of texts, to define.

The importance of this task will not be underestimated by the historian of ideas. The concept of liberty is the philosophic element subjacent to the theological disputes over grace.

1 Technical difficulties forced us to omit the tilde accent which usually appears in Bañes' name.

1   MOLINA AND LUTHER

The concept of free choice defended by Luis de Molina (1535-1600) is explained by him as follows. Liberty may be understood as opposed to servitude. In this sense St. Paul says: <u>ubi</u> <u>spiritus</u> <u>Domini</u>, <u>ibi</u> <u>libertas</u> (2 Cor. 3, 17.); <u>cum</u> <u>servi</u> <u>essetis</u> <u>peccato</u>, <u>liberi</u> <u>facti</u> <u>estis</u> <u>justitiae</u> (Rom. 6, 18.); <u>quia</u> <u>et</u> <u>creatura</u> <u>liberabitur</u> <u>a</u> <u>servitute</u> <u>corruptionis</u>, <u>in</u> <u>libertatem</u> <u>gloriae</u> <u>filiorum</u> <u>Dei</u> (Rom. 8, 21.). Secondly, liberty may be conceived as opposed to coercion. In this sense, whatever happens spontaneously, whether by natural necessity or not, happens freely. Thus, the generation of the Son by the Father is spontaneous, uncoerced, even though the Son be generated by natural necessity. Luther thought that the liberty of spontaneity was sufficient for free choice. But it is not. Even animals, which act spontaneously, are free in this sense. Lastly, liberty may be conceived as opposed to necessity, and in this meaning

> that agent is called free which, when all the requisites for acting are posited, can act or not act, or can so do one thing that it can also do the contrary. And it is by reason of this liberty that the faculty by which such an agent can so act

1

is called free. Since however it does not so act unless a
weighing and judgment of reason have preceded, thence it
is that, inasmuch as a judgment of reason is a prerequisite,
it is called free choice. Thus, free choice (wherever the
concession must be made) is nothing but the will, in which
the liberty explained, viz., as having been preceded by a
judgment, formally resides. In this sense a free agent is
distinguished from a natural agent, which has not the power
to act and not to act, but, when all the requisites for acting
are posited, acts necessarily and so does one thing that it
cannot effect the contrary.

*illud agens liberum dicitur, quod, positis omnibus
requisitis ad agendum, potest agere et non agere, aut
ita agere unum, ut contrarium etiam agere possit. Atque
ab hac libertate facultas, qua tale agens potest ita
operari, dicitur libera. Quoniam vere non ita operatur
nisi praevio arbitrio, judicioque rationis, inde est,
quod, quatenus ita praeexigit judicium rationis, liberum
appellatur arbitrium. Quo fit, ut liberum arbitrium
(si alicubi concedendum est) non sit aliud quam voluntas,
in qua formaliter sit libertas explicata, praevio
judicio rationis. Agens liberum in hac significatione
distinguitur contra agens naturale, in cuius potestate
non est agere et non agere, sed positis omnibus requisitis
ad agendum necessario agit, et ita agit unum, ut non
possit contrarium efficere. Concordia liberi arbitrii
cum gratiae donis, divina praescientia, providentia, et
reprobatione, D. Ludovico Molina Auctore, Lethielleux,
1876, pp. 10, 11. Cf. Ludovicus Molina, De Scientia Dei,
vid. F. Stedmüller, Neue Molinaschriften, in Beiträge
zur Geschichte der Philosophie und Theologie des
Mittelalters (Cl. Baeumker), Band XXXII, Geschichte des
Molinismus, Erster Band, Munster, 1935, p. 207, sqq.*

Whence, since the will is free only when it could have re-
frained from doing that which it actually does, there is implied
in its liberty a twofold aspect: the liberty to act or not to act
(libertas quoad exercitium actus), the liberty to act thus or so
(libertas quoad specificationem actus). In the last possibility is
had full and perfect liberty. It must be noted too that when the
will can choose but does not wish to, this also is an exercise of
its liberty; an unwillingness to act can quite well constitute a
sin of omission. Further, whenever the will does act, though it
might not have acted, its act is free, not because of an intrinsic

and inadmissible quality of the will itself but because it could
have nondetermined itself to the act which it actually chose.
The "free act, " that is, is so called because of the will's free
choice of the act. Obviously, when once the will has at any
instant determined itself--since it would be contradictory to say
that then it was undetermined--the will is no longer free in regard to its actual determination. Whatever is cannot--while it
is--not be, as Aristotle (1º de interpret., cap. ult.) and Boethius
(5º de Consolat. pr. ult.) taught.

*L. Molina, Concordia, pp. 11, 471, 370. For Aristotle
see De Interpretatione, C.9.19a, 23, Ed. Bekker, Berlin,
1831. For Boethius see De Consolatione Philosophiae,
Ed. A. Fortescue, Burns Oates, 1925, pp. 157-64.*

The fundamental position of Luther, Molina understood to be
the following. The Lutherans, Molina explains, posit a divine
influence by which God moves our wills and angelic wills, an
influence so efficacious that with it the will cannot but act
(whether naturally or supernaturally); without it the will cannot
act at all. The point, Molina continues, is this: it does not
depend upon the free cooperation of the will to render efficacious
the influence of God, a cooperation which the will could withhold
at the moment at which it does cooperate; rather, it is the efficacity of God's motion which moves the will to assent or to dissent, and this motion is such that with it the will cannot fail to
elicit the consent or dissent to which God moves it.

*L. Molina, Summa Haeresium Maior, presented to Card.
Gaspari Quiroga, May 26, 1594; vid. Stegmüller, op.
cit., p. 395.*

That the above was Luther's position Molina had learned from
St. John Fisher's (Bishop of Rochester, England) Assertionis
Lutheranae Confutatio, art. 36, and from Ruard Tapper's (Dean
of Louvain) Explicationis articulorum . . .controversia.

*Stegmüller, op. cit., cites the Paris edition, 1545, of
Fisher's text, and the Louvain edition, 1555, of Tapper's.
Molina refers to the Reformers' doctrine through these
and other secondary sources, e.g., Alfonsi a Castro's
Adversus omnes haereses, Cologne, 1539, and Thomas
Stapelton's Universa iustificationis doctrina Ed. Paris.,
1582. He complains that Dominic Banes . . . eorum (sc.,
Lutheranorum) errores typis habet mandatos in suis*

*commentariis atque in Hispaniam introductos; vid.
Stegmüller, op. cit., p. 445. If this is a complaint
that Banes had succeded where Luther had failed--viz.,
in getting Lutheranism spread throughout Spain, it
would explain why Molina had to have recourse to
secondary sources: he could not secure Luther's writings.*

In St. John Fisher's <u>Assertio</u> Molina saw the following doctrine
attributed to Luther.

There is no liberty in us for good or evil, or for indifferent
works, and so there is no free choice in us at all; free choice
is an illusion of Satan, since it is God who works everything
in us, even evil, the while our will is passive under the
action of God. Whence, these wretched men (the Catholics)
are deceived by the inconstancy, or, as they say, the contingency of human events; . . . things appear indeed to us
to be arbitrary and fortuitous, but . . . they are really all
necessary (i.e., not at all open to our choice); for not as
we will, but as God wills, so do we live, act, suffer.

*Stegmüller (op. cit., p. 396) cites Fisher's text
Assertionis Lutheranae Confutatio, art. 36 a J. Fisher,
episc. Roffensis, ed. Paris., 1545, f. 317, f. 320 r.
For Molina's text vid. Beiträge, op. cit., p. 396.
The texts from Luther upon which Fisher bases his
statements are taken from the Assertio omnium
articulorum M. Lutheri per bullam Leonis X damna-
torum, D. Martin Luthers Werke, ed. Weimar, vol. 7.
They would seem to be as follows: Liberum arbitrium
post peccatum res est de solo titulo, et dum facit,
quod in se est, peccat mortaliter. Est autem articulus
nixus primo in verbo Augustini de Spiritu et litera,
c.iiii, "Liberum arbitrium sine gratia non valet nisi
ad peccandum." Rogo, quae est ista libertas, quae non
nisi in alteram partem potest eamque peiorem? Est hoc
esse liberum, non posse nisi peccare? (p. 142).---
Hieremias quoque X. c [10.23.] sic dicit "Scio, domine,
quoniam non est hominis via eius, nec viri est, ut
dirigat gressus." Quid potuit apertius dicit? Si via
sua et gressus sui non sunt in potestate hominis, quo
modo via dei et gressus dei sunt in potestate eius? Via
enim hominis est ea, quam ipsi vocant naturalem
virtutem faciendi, quod est in se. Ecce haec non est in
arbitrio hominis seu liberi arbitrii: quid ergo liberum
arbitrium est nisi res de solo titulo. Quomodo potest
sese ad bonum praeparare, cum nec in potestate sit suas*

4

vias malas facere? Nam et mala opera in impiis Deus
operatur (p. 144) . . . adeo non est homo in manu sua,
etiam male operans et cogitans (p. 145). --- Periit ita-
que hic etiam generalis illa influentia, qua garriunt,
esse in potestate nostra naturales operationes operari.
. . . Qui ergo vitam nostram in manu sua retinuit,
motus nostros et opera nostra in manu nostra posuit?
Absit. Unde non est dubium, Satana magistro, in Ecclesiam
venisse hoc nomen "liberum arbitrium" ad seducendos
homines a via Dei in vias suas proprias (p. 145) . . .
nulli est in manu sua quippiam cogitare mali aut boni,
sed omnia . . . de necessitate absoluta eveniunt (p.
146). . . . Fallit hos miseros homines rerum humanarum
inconstantia seu (ut vocant) contingentia: oculos enim
suos mergunt in res ipsas operaque rerum, nec aliquando
elevant in conspectum dei, ut res supra res in deo
cognoscerent. Nobis enim ad inferna spectantibus res
apparent arbitrariae et fortuitae, sed ad superna
spectantibus omnia sunt necessaria, Quia non sicut nos,
sed sicut ille vult, ita vivimus, facimus, patimur
omnes et omnia (p. 146).

Luther means, Molina continues, that because God moves us
to all works, even evil, by an efficacious influx, there is choice
only in God, not in us; once posited the free and immutable
decision of God in our regard, everything happens necessarily
in virtue of that divine predetermination. This is the reason,
Molina adds, why Luther goes on to say:

Let us have no more of the free choice God-ward, which
is shown in respect to us and temporal things; for there,
as James says (1.17), there is no change or shadow of alter-
ation; whereas here everything changes and varies.

Fisher's text, from which Molina is quoting, is cited
in the Beiträge, op. cit., p. 397, from the Assertionis
..Confutation, f. 322 r. Fisher doubtless has in mind
the following text from Luther's Assertio omnium
articulorum. . ., ed. Weimar, vol. 7, p. 146; Cessat
liberum arbitrium erga deum, quod apparet erga nos et
temporalia: illic enim ut Jacobus ait, non est trans-
mutatio nec vicissitudinis obumbratio. Hic vero omnia
mutantur et variantur.

Still transcribing from Fisher, Molina continues:

For this reason [viz. that only God is free] Luther had asserted: "It is not within the power of man to make his ways
evil, for it is even evil that God works in the impious. Pro-
verbs (16.1): it is for man to prepare his heart, but God
controls the tongue. This means: man is accustomed to pro-
pose many things, but so far are his works from being in
his power that not even his words are, since he is forced by
God to speak and act otherwise that he had thought." Further
on Luther says: "Behold, not as man thinks, is his way, but as
God thinks." Still further on: "It was ill spoken of me to say
that before grace free choice was ours by mere title; I should
simply have said, free choice is a figment or an empty title;
for no man can think any good or evil whatsoever; rather,
everything, as Wycliffe rightly taught in an article condemned
at Constance, happens by absolute necessity.

*Fisher's text, op. cit., is cited in the Beiträge, op.
cit., p. 397, from f. 314 V, 318 r, 322 r. Part of
Luther's text which Molina is quoting from Fisher has
already been quoted, p. 8, n. 1: Hieremias quoque. . . .
Deus operatur. The remainder of Luther's texts which
Fisher had in mind here are from Luther's Assertio . . .
ed. Weimar, vol. 7. They run as follows: Sic rursus
Prover. XVI [1.], "Hominis est praeparare cor, domini
autem est gubernare linguam." Hoc est, homo multa solet
proponere, cum tamen adeo non sint in manu eius opera
eius, ut nec verba in hoc ipsum habeat in potestate sua,
coactus mirabili dei providentia et loqui et facere
aliter quam cogitavit . . . Ecce non, sicut homo cogitat,
via eius procedit, sed sicut dominus ordinat . . . (p.
145). ––– Male enim dixi, liberum arbitrium ante gratiam
sit res de solo titulo, sed simpliciter debui dicere
"liberum arbitrium est figmentum in rebus, seu titulus
sine re." Quia nulli est in manu sua quippiam cogitare
mali aut boni, sed omnia (ut Viglephi articulus Con-
stantiae damnatus recte docet) de necessitate absoluta
eveniunt (p. 146). For Wycliffe's condemnation see Conc.
Constant. art. Wicclefi damnati, art. 37, in Denzinger-
Bannwart, Enchiridion Symbolorum, 1928, n. 607.*

Before all this--Molina now transcribes from Tapper--which
Leo X's Bull occasioned, Luther wrote in a work he called
Operationes in Psalmos:

Accordingly it is an error to say that free choice comes into
play in good works, i.e., internal works: for I have already

said that the wish involved in faith, hope, and love is a
motion, a rapture, a leading of the Word of God; for though
such passivity is not always equally intense, it is nevertheless always passivity. Behold, says Jeremias (18.6), as
clay in the hands of the potter, so are ye, O house of Israel,
within my hand. What activity, I pray, has clay when the
potter forms it? See we not there mere passivity? But the
will made flesh, i.e., poured out in external work, can
rightly be said to cooperate and have activity; just as a
sword is not active in its motion, but only passive, yet
c ooperated withal in the wound it makes, just so, neither
does the will work anything in its wish--which is the motion
of the divine word, a mere passivity of the will--yet withal
cooperates in the works of its hands: prayer, walking, labor,
etc.

Tapper's text is found in his Explicationis articulorum
venerandae facultatis Sacrae Theologiae studii Lovani-
ensis circa dogmata Ecclesiastica . . . Tom. Lovan.,
1555, pp. 348-349. Molina's text is in the Summa
Haeresium Maior; vid. Stegmüller, op. cit., pp. 397, 398.
The text of Luther, from which Tapper quotes, is from
the Operationes in Psalmos, ed. Weimar, vol. 7, p. 177:
Error est itaque, liberum arbitrium habere activitatem
in bono opere, quando de interno opere loquimur. Velle
enim illud, quod credere, sperare, diligere iam diximus,
est motus, raptus, ductus verbi dei, et quaedam continua
purgatio et renovatio mentis et sensus de die in diem in
agnitionem dei. Licet non semper aeque intensa sit illa
passio, tamen semper est passio. "Ecce (inquit Hiere.
XVIII) sicut lutum in manu figuli, ita vos domus Israel
in manu mea." Nonne mera passio ibi cernitur? . . .
Voluntas vero incarnata seu in opus externum effusa potest
dici cooperari et activitatem habere, sicut gladius in
suo motu prorsus nihil agit, mere autem patitur. At in
vulnere facto cooperatus est per motum suum secanti per
ipsum. Quare sicut gladius ad sui motum nihil cooperatur,
ita nec voluntas ad suum velle, qui est divini verbi motus,
mera passio voluntatis, quae tum cooperatur ad opus
manuum, orando, ambulando, laborando, etc.

So far, then, we have seen Molina's notion of the doctrine of
Luther on free choice. That Molina saw that doctrine through the
eyes of Fisher and Tapper is perhaps unfortunate. At any rate,
an examination of Lutheran choice in the work in which it has
received its fullest and most authentic expression, the De Servo

Arbitrio, will make it clear that Molina did not miss Luther's point.

> *Luther always stood by his exposition of liberty con-*
> *tained in the De Servo Arbitrio: Magis cuperem eos*
> *(libros meos) omnes devoratos. Nullum enim agnosco*
> *meum iustum librum, nisi forte De Servo Arbitrio et*
> *Catechismum, Jul. 9, 1537, to Capito, Enders, T. Xi, p.*
> *247.*

The argument of Luther in the De Servo Arbitrio moves mainly in the supernatural plane. That is, he affirms the presence,
or denies the absence, of a certain kind of antecedent necessity
in the human choices pertaining to salvation: a man must, with
grace, choose a supernatural good; without grace a man must
do evil. Whether or not Luther also meant to affirm a natural
as well as supernatural determinism, Molina at any rate thought
that he did.

> *Como de lo arriba dicho de Luther, Calvino y Chemnitio,*
> *consta, el fundamento . . . . es que ad omnia opera causarum*
> *omnium secundarum . . . necessariam affirmant praemotion-*
> *em Dei . . . Hunc vero influxum sive naturalem ad opera*
> *naturalia, sive supernaturalem et gratiae ad opera natural-*
> *ia, sive supernaturalem et gratiae ad opera supernaturalia*
> *affirmant non cogere quidem voluntatem . . . quasi vio-*
> *lentiam illi inferant rationemque spontanei . . . ab ea*
> *tollant; attamen eam necessitare . . . L. Molina, Summa*
> *Haeresium Minor, vid. Stegmüller, op. cit., p. 439.*

And it is against any determinism of any antecedents, natural or
supernatural, that Molina will direct his doctrine. It will not be
necessary, therefore, to determine the disputed point about the
extent of Luther's determinism, in order to see the issue as
Molina saw it: are there any antecedents to human choice which
of themselves effect choice?

> *The texts of Luther against a natural determinism of*
> *human choice are mainly these: Non enim de esse naturae*
> *loquimur sed de esse gratiae (ut vocant). Scimus liberum*
> *arbitrium natura aliquid facere, ut comedere, bibere,*
> *gignere, regere, ne nos delirio illo velut argutulo*
> *rideat, quod nec peccare quidem liceret sine Christo, si*
> *vocem illam, nihil, urgeamus, cum tamen Lutherus donarit*
> *liberum arbitrium valere nihil nisi ad peccandum, adeo*
> *libuit sapienti Diatribe [Desiderii Erasmi, opera omnia,*

Lugduni Batavorum, 1706, T. 9] ineptire etiam in re seria (p. 752). ——— Quodsi omnino vocem eam [liberi arbitrii] omittere nolumus, quod esset tutissimum et religiosissimum, bona fide tamen eatenus uti doceamus, ut homini arbitrium non respectu superioris, sed tantum inferioris se rei concedatur, hoc est, ut sciat sese in suis facultatibus et possessionibus habere ius utendi, faciendi, omittendi pro libero arbitrio, licet ad idipsum regatus solius Dei libero arbitrio, quocunque illi placuerit (p. 638). De Servo Arbitrio, ed. Weimar, vol. 18.

Luther answered that question as follows: The nature of free choice cannot be ascertained unless we know what the human will can do, and what God does.

Nam fieri non potest, ut scias [Erasme, cf. n. 1, supra]; quid sit liberum arbitrium, nisi scieris, quid possit voluntas humana. Quid Deus faciat, an necessario praesciat. De Servo Arbitrio, ed. Weimar, vol. 18, p. 614.

Now, God's knowledge and will impose necessity upon human choice.

Deus nihil praescit contingenter, sed . . . omnia incommutabili et aeterna infallibilique voluntate et praevidet et proponit et facit. Hoc fulmine sternitur et conteritur penitus liberum arbitrium. . . . Si volens praescit, aeterna est et immobilis (quia natura) voluntas, si praesciens vult, aeterna est et immobilis (quia natura) scientia. Ex quo sequitur irrefragabiliter, omnia quae facimus, omnia quae fiunt, etsi nobis videntur mutabiliter et contingenter fieri, revera tamen fiunt necessario et immutabiliter, si Dei voluntatem spectes. Voluntas enim Dei efficax est, quae impediri non potest. . . Deinde sapiens, ut falli non possit. Non autem impedita voluntate opus (p. 615) ipsum impediri non potest, quin fiat loco, tempore, modo, mensura, quibus ipse et praevidet et vult (op. cit., p. 616).

We, on the other hand, can do nothing in the matter of our salvation. Without God we necessarily sin; with him we necessarily do good. Whence, nothing is done by our free choice; whatever we do is done only through necessity.

Alterum paradoxon, quicquid fit a nobis, non arbitrio
libero, sed mera necessitate fieri, breviter videamus
. . . Hic sic dico: Ubi id probatum fuerit, extra vires
et consilia nostra in solius Dei opere pendere salutem
nostram . . . nonne clare sequitur, dum Deus in opere
suo in nobis non adest, omnia esse mala quae facimus, et
nos necessario operari quae nihil ad salutem valent? Si
enim non nos, sed solus Deus operatur salutem in nobis,
nihil ante opus eius operamur salutare, velimus, nolimus.
. . . Rursus ex altera parte, si Deus in nobis operatur
mutata . . . voluntas (p. 634) . . . pergit . . . amando
bonum, sicut antea voluit et lubuit et amavit malum. . . .
Summa, si sub Deo huius saeculi sumus, sine opere et
spiritu Dei veri, captivi tenemur ad ipsius voluntatem.
. . . Si autem fortior supervenit et illo victo [deo,
sc., huius saeculi] nos rapiat in spolium suum, rursus
per spiritum eius servi et captivi sumus . . . ut velimus
et faciamus lubentes quae ipse velit (p. 635). Op. cit.

Thus only God is free; free choice in us does not exist.

Fixum ergo stat . . . Nos omnia necessitate, nihil
arbitrio libero facere dum vis liberi arbitrii nihil
est, neque facit, neque potest bonum absente gratia.
Sequitur nunc, liberum arbitrium esse plane nomen
divinum, nec ulli posse competere quam soli divinae
maiestati. Op. cit., p. 636.

In sum

if the prescience and omnipotence (of God) be admitted it follows . . . that we were not made by ourselves, nor do we
live, nor do anything, except by his omnipotence. And since
he foreknew us as we were to be, and now makes us such,
moves and governs us, what freedom, pray, can be im-
agined in us, that things be done now this way now that,
otherwise than as he has foreknown or now effects? The
prescience and omnipotence of God, then, are diametrically opposed to our free choice. For, either God will be
deceived by his prescience and also err in his action (which
is impossible), or else we shall act and be acted upon according to his prescience and action. . . . This omnipotence,
I say, and prescience of God, utterly destroy the dogma
of free choice.

Op. cit., p. 718.

To determine more closely what Luther meant by necessity
in human choice, it will be useful to recall certain notions commonly accepted in scholastic disputations.

*Cf. St. Thomas Aquinas, S.T.1.q.19a. a.3, resp; L. Molina,
De Scientia Dei, in Stegmüller, op. cit., pp. 230, sqq;
Quaestis de futuris contingentibus, ibid., pp. 5-7.*

Whatever must be is said to be necessary. Whatever is necessary
is either hypothetically or absolutely necessary. That is absolutely necessary which must be what it is, or which must exist. In
the first sense, the "essential" sense, everything is absolutely
necessary--a man, for example, must be a man. In the second
sense, the "existential" sense, only God is absolutely necessary.
That is said to be hypothetically necessary whose existence depends upon a condition not involved in its essence. Thus if Peter
sins, it is, only consequently upon the posited hypothesis of his
sin, necessary that he have sinned. There is nothing in the essence of Peter's sinning which places his sin among existents.
For that matter there is nothing in Peter either which places
him among existents. Hence, the existence of everything except
God is thus hypothetically necessary. Sometimes too the necessary is distinguished into the antecedently and the consequently
necessary. What is antecedently necessary causes existence;
what is consequently necessary is caused by an existent. Thus,
it is antecedently necessary that the sun rise; it is consequently
necessary that the sun be risen--if it rise. That is to say that
what is antecedently necessary arises either from violence or
coercion, or from some uncoerced principle of action within the
agent itself; whereas what is consequently necessary would arise
from the fact that what is done is done. So, lastly, and this will
be seen to be Luther's terminology, the necessary is divided into that which is necessary by the necessity of the consequent, and
that which is necessary by the necessity of the consequence.
Thus, two plus two is four is necessary by the necessity of the
consequent; for that proposition (the consequent) is in itself necessary. On the other hand John sits is a proposition necessary
by the necessity of the consequence of John's sitting. Obviously
these divisions of the necessary cut across each other.
Applying these notions to the matter in hand, it is clear that
human actions are consequently (or hypothetically) necessary,

or, to use the expression of Luther which we shall see in a moment, necessary by the necessity of the consequence. If Peter sins, it is, consequently upon the posited hypothesis of Peter's act, necessary that Peter have sinned . But the question is whether human actions are also necessary by the necessity of the consequent (or absolutely, or antecedently). Clearly, human choice--though not all human action--cannot be necessary by the necessity of a consequent (or absolutely, or antecedently necessary) arising from violence or coercion: a man can be forced to do many things; he cannot be forced to wish to do anything. Clearly too, it is necessary by the necessity of the consequent (or absolutely, or antecedently) that one who wills must will some good, for to will is to will some good. But, admitting that the will cannot be coerced and that when one chooses one must choose some good, the question arises of whether the absence of coercion is the only free element in choice. To put it in another way, granting that human choice is always spontaneous--that is, that choice arises from an uncoerced principle of action within the agent itself--is choice only this and nothing more? Granted that when I will, it is I who will, and that I will without any coercion of my wish (which would be inconceivable), the question is Must I will?"

Luther thought so. Choice for him was necessary, not indeed because choice is coerced, but because it is dominated by the foreknowledge and omnipotence of God. In short, choice for Luther is purely spontaneous; spontaneous because it issues from an uncoerced principle within the agent; purely spontaneous because by God's will and foreknowledge it issues thence necessarily. He writes:

The Sophists [these are Luther's adversaries] . . . have been forced to admit that everything happens necessarily, by the necessity, they call it, of the consequence, but not by the necessity of the consequent . . . They call it the necessity of the consequence . . . if God wills something, it is necessary that it [God's willing] be done, but it is not necessary that that which is done [in consequence of his willing] be. For only God necessarily is; everything else can, if God will it, not be. Thus they call the action of God necessary, if he will will; but what is done is not necessary. Yet what do they effect by that foolish talk? This forsooth: the thing that is done is not necessary, i.e., it has not a necessary essence, which is to say nothing except that what is done is not God.

Yet the point remains to the effect that everything is done necessarily if the action of God is necessary or if there be a necessity of the consequence; no matter how unnecessarily a thing once made may be, i.e., be not God, or have a necessary essence . . . Thence their foolishness: all things are done by the necessity of the consequence, but not by the necessity of the consequent, means nothing more than this: everything is done necessarily indeed, but not so done, is not God himself . . . Thus the statement stands . . . everything is done by necessity.

De Servo Arbitrio, pp. 616, 617.

According to Luther, then, everything happens necessarily, not indeed by the necessity of the consequent--since such necessity would make events have a necessary essence, which God alone has--

May not this persuasion of Luther's that only God has a necessary essence be the source of his refusal to admit that human nature can act freely? If there is no necessary essence, there is no nature; for essences are necessary, and nature is but essence considered as a principle of action. If there is no nature, there is no action; still less is there free action.

but by the necessity of the consequence of the action of God, the divine knowledge and will.

What is true of events--namely, that they happen necessarily in consequence of divine knowledge and will--is true also of choice.

This forsooth offends . . . common sense . . . that God damns . . . men as though he delighted in the eternal torments of the lost. . . . I myself have more than once taken such offense . . . before I realized how salutary was that despair and how close to grace. Therefore have men so labored and sweated to excuse the goodness of God. . . . it was there that the distinctions were formed . . . about the necessity of the consequent. . . .There always stuck withal, deeply fixed in the hearts of the learned and unlearned, the sting . . . that they felt the necessity we are under if God's prescience and omnipotence be believed. And natural reason itself is forced to admit it [the necessity]. . . . For all men acknowledge . . . first, that God is omnipotent . . . Secondly, that he knows

and foresees everything. . . . Admitting these two points . . .
they must admit . . . that we are not made by our will, but
by necessity; so, we do nothing by the right of free choice,
but according as God foresaw and acts by his counsel and
unfailing and changeless power. Whence . . . free choice
is found to be nothing.

Op cit., p. 719.

Yet, though events in general and choice in particular occur
necessarily, human choice is nevertheless free from coercion.
We choose willingly but necessarily. Choice is necessitated
willingness.

For if not we, but God alone works salvation in us, we, before his work, do nothing salutary, whether we will or no.
And I say we must do the works which avail nothing to salvation necessarily, not as though we were forced [coacte], but,
as they say, by the necessity of immutability, not by the
necessity of immutability, not by the necessity of coercion.
That is, when a man is without the spirit of God, it is not of
course by violence, or as though he were hurried along
against his will [raptus obtorto collo], or unwillingly, that
he does evil--as a robber or thief might be unwillingly led
to punishment--but he does it spontaneously and with a willing will. Now, of his own power he cannot omit, coerce, or
change this willingness or will to act, but he goes on gladly
willing [volendo et lubendo]. Even though he be forcibly coerced to do something else externally, still his inner will
remains averse and is angry at the force or resistance of-
fered it. Now, he would not be angry, if he were changed and
willingly followed force. This it is which we call the necessity of immutability, i.e., that the will cannot change itself
or turn elsewhere, but is rather the more aroused to will as
long as it is resisted. Its anger proves it. This would not
occur if it were free or had free choice. Interrogate experience. How little open to persuasion are they who, when affected by something, stick fast. Or, if they yield, they yield
to force or to the greater advantage of something else. Never
do they freely yield. But if they are unaffected, they allow
whatever takes its course and is done to take its course and to
be done.

14

Moreover, if, on the other hand, God works in us, the changed . . . will once more wills and acts merely by willingness, readiness, of its own accord, not under coercion; so that by no contrarieties, not even by the gates of hell . . . can it be changed to another course . . . but continues to wish, to be willing, to love the good, just as before, it wished, was willing in, loved, the bad. . . . In sum, if we are under the God of this world, without the work and spirit of the true God, we are held captive to his will. . . . so that we cannot will except what he wills. For he is that strong man, armed, who so keeps his house that they whom he possesses are in peace, lest they incite any movement or feeling against him; otherwise the kingdom of Satan divided in itself would not stand. And Christ asserts that it does stand. And this we do willingly, gladly, as is the nature of the will, which let it be forced, were not a will. For coercion is, if I may so call it, a "will" (voluntas). But if a stronger man comes upon the scene, and having conquered him [viz., the god of this world] seizes us as his spoil, we are once more by his spirit slaves and captives (yet this is royal liberty), so that we will and gladly do what he wishes. Thus the human will is between the two like a beast of burden. If God is in the saddle, it wishes and goes whither God wishes, as the Psalm says: [73.23]. I am like a beast before thee, yet I am always with thee. If Satan is in the saddle, it wills and goes whither Satan wishes. Nor does it lie within its choice to run to either of the two riders, or to seek him; rather the riders themselves strive to obtain and possess it.

Op. cit, pp. 634, 635.

Nothing could be clearer: choice is spontaneous, uncoerced, but necessitated. We like what we choose, but we must choose what we choose.

One more text will suffice to bring out the point which Luther makes: Choice is spontaneous; that is, it issues uncoerced from the one choosing. But choice is necessitated; that is, it must issue thence necessarily.

And now, how prettily does he [Erasmus] keep liberty together with necessity when he says: not every necessity excludes free will; for example, God the Father necessarily generates him, because not forced thereto.

15

Vid. Desiderii Erasmi opera omnia. Lugduni Batavorum, 1706, T. 9, p. 1234. Not being primarily concerned with Erasmus I have merely verified Luther's statements about him.

I pray, are we arguing now about coercion and force? Have we
not witnessed in so many books that it is about the necessity of
immutability that we are speaking? We know that the Father
generated by willing, that Judas betrayed Christ by willing,
but we say that this wish in Judas himself was certainly and
infallibly to come to pass if God foreknew it. Or, if what I
say is not yet understood, let me relate one kind of coercive
necessity for a work, another sort of infallible necessity for
a time. . . . That is, I am not arguing whether Judas was an
unwilling or willing traitor, but whether, at a time predefined
by God, it had infallibly to be that Judas willingly betrayed
Christ. But see what the Diatribe says here: if you consider
the infallible prescience of God, Judas was necessarily to be
a traitor, and yet Judas could have changed his wish. . . .
How could Judas have changed his wish against the infallible
prescience of God? Could he have changed the prescience of
God and made it fallible? . . .

Even the Sophists had felt the force . . . of this argument:
Thence did they imagine the necessity of the consequence and
of the consequent . . . For if you admit the necessity of the
consequence, overthrown . . . is free choice, nor does either
the necessity or the contingence of the consequent help matters at all. What is it to me if free choice be not forced, but
willingly do what it does? It is enough for me that you admit
that it must needs be that it willingly do what it does and that
it cannot bear itself otherwise if God have so foreknown. If
God knows that Judas will betray or changes his will to betray,
whichever God has foreknown will necessarily occur, or else
God will be deceived . . . For this is the result of the necessity of the consequence; namely, if God foreknows, that
must necessarily be done. This means, free choice is nothing.
. . . And the necessity of the consequent, by which they
console themselves . . . is diametrically opposed to the
necessity of the consequence. For example, there is necessity
of the consequence if I say: God foreknows that Judas will be
a traitor; therefore it will certainly and infallibly happen
that Judas will be a traitor. Opposed to this necessity and

consequence you console yourself thus: but because Judas can change his will to betray, therefore, there is no necessity of the consequent. I ask you, how agree these two: Judas is able to wish not to betray, and it is necessary that Judas wish to betray? Are they not directly contradictory and repugnant? He is not, you say, forced to betray unwillingly. What has that to do with it? You spoke of the necessity of the consequent, to the effect that it was not induced by the necessity of the consequence; you said nothing of the coercion of the consequent. The answer was about the necessity of the consequent, and you trot out an example of the coercion of the consequent. I ask one question, and you answer another.

Op. cit., pp. 720, 721, 722.

It looks as though Luther had the better of this brush with Erasmus. Erasmus had tried to exempt choice from necessity by asserting a willingness in the choice of one who must nevertheless choose.

vid. supra, p. 29, n. 1.

Luther seized upon the statement and pointed out that he never denied that choice was always willing choice. Luther's point is that choice, though always willing, is nevertheless, in consequence of God's knowledge and will, necessary. That choice was in consequence of God's will, and knowledge made little difference for Luther as to its necessity. Even though choice was not according to the necessity of the consequent, it was withal necessary, not indeed because it was coerced, but because the knowledge and will of God made it to be what it is. Erasmus seems to have been aware that according to Catholic theology choice must be spontaneous (willing) and unnecessitated. But, he offers no reason to show why it is both, unless, being neither a philosopher nor a theologian, the fact that choice be uncoerced be a reason. Luther answers: You deny the necessity of the consequent in free choice. Good. So do I. But I say that choice is nevertheless necessary, because, though uncoerced, choice is made necessary by divine antecedents. You say: Free choice need not be, since it is not coerced. But this is not a sufficient reason why choice should not be necessary. In short, the spontaneity of choice does not exempt it from necessity.

The conclusion from all this is that Luther means by "choice" the election of good or of evil. Of himself a man can elect neither. He is always necessitated to one or the other, and he is so necessitated by the omnipotence and foreknowledge of God. Of course there is no coercion of man's will in these necessitated choices.

Satan et homo lapsi et deserti a Deo non possunt velle bonum, hoc est ea quae Deo placent aut quae Deus vult. Sed sunt in sua desideria conversi perpetuo, ut non possint non quaerere quae sua sunt. Haec igitur eorum voluntas et natura sic a Deo aversa non est nihil. Neque enim Satan et impius homo nihil est aut nullam naturam aut voluntatem habet, licet corruptam et aversam naturam habeant. Illud igitur reliquum quod dicimus naturae in impio et Satan ut creatura et opus Dei non est minus subjectum omnipotentiae et actioni divinae quam omnes aliae creaturae et opera Dei. Quando ergo Deus omnia movet et agit, necessario movet etiam et agit in Satana et impio. Agit autem in illis taliter, quales illi sunt et quales invenit, hoc est, cum illi sint aversi et mali et rapiantur motu illo divinae omnipotentiae, non nisi aversa et mala faciunt, tamquam si eques agat equum tripedem vel bipedem, agit quidem taliter, qualis equus est, hoc est equus male incedit. Sed quid faciat eques? equum talem simul agit cum equis sanis, illo male, istis bene, aliter non potest, nisi equus sanetur. Hic vides Deum, cum in malis, et per malos operatur, mala quidem fieri, Deum tamen non posse mala facere, licet mala per malos faciat . . . Vitium ergo est in instrumentis, quae odiosa Deus esse non sinit, quod mala faciunt, movente ipso Deo. Non aliter quam si faber securi serrata et dentata male secaret.
Haec rata et certa sunt, si credimus omnipotentem esse Deum, Deinde impium esse creaturam Dei . . . Omnipotentia Dei facit, ut impius non possit motum et actionem Dei evadere, sed necessario illi subiectus paret. Op. cit., pp. 709, 710.

Since, then, choice is uncoerced, spontaneous (concretely, since when I choose I choose, and I choose willingly)--since, further, choice though spontaneous is effected by antecedents which of themselves cause choice--it follows that for Luther choice is necessitated spontaneity. Corrupted in his nature by sin, man's will is also corrupted. Obviously there is no constraint in human choice; it is always voluntary. But left to itself, choice will always elect evil, and if grace supervene, with the same necessity it will elect the good. Quite exact, in his system, is Luther's comparison of the will to a horse which two riders, God and the devil, strive to mount. If God mounts the will, choice must be voluntarily made of the good; if the devil mounts it, choice must be of evil. Subject to immutable necessity which holds it changelessly captive, the will is really a slave to necessity, and its liberty is a titulus sine re.

vid. Assertio . . . . Werke, Weimar, vol. 7, p. 146.

The argument, then, of the De Servo Arbitrio may be stated simply thus: antecedents to human choice which of themselves effect choice, are incompatible with the immunity of choice from necessity but are not incompatible with the immunity of choice from coercion. Now, there are such antecedents. Human choice, therefore, is not immune from necessity, but it is immune from coercion. Whence, liberty is pure spontaneity: choice arises from an uncoerced but necessitated principle of action. The supposition of the argument is of course that human nature is corrupted by original sin to the extent that even under grace it remains vitiated but is reputed just by God.

Est tamen naturaliter et inevitabiliter mala et viciata natura, Disputatio contra scholasticam theologiam, th. 9, Weimar, vol. 7, p. 146.

It has been already noted that Luther denies the applicability of this argument to natural choices. How consistent that denial was, the reader must judge for himself from the texts quoted which bear the opposite sense. At any rate, Molina thought that Luther meant what he said, not the denial of what he said. Anyhow, whatever be the extent of Luther's determinism, the point is unessential to the understanding of the theory of Molina. Molina directs his theory against the determinism of any antecedents to choice, whether natural or supernatural. That Luther may have limited his determinism to supernatural choices is not essential to the understanding of a theory which opposes the determinism of all antecedents.

The position which Molina might have adopted in opposition to the Lutheran position was either one of two. He might have denied the first part of the major thus: antecedents to human choice which of themselves effect choice are not incompatible with immunity of choice from necessity. (He could not deny the second part of the

Lutheran major: such antecedents are not incompatible with spontaneity; after all, a man cannot will and not will in the same act. Nor could he deny that antecedents to choice are necessary. Homo sine gratia non potest velle bonum is a constant assertion of Molina's theology. And in the natural order, too, a man cannot act without the natural concourse of God.) Having denied the first part of the major, Molina might have conceded the minor: there are such antecedents. He would then have been able to deny the conclusion and to say: liberty is not pure spontaneity. His theory of liberty, then, would have had to render some reason why antecedents which of themselves effect choice do not nevertheless necessitate choice. That is, his theory of liberty must then have shown that the conditions or causes necessary for the exercise of human spontaneity excluded necessity. The other position which Molina might, and did, adopt was this: he conceded the major (antecedents which of themselves effect choice necessitate choice), denied the minor and the conclusion.

Como de lo arriba de Luthero . . . consta, el fundamento . . . es que ad omnia opera causarum omnium secundarum, necessariam affirmant praemotionem Dei. . . ut sine illo operari non possint et cum illo non possint non operari . . . Hunc vero influxum . . . affirmant non cogere quidem voluntatem . . . quasi violentiam illi inferant rationemque spontanei . . . tollant: attamen eam necessitare . . . (p. 439). ---Si vero tales [sc., conditiones praeexistentes, aut concomitantes] sint, quae voluntatem creatam non sinant facere contrarium aut contradictorium perinde ac si illae non fuissent, utique libertatem a voluntate creata circa id tollunt, eamque ad id efficiendum necessitant, esto eam non cogant sed spontaneum in eam relinquunt (p. 448). ---Dicimus . . . Deum ita cum voluntate . . . concurrere . . . tum ad actus naturales tum etiam ad supernaturales . . . ut semper integrum voluntati relinquat non elicere huius modi actus . . . aut etiam elicere actum contrarium . . . ac proinde influxum Dei sive naturalem . . . sive supernaturalem . . . non esse ita ex se efficacem, quin integrum voluntati relinquat non consentire . . . ut Concilium Tridentinum sess. 6. c. 5 et can. 4 adversus Lutheranos dilucide definivit (p. 446). L. Molina, Summa Haeresium Minor, vid. Stegmüller, op. cit.

What result this position was going to have upon Molina's theory of liberty we shall see more fully later. Suffice it for the present to remark first that Molina saw clearly Luther's point: human

20

choice is necessitated but not coerced. Second, he saw that Luther's position was opposed to Catholic dogma. Third, he thought that the denial of the Lutheran minor (there are antecedents to choice which of themselves effect choice) was dictated to him by his theology.

inferunt (sc., Lutherus, Calvinus, Chemnitius), voluntatem angelicam et humanam habere quidem rationem spontanei minimeque coacti . . . non tamen habere rationem liberi arbitrii . . . quoniam, inquiunt, licet ad eos (actus) eliciendos non cogatur, necessitatur tamen ab efficaci praemotione divina ordineve efficaci divinae providentiae . . . L. Molina, Summa Haeresium Minor, vid. Stegmüller, op. cit., p. 440. On the opposition of Luther's position to Catholic dogma see n. 1, p. 39, supra, and cf.: haec autem opinio [quod quidam posuerunt quod voluntas hominis ex necessitate movetur ad aliquid agendum; nec tamen ponebant quod voluntas cogeretur] est heretica: tollit enim rationem meriti et demeriti in humanis actibus. St. Thomas Aquinas, De Malo, q. 6, a. 1, resp. That Molina thought he must, from revelation, deny Luther's minor is clear from: Nos autem cum Concilio Tridentino [Sess. 6, c. 5 et can. 4], fide catholica . . . asseveramus Deum . . . ita nos adiuvare . . . ut nunquam conversio nostra stet per ipsum sed semper stet per nos . . . Auxilium vero . . . quo nos . . . praemovet, excitat, allicit et invitat, tale esse ut integrum nobis relinquat consentire . . . vel non consentire aut etiam dissentire, ut Concilium Tridentinum definit. L. Molina, Summa Haeresium Maior, vid. Stegmüller, op. cit., p. 432.

As a matter of fact the theology of Molina truly did dictate to him the denial of necessity in choice. But it is far from apparent that Catholic theology dictated his denial of the Lutheran minor (there are antecedents to choice which of themselves effect choice). As we shall see, many theologians of the Church denied the Lutheran major. Antecedents to choice which of themselves effect choice are not, they said, incompatible with the immunity of choice from necessity. Having admitted, then, the minor, the theologians of this latter position attempt to show from the nature of the antecedents themselves that Lutheran conclusion (choice is necessitated spontaneity) is false. These theologians thus attempt to secure a metaphysic--whether triumphant or not is not the point; the point is that an explanation per causas is attempted, and this is a metaphysic--of liberty. Molina, having denied the Lutheran

minor, had on his hands a theory of a liberty--or of a free act--
which, not being caused by the antecedents themselves of choice,
cannot be explained by those antecedents. If then Molina wishes
to, and does, assert the absence of necessity in choice, he has
no explanation per causus of the absence of necessity in choice,
since according to Molina no antecedents of themselves cause
choice, Molina can recur only to facts to make good his case.
The facts to which he recurs are experience and revelation.

*Molina in his De Scientia Dei (vid. Stegmüller, op. cit.,
pp. 208 et sqq.) thus proves the absence of necessity
in choice . . . quando non esset aliud argumentum ad
probandum libertatem arbitrii quam experientia, qua
quivis experitur in se ipso, in potestate sua esse stare
aut sedere . . . insania profecto est negare ab hominibus
libertatem arbitrii, neque minus stultum est adhibere
fidem neganti libertatem arbitrii quam experimur, quam
adhibere fidem persuadenti papyrum hanc quam cernimus
non esse albam. Cf. L. Molina, Concordia, p. 125. Iam
vero veniamus ad testimonia Scripturae sacrae, ex quibus
apparebit, hereticos negantes libertatem arbitrii in
media luce caecutire (p. 209). Cf. L. Molina, Concordia,
p. 128. Veniamus ad definitiones Ecclesiae (p. 212). Cf.
L. Molina, Concordia, p. 130. Unanimem sanctorum Patrum
hac in parte videre poteris apud Castrum verbo libertas
. . . Cf. L. Molina, Concordia, pp. 131-44. And these
are his only proofs. That Molina thought that antecedents
to choice do not of themselves effect choice appears from
his Summa Haeresium Minor (vid. Stegmüller, op. cit., p.
446). Dicimus . . . influxum Dei sive naturalem . . .
sive supernaturalem . . . non esse ita ex se efficacem,
quin integrum voluntati relinquat non consentire, non
cooperari et non converti in instanti in quo consentit,
cooperatur et convertitur, ut Concilium Tridentinum
sess. 6.c.5 et can. 4 adversus Lutheranos dilucide
definit et in nobis ipsis experimur; ac proinde ab
eiusmodi ita libero consensu et cooperatione pendere,
quod auxilium gratiae . . . efficax sit nec cassum et
inefficax maneat. Throughout, as it is apparent, Molina
realises that necessitated choice is opposed to his
theology, and he thinks that antecedents efficacious
of choice necessitate it; . . . esse efficax huismodi
auxilium . . . provenit ex eo quod expediat Deum at-
temperare et moderari suum influxum, ne inferat voluntati
necessitatem . . . Ac sane si Deus . . . praemotione
efficaci quam Lutherani et Bannes constituunt, influeret,
non solum libertas arbitrii a voluntate creata ad omnes*

actus auferretur, sed etiam multum, immo omnino,
derogaretur iustitiae divinae circa homines . . . ac
Dei causae adversus reprobos et malos, qui eo ipso
culpa carerent quod non aliter vixerint, quando qui-
dem iuxta Lutheranos et Bannes denegavit illis auxilia
efficacia et praemotiones efficaces ad aliter operandum
atque ad aliter se gerendum sine quibus gerere se aliter
ac cooperari nequiverunt . . . Quare ordo divinae pro-
videntiae necessitatem non infert voluntati creatae
. . . contrariumque Lutheranorum et Bannes assertum
error est in fide. L. Molina, Summa Haeresium Minor,
vid. Stegmüller, op. cit., pp. 446, 447.

2   MOLINA AND CALVIN

Adressing himself to Calvin, whose doctrine he transcribes from Tapper, Molina writes as follows.

Calvin taught after Luther that everything happens by reason of the efficacious providence of God by which he works all in all. Nor does Calvin admit liberty in man even in civil or natural matters (inasmuch, i.e., as what is free means that which can turn itself to whichever of two courses it pleases, but only inasmuch as what is free is distinguished from what is coerced, and is the same as the spontaneous). Whence in the second chapter of his Institutes he speaks as follows: "I am of the opinion that the words which sound absurd should be avoided, especially when their falsity is pernicious. Now, would not anyone at all, who hears that man is free, think forthwith that he is master of his mind and will, and can, of himself, turn himself to whichever of two courses he pleases?"

Tapper's text is found in Explicationis Articulorum venerandae facultatis Sacrae Theologiae studii Lovaniensis circa dogmata Ecclesiastica . . . T. I. D. Ruard Tapper, Lovanii, 1555, pp. 358, 359, 360. Molina's text is from his Summa Haeresium Maior, vid.

Stegmüller, op. cit., p. 398. The text of Calvin which Tapper is quoting may be found in J. Calvini . . . Institutionum Christianae Religionis, Amstelodami, 1667, l. 2, c. 2, n. 7, p. 63 . . . sed religiose censeo cavendas eas voces, quae absurdum aliquid sonant: prae-sertim ubi perniciose erratur. Quotus, autem, quaeso, quisque est, qui dum assignari homini liberum arbitrium audit, non statim concipit illum esse et mentis suae et voluntatis dominum, qui flectere se in utramvis partem a se ipso possit? For Calvin on liberty in civil and natural matter vid. Calvin, op. cit., l. 2, c. 2, pp. 65, 66.

Calvin [continues Molina] strives in many ways to show that there is not such liberty in man, not even to sin, though he admits that the philosophers, and after them the Fathers, admitted such liberty in man. In his second book against Pighius, Calvin says:

If liberty is opposed to coercion, I both admit there is free choice and steadily assert it; and I hold to be a heretic whoso-ever thinks otherwise--provided that be called free which is not forced or violently drawn by an external motion, but acts of its own accord. But since they commonly think of something quite different when they hear or read of this epithet being ap-plied to man, and since they refer it to his faculties and powers, and get the notion that he has good and evil within his power in such wise that he can do either by his own nature, this is the reason I am displeased. Yet that the will be by necessity led or drawn to evil, since its liberty has been abdicated, offends those who know not how to distinguish between necessity and coer-cion. Yet if someone should ask them: is not God necessarily good? is not the devil necessarily bad? what would they an-swer? For God's goodness is so linked with his divinity that it is no more necessary that he be God than that he be good. And the devil through his fall is so estranged from the participation in good, that he cannot but do evil. And if some sacrilegious person sneers that small praise is due to God because of his goodness, since he is forced to preserve it, who will not have the answer ready that it is by reason of God's immense goodness that he is unable to do evil, not by reason of violent impulsion. Wherefore, if it is no obstacle to the free will of God in his doing good that he must do good; if the devil, who can do only evil, never-theless sins by his will, who teaches that therefore a man sins less voluntarily because he lies under the necessity of sinning? Let, then, the sum of this distinction be observed: man, vitiated as he is by the fall, sins willingly indeed, not as one coerced or unwilling; he sins by the readiest affection of his mind, not by violent coercion, by the motion of his own list, not by extreme coercion. Yet such is the depravity of his nature that he cannot but be moved and driven to evil. And if this be true, he is, in no uncertain terms, certainly subject to the necessity of sinning.

For the text of Molina vid. op. cit. in Stegmüller, op. cit., pp. 398, 399; Tapper's text is from the op. cit., pp. 358, sqq. Tapper is quoting first from the Response to Pighius which may be found in J. Calvini, Responsio ad Pighium, l. 2, Amstelodami, 1667, p. 133. Si coactioni opponitur libertas, liberum esse arbitrium et fateor, et constanter assevero: ac pro heretico habeo, quisquis secus sentiat. Si hoc, inquam, sensu liberum vocatur, quia non cogatur, aut violenter trahatur externo motu, sed sponte agatur sua, nihil moror. Sed quum aliud prorsus vulgo concipiant, dum hoc epitheton hominis voluntati attributum, vel audiunt, vel legunt, haec causa est cur mihi displiceat. Si quidem ad facultatem vires-que referunt: nec impedire possis, quin simulac libera fuerit voluntas dicta, haec pluribus imaginatio protinus in mentem veniat: habere igitur sub potestate sua bonum et malum, ut ad alterutrum eligere suapte virtute queat. Tapper is quoting, secondly, from J. Calvini, Institutionum Christianae Religionis; the text may be found in l. 2, c. 3, n. 5, pp. 71, 72, of the Amsterdam edition, 1667. Of-fendit autem eos, qui inter necessitatem et coactionem distinguere nesciunt. At si quis eos interroget, Annon Deus necessario bonus est: annon diabolus necessario malus: quid respondeant? Si enim connexa est Dei bonitas cum divinitate, ut non magis necessarium sit ipsum esse Deum, quam bonum. Diabolus autem per lapsum sic a bini communicatione alienatus est, ut nihil quam male agere possit. Quod si quis sacrilegus obganniat, Deo parum laudis ex sua bonitate deberi, ad quam servandam cogatur: cui non erit prompta responsio, Immensa eius bonitate fieri ne male agere possit, non violenta impulsione? Ergo si liberam Dei voluntatem in bene agendo non im-pedit, quod necesse est illum bene agere: si diabolus, qui nonnisi male agere potest, voluntate tamen peccat: quis hominem ideo minus voluntarie peccare dicet, quod sit peccandi necessitati obnoxius? --- Haec igitur distinctionis summa observetur, hominem, ut vitiatus est ex lapsu, volentem quidem peccare non invitum nec coactum:

26

affectione animi propensissima, non violenta coatione:
propriae libidinis motu, non extraria coatione: qua
tamen est naturae pravitate, non posse nisi ad malum
moveri et agi. Quod si verum est, peccandi certe
necessitati subjacere non obscure exprimitur.

Still transcribing from Tapper, Molina continues:

From the Institutes of the same Calvin Tapper also relates
that Calvin teaches man has not free choice, i.e., that it is
not in his power to do what he does; that it is not in his power
not to sin when he sins, not to be converted when he is converted to the Lord; and contrariwise, that it is not in his
power to act when he does not act, to be converted and peni-
tent when he is not converted; but it is by an efficacious
providence by which God works all in all, and by the strong
inclination of his will, that all things are done necessarily and
that nothing is left to our power; that free choice, as a horse
by its rider, is led and drawn to good or evil; and therefore,
just as by the necessity coming from the evil dwelling in him
he does evil, so, acted upon by God's grace and doing nothing
by his own power, he necessarily does good. Whence, in
paragraph 53 of his Institutes he says: "some will perhaps
admit that the will, turned from the good by its own nature,
is converted only by God's power; yet with the proviso that
thus got ready it has thereafter its own part to play in its
activity; just as Augustine taught (ep. 106 ad Bonifat.): the
grace of God precedes every good work, which the will
accompanies but does not go before, follows after but does
not precede." And, departing from this opinion of Augustine's,
he adds in the same place: "but because a reformed will is the
work of the Lord this is wrongly attributed to man that he
yields to prevenient grace with a subject will." And in paragraph 56 he subjoins: "grace moves the will, not as the tradi-
tion and belief of many centuries would have it, viz., in such
wise that it is thereafter dependent upon our election to follow
or refuse its motion, but by efficaciously effecting that will.
And so, the saying so often repeated by Chrysostom (Serm.
de invent. S. Crucis) must be repudiated: whomsoever he
draws is drawn according to his will."

The first text of Calvin may be found in the Instit.
Christ. Relig., Amstelodami, 1667, l. 2, c. 3, n. 7, p.

27

72. Erunt forte, qui concedent voluntatem a bono suopte ingenio aversam, sola Domini virtute converti: sic tamen, ut praeparata, suas deinde in agendo partes habeat: quemadmodum docet Augustinus, omne bonum opus, gratiam praecedere, et id comitante, non ducent, pedissequa, non praevia voluntate. The second text, ibid., n. 10, p. 74: Ac voluntatem movet [Deus], non qualiter multis seculis traditum est et creditum, ut nostrae postea sit electionis, motioni abtemperare aut refragari: sed illam efficaciter efficiendo. Illud ergo toties a Chrysostomo repetitum repudiari necesse est, Quem trahit volentem trahit. I have been unable to find Chrysostom's text. The reference is from the editors of Calvin.

The <u>universa</u> <u>iustificationis</u> <u>doctrina</u> of Thomas Stapelton supplied Molina with more texts from Calvin. According to Stapelton, Calvin denies that the providence of God is an otiose providence of mere prescience. Rather, God so directs all events by it that it belongs no less to his hands than to his eyes; that is, it is not only prescient but also directive, and so lies in the act of his will and not in bare prescience, according to the text of Genesis (22:8) "The Lord will provide for himself the victim." Then Calvin posits that the providence of God reaches to all acts and effects by a destined order and definite plan and influence, even to the plans and wills of men, the good as well as the bad, with the result that they are borne straight to the end fixed by the same divine providence. Thus the human mind depends rather on the motion of God than on the choice of its own election. Wherefore Calvin says that the will of God is the cause of all things in such wise that it not only rules by the Holy Spirit the elect but also forces the reprobate to obedience. And he teaches that the fall of the first man and of the angels pertains to their destination, by God's providence, to evil. Whence Calvin says: "I admit that it was by God's will that all the sons of Adam fell, and that we must always come back to the sole choice of the will of God, the cause of which is hidden in himself." And he adds that no other cause for the angels' fall can be adduced except the reprobation which is hidden in the secret counsel of God. Calvin distinguishes prescience from providence, and confesses that prescience causes no necessity in things, but affirms that providence does. For he says that God provides what he has decreed will happen; he does not merely foresee it. And therefore does Calvin praise Laurence Valla's opinion, who teaches that life and death, salvation and damnation are actions rather of the divine will than of prescience.

*Molina's text is from the Summa Haeresium Maior, vid.
Stegmüller, op. cit., pp. 401, 402. Stegmüller, ibid.,
cites Stapelton's text from the universa iustificationis
doctrina, l. 11, c. 7, ed. Paris, 1582, pp. 380, 381.
The texts of Calvin may be found in J. Calvini, Instit.
Relig. Christ., Amstelodami, 1667, on the pages to be
indicated. Principio igitur teneant lectores providentiam
vocari, non qua Deus e coelo otiosus speculatur quae in
mundo fiunt, sed qua veluti clavum tenens, eventus omnes
moderatur. Ita non minus ad manus, quam ad oculos pertinet.
Nec enim cum filio suo dicebat Abraham, Deus providebit,
tantum volebat praescium futuri eventus asserere: sed
curam rei incognitae in eius voluntatem rejicere, qui
rebus perplexis et confusis exitum dare solet. Unde
sequitur, providentiam in actu locari: nimis enim in-
scite nugantur multi de nuda praescientia (l. 1, c. 16,
n. 4, p. 46). ---Neque tamen hic etiam error tolerabilis
est: Hac enim Providentia quam universalem appellant,
nihil impediri tradunt, vel creaturas omnes, quominus
contingenter moveantur, vel hominem, quominus libero
voluntatis suae arbitrio huc atque illuc se convertat,
atque ita inter Deum et hominem partiuntur: ut ille
motionem huic sua virtute inspiret, qua agere possit
pro naturae sibi inditae ratione: hic autem actiones
suas voluntario consilio moderetur. Breviter: Dei
potentia, sed non destinatione, mundum, res hominum,
ipsosque homines gubernari volunt (ibid.). ---Unde eius
providentia, non coelum modo ac terram, et creaturas
inanimatas, sed hominum etiam consilia et voluntates
gubernari sic asserimus ut ad destinatum ab ea scopum
recta ferantur (l. 1, c. 16, n. 8, p. 47). ---Ego vero
dico . . . Deum, quoties viam facere vult suae providentiae etiam in rebus externis hominum voluntates
flectere et versare, nec ita esse liberam ipsorum
electionem quin eius libertati Dei arbitrium dominetur.
Velis, nolis, animum tuum a motione Dei potius, quam ab
electionis tuae libertate pendere, haec quotidiana experientia reputare coget . . . (l. 2, c. 4, n. 7, p. 77).
---Summa haec sit: quum Dei voluntas dicitur rerum omnium
esse causa, providentiam eius statui moderatricem in
cunctis hominum consiliis et operibus, ut non tantum
vim suam exerat in electis, qui Spiritu Sancto reguntur,
sed etiam reprobos in obsequium cogat (l. 1, c. 18, n. 2,
p. 55).---Fateor sane in hanc qua nunc illigati sunt,
conditionis miseriam, Dei voluntate decidisse universos
filios Adam: atque id est quod principio dicebam, rede-
undum tandem semper esse ad solum divinae voluntatis*

It will have been clear from the above that Colvin's notion of
choice is practically the same as the notion of Luther. And Calvin
arrives at it in pretty much the same way. Starting from the
position that man could originally choose the good,

*How this is to be reconciled with his general doctrine
that providence imposes necessity on choice Calvin does
not say. But his meaning is clear from this passage, J.
Calvini, Instit. Relig. Christ., Amstelodami, 1667, l. l,
c. 15, n. 8, p. 44: Ergo animam hominis Deus mente in-
struxit, qua bonum a malo, justum ab injusto discerneret:
ac quid sequendum vel fugiendum fuit, praeeunte rationis
luce videret. Unde partem hanc directricem
dixerunt Philosophi. Huic adjunxit voluntatem, penes quam
est electio. His praeclaris dotibus excelluit prima hominis
conditio, ut ratio, intelligentia, prudentia, judicium non
modo ad terrenae vitae gubernationem suppeterent, sed quibus transcenderent usque ad Deum et aeternam felicitatem.
Deinde ut accederet electio, quae appetitus dirigeret,
motusque omnes organicos temperaret: atque ita voluntas
rationis moderationi esset prorsus consentanes. In hac
integritate libero arbitrio pollebat homo, quo, si vellet,
adipisci posset aeternam vitam.*

Calvin concludes that since sin has quite vitiated him,

*Cf. op. cit., l. 2, c. 1, n. 9, p. 60: Quamobrem dixi
cunctas animae partes a peccato fuisse possessas ex
quo fonte justitiae descivit Adam. Neque enim appetitus
tantum inferior eum illexit, sed arcem ipsam mentis oc-
cupavit nefanda impietas, et ad cor intimum penetravit
superbia: ut frigidum sit ac stultum, corruptelam quae
inde manavit, ad sensuales tantum (ut vocant) motus
restringere . . . et Paulus omnem dubitationem tollit,
corruptionem docens, non in una tantum parte subsidere
sed nihil mortifera eius tabe purum esse aut sincerum.*

there is now left him only the necessity either of sinning without
grace or, with grace, of doing good. Man must, as a consequence
of original sin, either do good or do evil.

*Op. cit., l. 2, c. 3, n. 13, p. 75: Audiamus nunc
Augustinum suis verbis loquentem, ne aetatis nostrae
Pelagiani, hoc est, Sorbonici sophistae totam vetustatem
nobis adversari pro suo more criminentur . . . Libro de
correptione et gratia . . . exequitur, quod breviter,
eius tamen verbis referam gratiam persistendi in bono,
Adae fuisse datam, si vellet; nobis dari, ut velimus, ac
voluntate concupiscentiam superemus. Habuisse ergo illum
posse, si vellet: sed non velle, ut posset: nobis et velle
dari et posse. Primam fuisse libertatem, posse non peccare:
nostram multo majorem, non posse peccare. Ac ne de futura
post immortalitatem perfectione loqui putaretur . . .
scrupulum hunc paulo post eximit. Tantum quippe, inquit,
Spiritu Sancto accenditur voluntas sanctorum: ut ideo
possint, quia sic volunt: ideo velint, quia Deus operatur
ut sic velint . . . Subventum est ergo infirmitati voluntatis humanae, ut gratia divina indeclinabiliter et insepara-
biliter ageretur, ideoque quantumvis infirma non deficeret
. . . Habemus nunc Augustini ore testatum, quod in primis
obtinere volumus, non offerri tantum a Domino gratiam,
quae libera cuiusque electione aut recipiatur, aut
respuatur: sed ipsam esse quae in corde et electionem et
voluntatem formet: ut quicquid deinde sequitur boni operis,
fructus sit ipsius ac effectus, nec aliam habeat sibi ob-
sequentem voluntatem, nisi quam fecit. Sunt enim eius quoque vera ex alio loco, omne bonum in nobis opus, nonnisi
gratiam facere.*

What Calvin leaves to choice is exactly what Luther left to it: spontaneity, the willingness by which a man is ready to choose that
which he must choose.

*Ibid.: Quod autem alibi dicit Augustinus non tolli
gratia voluntatem, sed ex mala mutari in bonam: et
quum bona fuerit, adjuvari: significat tantum hominem
non ita trahi, ut sine motu cordis, quasi extraneo
impulsu feratur: sed intus sic affici, ut ex corde
obsequatur . . . Ita homini tale relinquitur liberum
arbitrium (si appellare ita libet) quale alibi scribit,
quod nec ad Deum converti, nec in Deo persistere, nisi
per gratiam possit: a gratia valeat, quicquid valeat.*

The capital text, explicative of Calvin's whole mind on the
subject, is found in his <u>Responsio</u> ad <u>Pighium</u>. If by liberty,
Calvin there explains, is meant immunity from coercion, man
is free. Now coercion means force, violence. In the sense of
not being coerced or impelled by external force, the choice of
man is certainly free, since whatever he chooses to do he
chooses of his own accord. But commonly choice is supposed
to be more than mere willingness; it is supposed to be the power
of choosing not merely willingly, not merely spontaneously, but
the power also, innate in man, of choosing good and evil. Man
of himself has not this power. And because he has not, to refuse
to call him free, even though he act spontaneously, is not to be
a meticulous word pedant; rather, it is to relieve nearly every-
one of a dangerous error. Freedom, in fact, and servitude are
contradictory. If, then, the will of man is in servitude, it cannot except by improper usage be called free. Of course, if coercion be confused with necessity and <u>that</u> be called free from
necessity which is only free from coercion, it is small wonder
that man is thought to be free from necessity. Pighius by astutely
confusing necessity and coercion succeeds in perpetuating this
error. But it is time to call a halt to the confusion, by drawing
some necessary distinctions. The will is either free or slave,
either spontaneous or coerced. A free will is usually thought to
be one which can, of itself, elect good and evil. A coerced will
is a contradiction; for if coerced, it would not act of its own accord or by the inward motion of its election but would be violently
drawn by some external impulse. But the will cannot be forced.
A spontaneous will is one which turns willingly whither it is led,
but it is not drawn thither unwillingly. Lastly a slave will is one
which because of its corruption is held captive to its desires, so
that it can choose nothing but evil, even though it do so spontaneously and willingly, not driven thereto by external impulsion.
According to these distinctions it may be said that a man chooses.
But his choice is spontaneous, and the evil he does is imputable

to his voluntary election. The point is that there is no violence
or coercion which can be brought to bear on choice. But choice
is not free, and the reason is that man because of his ingrained
depravity is necessarily borne to evil and only to evil. Whence
the great importance of distinguishing between necessity and
coercion. Man is not unwillingly drawn to evil, but because his
will is captive under the yoke of sin, therefore does he sin
necessarily. The two, slavery and necessity, go together. On
the other hand, this slavery is voluntary, not forced. Its source
is in the vitiated will itself. Though the will must sin, it sins
willingly, and in this willingness lies its spontaneity. The spontaneous, then, can be necessary. Pighius, confusing the two,
thinks that if choice be spontaneous, it is not necessary. The
fact is that choice is both spontaneous and necessary.

*Part of this text has been already quoted, vid., p. 47,
n. 1. Its continuation (from J. Calvini, Responsio ad
Pighium, l. 2, Amstelodami 1667, p. 133) is as follows:
Non igitur unius voculae causa frustra litigo: sed
causam mihi justam habere videor, cur voculam optem
sublatam e medio, ad quam major prope mundi pars tanto
periculo impingit. Quamquam ne cum Scriptura quidem usu
videtur admodum bene convenire. Libertas enim et servitus
inter se pugnant. Proinde, si serva est hominis voluntas,
libera simul, nisi improprie, dici non potest . . . Sed
quoniam astute Pighius cum necessitate coactionem perpetuo
confundit, quarum discrimen tenere, et diligenter memi-
nisse, plurimum ad propositam quaestionem refert, haec
quattuor quid inter se differant, observare convenit:
voluntatem, aut liberam esse, aut servan, aut spontaneam,
aut coactam. Liberam voluntatem vulgo intelligunt, et sic
Pighius quoque definit, quae bonum aut malum eligere,
habeat in sua potestate. Coacta voluntas nulla esse potest
quum alterum alteri repugnet. Verum, docendi causa, quid
significet, dicendum erit, ut intelligatur, quid sit co-
actio. Eam ergo sic vocamus, quae non sponte sua, nec
interiore electionis motu, inclinatur huc vel illuc, sed
externo motu violenter fertur. Spontaneum dicimus, quae
ultro se flectit, quocunque ducitur, non autem rapitur,
aut trahitur invita. Serva postremo voluntas est, quae
propter corruptionem sub malarum cupiditatum imperio
captiva tenetur, ut nihil quam malum eligere possit,
etiamsi id sponte ac libenter, non externo motu impulsa
faciat. Secundum has definitiones, homini arbitrium
concedimus, idque spontaneum, ut si quid mali facit,
sibi ac voluntariae suae electioni imputare debeat.
Coactionem et violentiam tollimus, quia pugnat cum*

33

*natura voluntatis, nec simul consistat. Liberum
autem negamus, quia propter ingenitam homini pra-
vitatem ad malum necessario feratur, nec nisi malum
appetere queat. Atque hinc colligere licet, quantum
sit necessitatis et coactionis discrimen. Neque enim
hominem dicimus invitum trahi ad peccandum, sed quoniam
vitiosa sit eius voluntas, sub peccati jugo teneri
captivam, ideoque necessario male velle. Ubi enim
servitus, illic necessitas. Sed plurimum interest,
voluntariane sit servitus, an coacta. Nos autem non
alibi statuimus peccandi necessitatem quam in vitio
voluntatis: unde spontaneam esse ipsam sequitur. Nunc
vides spontaneum et necessarium simul convenire posse,
quod astu tegere conatur Pighius, dum liberum hominem
in eo aestimat, si non necessario faciat, aut bene,
aut male.*

Molina lumps together the theories of Calvin and Luther. They
both, he explains, posit a divine influence upon the operation of
second causes so efficacious that without that influence these
causes cannot act, that with it they cannot fail to act. Moreover
this divine influence does not indeed force the will in the sense
that it imposes violence upon the will (as a man, for example,
might be violently led to prison), but this influence does necessitate human choice. Such being the part of God in the causality
of human choice, it follows that all natural and supernatural
actions are brought about by the efficacity of the promotion of
God by which second causes cannot act otherwise than as they do.
Whence both Calvin and Luther hold that the providence of God--
that is, his prevision and his free ordinance--imposes necessity
upon all human actions. From these two positions, upon pre-
motion and providence, it follows that choice though spontaneous
is necessitated. The only difference, if any, between Calvin and
Luther seems to Molina to be that the choice defended by Luther
is more passive than it is in Calvin.

*L. Molina, <u>Summa Haeresium Minor</u>, Stegmüller, op. cit.,
pp. 439-41: el fundamento, en que estos tres hereges
[Luther, Calvin, Chemnitz] convienen y se apartan de la
verdad Catholica, es que ad omnia opera causarum secundarum,
necessariam affirmant praemotionem Dei seu influxum . . .
ita efficacem, ut sine illo operari non possint et cum
illo non possint non operari id quod numero operantur.
Hunc vero influxum . . . affirmant non cogere quidem
voluntatem . . . quasi violentiam illi inferant [in-
fluxum sc., sive naturalem sive supernaturalem] ration-*

*emque spontanei ab ea tollant; attamen eam necessitare
. . . Et quia, si Deus hoc modo operatur . . . affirmant, omnia . . . evenire . . . necessario . . . ex
efficacia praemotionis . . . Hinc confitetur [Calvinus]
ex sola praescientia nullam inferri necessitatem in
rebus. Affirmat tamen, ex providentia necessitatem . . .
inferri . . . Atque cum eo conveniunt Lutherus et
Chemnitius . . . Ex his duobus erroribus . . . inferunt
Lutherus, Calvinus, Chemnitius, voluntatem . . . habere
quidem rationem spontanei minimeque coacti . . . non tamen
habere rationem liberi arbitrii . . . Si quod est discrimen inter Lutherum . . . et Calvinum . . . hoc sane
dumtaxat est, quod Lutherus affirmat voluntatem . . .
solum se habere passive.*

The following statement, then, may summarize Calvin's
thought upon human choice. Antecedents to choice which of themselves effect choice, make choice necessary though they leave it
uncoerced. Now, there are such antecedents: the providence of
God, the vitiated will of man. Choice, therefore, is uncoerced
but necessitated. It is the same position as that of Luther.

Against the two men Molina takes the same attitude. He knows
that, according to his theology, choice is spontaneous and unnecessitated.

Vid., p. 40, n. 1.

He does not see how antecedents which of themselves effect choice
leave choice unnecessitated. Hence he feels called upon to deny the
premise to the argument of the Reformers. If choice be both spontaneous and unnecessitated; if, further, choice cannot be such
upon the supposition that its antecedents of themselves effect it;
the only way out, Molina thinks, is to deny that there are such
antecedents.

*L. Molina, Censura contra Dominicum Bannes, vid.
Stegmüller, op. cit., p. 482. Contra hanc Calvini . . .
doctrinam [Deum sc., solum esse causam actus voluntatis,
quoniam licet voluntas active concurrat, ita tamen
determinata concurrit, ut Dei motioni quae efficaciter
illum actum operatur, refragari non possit] est expressa
definitio Concilii Tridentini esse. 6, c. 5. In quo
habetur, homines per excitantem et adiunvantem gratiam
disponi ad convertendum se, assentiendo et cooperando
eidem gratiae, ipsumque hominem agere inspirationem
recipientem, atque ita agere, ut ipsam abicere possit.*

35

*Et canone 4 damnantur . . . qui dixerint, liberum
arbitrium a Deo motum nihil cooperari assentiendo Deo
excitanti . . . neque posse dissentire si velit. Ergo
si liberum arbitrium ex sententia et definitione Concilii cooperatur assentiendo gratiae, atque ita agit
ut inspirationem abicere possit et dissentire si velit,
dici non potest, collationem auxilii efficacis solam
esse causam et adaequatam assensus et conversionis nec
liberum arbitrium ab ea causalitate prorsus excludi.*

Hence we see once more the reason why, if antecedents cannot
of themselves cause choice and leave it free, Molina has cut
from beneath his feet the ground upon which is based the explanation (not the assertion) that choice is without necessity.
Philosophy attempts to explain through causes. Molina will assert without giving antecedent reasons. He will assert the absence of necessity in choice because experience and revelation
so attest.

3 MOLINA AND ST. THOMAS

Thus far we have seen that Molina denies there are any antecedents to free choice which of themselves effect that choice.
The words to be emphasized in this denial are any and of themselves. By any Molina excludes both divine (natural and supernatural) as well as human antecedents. These are respectively
in the divine order, the knowledge and the will of God, together
with their executive instruments, grace and (in the natural order)
natural concourse; in the human order, the practical judgment
by which is presented some good to be chosen. By of themselves
he means that there is no intrinsic causal nexus between antecedents and choice; that is, he denies that it is solely by reason
of the nature of the antecedents that choice is posited.

Cf. p. 3, n. 1.

Positis omnibus ad agendum requisitis, potest agere et non agere
. . . No antecedent to free choice is of such a nature as to pre-
determine choice. We have further seen that Molina adopted this
position because he thought that the Reformers' major was true:
antecedents to choice which of themselves effect choice impose

37

necessity upon, but do not coerce, the will. And if that major be true, the only element left to liberty, he thought, is spontaneity. It all seemed to destroy the Christian notion of imputability.

> *L. Molina, Summa Haeresium Maior, vid. Stegmüller, op. cit., pp. 446, 447. Ac sane si Deus tam ad opera voluntatis creatae naturalia quam ad supernaturalia praemotione efficaci, quam Lutherus et Bannes constituunt, influeret, non solum libertas arbitrii a voluntate creata ad omnes eos actus auferretur, sed etiam consequenter multum, immo omnino, derogaretur iustitiae divinae circa homines et angelos, ac Dei causae adversus reprobos et malos, qui eo ipso culpa carerent, quod non aliter vixerint, quando quidem iuxta Lutheranos et Bannes denegavit illis auxilia efficacia et praemotiones efficaces ad aliter operandum atque ad aliter se gerendum, sine quibus gerere se aliter ac cooperari nequiverunt.*

Hence his denial of the Reformers' minor: there are antecedents to choice which of themselves effect choice.

In consequence of this denial Molina had himself to establish a theory of the relations between choice and its antecedents which he thought would leave to choice its spontaneity and its immunity from necessity. That this was Molina's purpose is beyond question.

> *L. Molina, Epitome de Praedestinatione, vid. Stegmüller, op. cit., p. 336. Y aunque de ordinario ay inconueniente en verse fragmentos solos de obras, y mucho mas en dezirse en summa lo prouado y deduzido de principios parece otra cosa, supponiendo que ad arbitrii libertatem no basta sponte operari ut Lutherani voluerunt, id namque bestiis convenit, mas ser necessario nihil impedientibus circumstantiis omnibus concurrentibus, esse in facultate hominis, quando aliquid libere uult, illud non uelle aut etiam nolle, vel uelle contrarium, prout fuerit libertas vel ad solum exercitium vel etiam ad speciem actus. Lo que digo en breues palabras es lo siguiente . . .*

It is the theory which he though would accomplish his purpose that interests us. And the important point to remember for the understanding of that theory is that it starts off by excluding the determination of choice by the antecedents themselves.

*L. Molina, Epitome de Praedestinatione, vid. Stegmüller,
op. cit.: Ex dictis intelligetur facile, certitudinem
seu infallibilitatem, quod eiusmodi adultus [prae-
destinatus] perveniet in vitam aeternam, non esse in
mediis, quae Deus ex sua parte illi conferre statuit qui-
busque illum praedestinavit (p. 343) . . . Et quoniam
idem est de ratione mediorum, quae se tenet ex parte
divini intellectus, quod de decreto voluntatis eam ex
parte sua mandandi executioni, per quod ratio providentiae
in beatitudinem completur, quod de decreto fuit dictum
de tota ratione providentiae simili modo intelligatur
(p. 347). We shall see later Molina's concept of the
relation of human antecedents to choice. Suffice it for
the present to observe that for Molina human antecedents
do not determine choice: positis omnibus ad agendum requisitis, potest agere vel non agere: cf. pp. 1, 2, 3.*

In order to explain Molina's theory we may as well begin by
contrasting it with the theory of the man whom Molina often uses
as his point of reference, St. Thomas Aquinas.

*Cf. L. Molina, Concordia, ed. cit., p. 288: D. Thomam
quem in omnibus patronum potiusquam adversarium habere
percupio . . .*

St. Thomas' theory comprises, as was the theory of Molina to
comprise, three points: first, the relation between divine prescience and the free act; second, the relation between the causality of God and the free act; last, the theory of liberty implied in
these relations.

The first question, then, is: How does God know the future
free acts of man? (That God does know these acts does not
touch the present question.) To this question the constant answer
of St. Thomas is that God knows the future free acts of man in
the divine efficient causality.

In evidence of this the following texts may be adduced. Future
free acts can be considered a) as acts whose realization is contingent. There are therefore three questions: How does God
know things a) distinct from himself? b) things which do not
exist? c) things whose realization is contingent? To the first
question (How does God know things distinct from himself?)
the answer is as follows. God knows these things inasmuch as
they exist in him as in their immaterial principle.

We must further see how God knows creatures. Whence we must know that, since every agent acts in so far as it is in act, the thing effected by an agent must in some way be in the agent. Now whatever is in something else is in it after the manner of the recipient. Whence if an active principle be material, its effect is in it as though materially, because [it is there] as though in a kind of material virtue. But if the active principle be immaterial, its effect also will be in it immaterially. Moreover it was said above that something is known by another in so far as it is received immaterially in it. Thence it is that active material principles do not know their effects, because their effects are not in them as they (the effects) are cognoscible. But their effects <u>are</u> in active immaterial principles in so far as they are cognoscible, because they are there immaterially. Whence every active immaterial principle knows its effect. Thence it is said in the eighth proposition of the book of causes that intelligence knows what is beneath it in so far as it is its cause. Thus, since God is the active immaterial principle of things, it follows that in him is the knowledge of them.

Vid. [author's translation] De Veritate, 2, a. 3, resp. ad fin.

To the same question (How does God know things distinct from himself?) is given the same answer in the <u>Summa</u> <u>Contra</u> <u>Gentiles</u>.

1. 1, c. 49.

God knows things distinct from himself, first because God <u>est</u> <u>per</u> <u>suam</u> <u>essentiam</u> <u>causa</u> <u>essendi</u> <u>aliis</u>, second because <u>si . . .</u> <u>Deus</u> . . . <u>est</u> <u>causa</u>, <u>quum</u> <u>ipse</u> <u>sit</u> . . . <u>intellectualis</u>, <u>simil-</u> <u>itudo</u> <u>causati</u> <u>sui</u> <u>in</u> <u>eo</u> <u>erit</u> <u>intelligibiliter</u>, lastly <u>quum . . .</u> <u>perfecte</u> <u>se</u> <u>ipsum</u> <u>cognoscat</u>, <u>cognoscit</u> <u>se</u> <u>esse</u> <u>causam</u>; <u>quod</u> <u>esse</u> <u>non</u> <u>potest</u>, <u>nisi</u> <u>cognoscat</u> . . . <u>causatum</u> . . . <u>aliud</u> <u>ab</u> <u>ipso</u>. All three minors--namely, God is the intellectual cause of things distinct from himself--are the same.

So too in the <u>Summa</u> <u>Theologica</u> is given the same answer to the same question. "By the fact that itself [the divine power] is the first effective cause of all beings, it must needs be that God knows things distinct from himself."

1. q. 14, a. 5, resp.

In the next paragraph St. Thomas goes on to say that God knows creatures in himself inasmuch as his essence contains the similtude of things distinct from himself.

The answer, then, to the first question (cf. a] supra.) would seem to be The reason God knows creatures is that he is their efficient cause. The reason for divine knowledge is the efficient causality of God.

To the second question (How does God know that which is non-existent?) the following is the answer.

Nonexistent things are past, future, or purely possible (the last neither have existed, nor do exist, nor will exist). Cf. De Veritate, 2, a. 8.

God knows some nonexistents as an artist knows the products of which he is the cause. The knowledge of an artist antecedes the work of which he has the knowledge. Just so, the knowledge of God antecedes its objects. Now, an artist can know many things which he will never realize. So too, then, can God. It follows that God can know some nonexistents. Moreover, among these nonexistents are things which were or will be. Of these God has a practical knowledge--namely, a knowledge which is their cause--since ex eius scientia prodeunt secundum eius dis-positionem. Of the purely possible things God has only specu-lative knowledge, and though it can be said that this speculative knowledge views those purely possible things in the potency of God, still it is best to say that such knowledge views the pure-ly possible in the goodness of God, which is the final end of everything. God's goodness, in fact, is communicable in many ways different from those in which it is actually communicated to past, present, and future things. Purely possible nonexistents, therefore, exist in the potency of God as in their active principle or in the goodness of God as in their final cause. Past and future nonexistents exist in God's practical knowledge, which is their cause.

De Veritate, 2, a. 8, resp. et ad 1um.

Clearly the basis of this reasoning is the divine causality. "The cognition of the divine intellect about other things is like the artist's cognition of his products of art, since it is by his knowl-edge that he is the cause of things."

"But God's knowledge is about all things through a cause; for knowing himself, the cause of all things, he knows other things as being his effects. . . There is no difficulty, then, in that he knows even those things which are not."

Ibid.

There is not even an insuperable difficulty against the immutability of God's knowledge of future things. For his knowledge has no succession, no more than has his being; it is eternal knowledge. Now, eternity is related to time as is the proportion of what is indivisible related to the continuous. Whatsoever, therefore, is at any point of time, coexists with the eternal as being present to eternity. True, what is at any given point of time is past or future with respect to another portion of time. But nothing can coexist as being present to eternity unless it coexist with the whole of eternity. Eternity has not the duration of succession. Whatever, then, is done throughout the whole course of time the divine intellect sees as though it were present within that intellect's whole eternity; nevertheless that did not always exist which occurs at a given time. There is left the conclusion that God knows things which are not yet in time.

Cont. Gent. 1. 1, c. 66: Intelligere Dei successionem non habet, sicut nec eius esse. Est igitur totum simul, semper manens, quod de ratione aeternitatis est. Temporis autem duratio successione prioris et posterioris extenditur. Proportio igitur aeternitatis ad totam temporis durationem est sicut proportio indivisibilis ad continuum; non quidem eius indivisibilis quod terminus continui est, quod non adest cuilibet parti continui (huius enim similitudinem habet instans temporis), sed eius indivisibilis quod extra continuum est, et cuilibet tamen parti continui sive puncto in continuo signato coexistit. Nam, quum tempus motum non excedat, aeternitas, quae omnino extra motum est, nihil temporis est. Rursum, quum esse aeterni nunquam deficiat, cuilbet tempori vel instanti temporis praesentialiter adest aeternitas . . . Quidquid igitur in quacumque parte temporis est, coexistit aeterno, quasi praesens eidem, etsi respectu alterius partis temporis sit praeteritum vel futurum. Aeterno autem non potest aliquid praesentialiter coexistere, nisi toti: quia successionis durationem non habet. Quidquid igitur per

*totum temporis decursum agitur, divinus intellectus in
tota sua aeternitate intuetur quasi praesens; nec tamen
quod quadam parte temporis agitur semper fuit existens.
Relinquitur igitur quod eorum quae secundum decursum
temporis nondum sunt Deus notitiam habet.*

St. Thomas then resumes his thought upon the divine knowledge
of nonexistents. God knows nonexistents, though not all nonexistents are related to his knowledge in the same way. The purely
possible nonexistents (quae non sunt, nec erunt, nec fuerunt)
are known by him only in his divine power. His knowledge of
these is called, technically, the knowledge of simple intelligence.
The present, past, and future are known in their causes and in
themselves, by God in his power, with a knowledge called the
knowledge of vision. And we must not think that God knows the
future (quae nondum sunt) only in its causes; he knows the future
in itself, inasmuch as his eternity is present to all time. Yet
it is by his essence that God knows everything, for his essence
is representable by much that is not, was not, and will not be.
Further, his essence is the similitude of the virtue of each cause,
of the virtue according to which effects preexist in their causes.
Last, the essence of God is the exemplary cause of everything.
Thus God knows all nonexistents according to the being which
they have, whether that being be in the power of God, in the
causes of nonexistents, or in nonexistents themselves.

*Ibid. Per has igitur rationes apparet quod Deus non-
entium notitiam habet. Non tamen omnia non entia eam-
dem habent habitudinem ad eius scientiam. Ea enim quae
non-sunt, nec erunt, nec fuerunt, a Deo sciuntur, quasi
eius virtuti possibilia; unde non cognoscit ea ut
existentia aliqualiter in seipsis, sed existentia solum
in divina potentia; quae quidem a quibusdam dicuntur a
Deo cognosci secundum notitiam simplicis intelligentiae.
Ea vero quae sunt praesentia, praeterita vel futura nobis,
cognoscit Deus secundum quod sunt in potentia sua, et in
propriis causis, et in seipsis; et horum cognitio dicitur
notitia visionis. Non enim Deus rerum, quae apud nos
nondum sunt, videt solum esse quod habent in suis causis,
sed etiam illud quod habent in seipsis, in quantum eius
aeternitas est praesens, sua indivisibilitate, omni
tempori. Et tamen omne esse cuiuscumque rei Deus cognoscit
per essentiam suam; nam sua essentia est repraesentabilis
secundum multa quae non sunt, nec erunt, nec fuerunt.
Ipsa etiam est similitudo virtutis cuiuslibet causae,
secundum quam praeexistunt effectus in causis; esse etiam*

cuiuslibet rei, quod habet in seipsa, est ab ea exemplar-
iter deductum. Sic igitur non-entia cognoscit Deus, in
quantum aliquo modo habent esse vel in potentia Dei, vel
in causis suis, vel in seipsis; quod rationi scientiae
non obsistit.

The same answer to the same question (How does God know
nonexistents?) is given in the Summa Theologica.

1a. q. 14, a. 9.

St. Thomas objects to himself: the knowledge of God is the cause
of what he knows; but there is no cause of nonexistents, for non-
being has no cause.

Obj. 3.

He answers: God knows whatsoever is, in whatsoever way it is.
And there is no difficulty in that those things which simply are
not in some sense are. For what simply is actually is; what actually is not is either in the power of God himself or in that of the
creature. Yet some difference in those things which actually are
not must be noted. For some things, though they actually are not,
yet either were or will be. All these things God knows by the knowledge of vision. The reason is that since God's knowledge, which
is his being, is measured by eternity--which existing without succession comprehends all time--the present vision of God stretches
to all time and to everything in whatsoever portion of time, as
being presently subject to that vision. Other things there are which
are in the power of God, or of the creature, and yet they are not,
they will not be, nor were they. With respect to them God is not
said to have the knowledge of vision, but of simple intelligence.
As to the objection--namely, that God's knowledge cannot be the
cause of nonbeing--it must be said that divine knowledge is the
cause of things inasmuch as his will is adjoined to it.

Obj. 3.

Whence it is not necessary that whatsoever God knows should be,
have been, or be. Only those things which he wishes or permits
will be, have been, or are. Thus, once more, it is not in the
knowledge of God that they be, but that they can be.

44

Summa Theologica, 1a, q. 19, a. 9. The objection runs:
scientia Dei est causa scitorum ab ipso. Sed non est
causa non entium, quia non ens non habet causam. Respondeo
. . . Deus scit omnia quaecumque sunt quocumque modo.
Nihil autem prohibet ea quae non sunt simpliciter, aliquo
modo esse. Simpliciter enim sunt quae actu sunt; ea vero
quae non sunt actu, sunt in potentia vel ipsius Dei, vel
creaturae . . . Sed horum quae actu non sunt, est at-
tendenda quaedam diversitas. Quaedam enim licet non sunt
nunc in actu, tamen vel fuerunt, vel erunt; et omnia ista
dicitur Deus scire scientia visionis. Quia cum intelligere
Dei, quod est eius esse, aeternitate mensuretur, quae sine
successione existens totum tempus comprehendit, praesens
intuitus Dei fertur in totum tempus et in omnia quae sunt
in quocumque tempore, sicut in subjecta sibi praesential-
iter. Quaedam vero sunt, quae sunt in potentia Dei vel
creaturae, quae tamen nec sunt nec erunt neque fuerunt;
et respectu horum non dicitur habere scientiam visionis,
sed simplicis intelligentiae . . . Ad tertium dicendum
[the objection above], quod scientia Dei est causa rerum
voluntate adjuncta. Unde non oportet quod quaecumque scit
Deus, sint vel fuerint vel futura sint; sed solum ea quae
vult esse, vel permittere esse. Et iterum non est in scientia
Dei quod illa sint, sed quod esse possint.

From all this it appears that the reason, according to St. Thomas,
why God knows non-entia, is the divine causality. Such is his formal
statement in the De Veritate and the Contra Gentiles.

Vid. supra p. 40.

Vid. supra p. 40.

Such too is the presupposition of the arguments presented by him in
the Contra Gentiles and the Summa Theologica.

Vid. supra pp. 40 ff.

Further, the divine knowledge of non-entia is the knowledge either of
vision or of simple intelligence. Vision such knowledge is called when
and because it is of the past, present, and future as being totally
present (as is present the object of any, even human, vision) to the
eternity of God's knowledge. Simple intelligence it is called when and
because it is purely of what can be (as when, for example, we simply
understand what a circle is without seeing any instance of it). Moreover, the knowledge of God which is the cause of things lies in his
knowledge of what can be together with his knowledge of what--

45

because God wills it--will be. Not everything that God knows--
or is--will be; only that which he wills to be will be, though many
things are (in the sense of being able to be) which are not (in the
sense of existing now or in the future).

There is enough in the above exposition to elaborate the theory
of St. Thomas upon the divine knowledge of contingent future
events. But he has gone to this trouble for us. It is his answer to
the third question, proposed above under the general problem of
the relations between divine prescience and human acts, How
does God know contingent future events?

The reason for a separate treatment of this question is this:
a contingent event is in its cause in such wise that, as far as its
cause is concerned, it can be and it can not be; yet the divine
knowledge even of the contingent is infallible; how, then, can contingency be reconciled with the infallibility of divine prescience?

St. Thomas' answer to the problem amounts to this: the reason
why the infallibility of divine prescience does not hinder the contingency of future events lies in the fact that contingent futures,
since they simultaneously present in the eternity of God, are seen
by him as though actually realized.

Summa Theologica, 1a. q. 14, a. 13. Respondeo dicendum:
. . . quod Deus contingentia futura cognoscit . . . contingens
aliquod dupliciter potest considerari: uno modo in seipso,
secundum quod iam in actu est; et sic non consideratur ut
futurum, sed ut praesens, neque ut ad utrumlibet contingens,
sed ut determinatum ad unum; et propter hoc sic infallibiliter
subdi potest certae cognitioni, utpote sensui visus, sicut
cum video Socratem sedere. Alio modo potest considerari con-
tingens ut est in sua causa; et sic consideratur ut futurum,
et ut contingens nondum determinatum ad unum, quia causa con-
tingens se habet ad opposita; et sic contingens non subditur
per certitudinem alicui cognitioni. Unde quicumque cognoscit
effectum contingentem in causa sua tantum, non habet de eo
nisi conjecturalem cognitionem. Deus autem cognoscit omnia
contingentia non solum prout sunt in suis causis, sed etiam
prout unumquodque est actu in seipso. Et licet contingentia
fiant in actu successive, non tamen Deus successive cognoscit
contingentia, prout sunt in suo esse, sicut nos, sed simul;
quia eius cognitio mensuratur aeternitate, sicut et suum
esse; aeternitas autem tota simul existens ambit totum
tempus . . . Unde omnia quae sunt in tempore, sunt Deo ab
aeterno praesentia, non solum ea ratione quia habet rationes
rerum apud se praesentes, ut quidem dicunt, sed quia eius
intuitus fertur ab aeterno supra omnia, prout sunt in sua
praesentialitate. Unde manifestum est quod contingentia in-
fallibiliter a Deo cognoscuntur, in quantum subduntur divino

46

*conspectui secundum suam praesentialitatem, et sunt future
contingentia, suis causis comparata.*

The difficulty on this point lies, of course, in our thinking of the
divine knowledge after the fashion of our own.

*The difficulty in the field of causality which the divine
prescience occasions will be touched later. See pp. 48 ff.*

We think of future things as future; God knows them as they are
rather than as they will be. With him there is no future; all is
present.

*De Veritate, q. 2, a. 12. Quidem enim de divina scientia
judicare volentes ad modum scientiae nostrae, dixerunt
quod Deus futura contingentia non cognoscit. Sed hoc non
potest esse; quia secundum hoc non haberet providentiam
de rebus humanis, quae contingenter eveniunt. Et ideo
alii dixerunt, quod Deus omnium futurorum scientiam
habet; sed cuncta ex necessitate eveniunt, alias scientia
Dei falleretur de eis. Sed hoc esse etiam non potest; quia
secundum hoc periret liberum arbitrium. . . Difficultas
autem in hoc accidit, eo quod divinam cognitionem signi-
ficare non possumus nisi per modum nostrae cognitionis con-
significando differentias: si enim significaretur ut est
Dei scientia, magis dici deberet quod Deus scit hoc esse,
quam quod sciat futura, quia sibi numquam sunt futura, sed
semper praesentia . . .*

As to the divine, infallible prescience of those contingent future
events emanating from free causes, St. Thomas' answer is the
same. God knows free future events cum ipse sit universale essendi principium.

*Contra Gent., 1. 1, c. 68. Deinde oportet ostendere quod
Deus cogitationes mentium et voluntates cordium cognoscat
in virtute causae, quum ipse sit universale principium
essendi. Omne enim . . . cognoscitur a Deo, in quantum
suam essentiam cognoscit . . . Sic Deus cognoscendo suam
essentiam alia cognoscit, sicut per cognitionem causae
cognoscuntur effectus. Omnia Deus cognoscit, suam essentiam cognoscendo, ad quae sua causalitas extenditur.
Extenditur autem ad operationes intellectus et voluntatis;
nam, quum quaelibet res operetur per suam formam . . .
oportet fontale principium, a quo est etiam omnis forma,
omnis operationis principium esse; quum effectus causarum*

47

secundarum in causas primas principalius reducantur.
Cognoscit igitur Deus cogitationes et affectiones
mentis.

Nor does the freedom of human acts make it impossible that God
know those acts in their divine cause.

> The dominion which the will has over its acts, in that it is
> within its power to will or not to will, excludes the deter-
> mination of its power to one thing and the violence of an ex-
> ternally acting cause; but it does not exclude the influence of
> a superior cause from which the will has being and operation;
> thus there remains causality in the first cause, which is God,
> with respect to the movements of the will, so that God, thus
> knowing himself, can know such movements.

> *Cont. Gent., 1. 1, c. 68. Dominium autem quod habet*
> *voluntas supra suos actus, per quod in eius est potestate*
> *velle vel non velle, excludit determinationem virtutis*
> *ad unum et violentiam causae exterius agentis; non autem*
> *excludit influentiam superioris causae, a qua est ei esse*
> *et operari. Et sic remanet causalitas in causa prima, quae*
> *Deus est, respectu motuum voluntatis, ut sic Deus, seipsum*
> *cognoscendo, huismodi cognoscere possit.*

More texts to the same effect--namely, that it is in the divine
causality that God sees the future free acts of men--might easily
be adduced.

> *E.g., Summa Theol., 1a q. 57, a. 4: Solus Deus . . . af-*
> *fectiones voluntatum cognoscere.potest. Cuius ratio est,*
> *quia voluntas . . . soli Deo subjacet, et ipse solus in*
> *eam operari potest . . .; De Veritate, q. 8, a. 13:*
> *motus voluntatis . . . non potest cognosci in aliquibus*
> *similitudinibus rerum naturalium, sed solum in essentia*
> *divina quae in voluntatem [humanam] imprimit; De Malo,*
> *q. 16: cum voluntas interius non possit ab alio nisi a*
> *Deo moveri . . . non potest cognosci . . . nisi ab ipso*
> *Deo . . .*

But it seems clear enough that according to St. Thomas the reason
why God knows all things created, including free acts, is this: he
is the cause of all things.

The second point in St. Thomas Aquinas' theory touching the
relations between choice and its antecedents deals with the relation

48

between divine causality and choice. That the causality in a
question is efficient is clear.

Summa Theol., 1a q. 14, a. 5: *eo quod ipsa (virtus divina)
est causa prima effective omnium entium, necesse est quod
Deus alia a se cognoscat. Cf. De Veritate, 2, a. 3, where
God is called the immateriale principium activum; Cont.
Gent., 1. 1 c. 49, where he is spoken of as the causa es-
sendi aliis.*

The problem is to determine the constituents of the divine causality. And the first question which presents itself, What constitutes
the divine causality in itself? is answered, The divine intellect
and will. The role of each is thus described.

An intelligible form does not designate a principle of action
according as the form is merely in the intelligent agent, unless there be adjoined to the form an inclination to the effect.
This inclination is through the will. For, since an intelligible
form is related to opposites--since the knowledge of opposites
is the same--it would not produce a determinate effect unless
it were determined to one effect through appetite . . . Whence,
the knowledge of God must be the cause of things according as
it has in conjunction with it his will. This is why the knowledge
of God which is the cause of things is used to be named the
knowledge of approbation.

Summa Theol., 1a q. 14, a. 8, resp. ad fin. [I shall quote
the whole passage]: scientia Dei est causa rerum. Sic
enim scientia Dei se habet ad omnes res creatas, sicut
scientia artificis se habet ad artificiata. Scientia autem
artificis est causa artificiatorum, eo quod artifex operatur
per suum intellectum. Unde oportet quod forma intellectus
sit principium operationis, sicut calor est principium
calefactionis. Sed considerandum est quod forma naturalis,
in quantum est forma movens in eo cui dat esse, non
nominat principium actionis, sed secundum quod habet in-
clinationem ad effectum; et similiter forma intelligibilis
non nominat principium actionis secundum quod est tantum in
intelligente, nisi adjungatur ei inclinatio ad effectum;
quae est voluntas. Cum enim forma intelligibilis ad opposita
se habet, cum sit eadem scientia oppositorum, non produceret
determinatum effectum, nisi determinaretur ad unum per appetitum, ut dicitur in IX Metaph., text 10. Manifestum est
autem quod Deus per intellectum suum causat res, cum suum
esse sit suum intelligere; unde necesse est quod sua scientia

*sit causa rerum, secundum quod habet voluntatem conjunctam.
Unde scientia Dei, secundum quod est causa rerum, con-
suevit nominari scientia approbationis. Cf. ad 1um . . .
scientiae non competit ratio causalitatis, nisi adjuncta
voluntate.*

Knowledge, in fact, is a directive cause, for by it is conceived
the form of the work; the will is the commanding cause, because
the form--as being merely in the intellect--is not determined to be
in or not to be in effect except through the will.

*Summa Theol., 1a q. 19, a. 4, ad 4um: unius et eiusdem
effectus etiam in nobis est causa scientia ut dirigens,
quia concipitur forma operis; et voluntas ut imperans;
quia forma ut est in intellectu tantum, non determinatur
ad hoc quod sit vel non sit in effectu, nisi per voluntatem. Unde intellectus speculativus nihil dicit de
operando. Sed potentia est causa ut exequens, quia
nominat immediatum principium operationis. Sed haec omnia
in Deo unum sunt. Cf. De Veritate, q. 5, a. 6.*

Divine causality in itself is thus, according to St. Thomas, con-
stituted by two factors: the intellect of God, which furnishes the
idea of an effect; the will of God, which commands and determines the realization of that idea. The comparison, often made
by St. Thomas, between the causality of an artist and the causality of God is here in point. Simply to think what he will do will
not get done for him an artist's work. He must also, besides conceiving his work, will to do it.

We come now to the central and delicate point in the theory of
St. Thomas concerning the relation between divine causality and
human choice. The problem: how is the instrument (natural concourse or, if given, grace) of that causality (the divine intellect
and will) related to the contingency of second causes and in
particular to choice?

The function of the instrument of divine causality is described
by the general terms of movere, motio. The nature of this motio
with regard to its effect, first, on all second causes can be ascertained from the De Potentia.

q. 3, a. 7.

In this article St. Thomas put himself the following objections. 1) In whatsoever operation of the creature God operates,
God and nature will operate either by one and the same operation

or by different operations. But not by one and the same operation, for the unity of operation attests the unity of a nature; for example, since in Christ there are two natures, there are also two operations. Now the nature of a creature and the nature of God are not one. Nor, similarly, can there be diverse operations for diverse operations cannot terminate in the same effect since notions and operations are distinguished by their terms. Therefore in no way is it possible that God work in nature.

Obj. 3.

2) If God operates in a nature which operates, he must by his operation contribute something to a natural thing, for an agent by acting actually does something. Either, therefore, that which God does suffices that nature operate of itself, or it does not suffice. If God's action suffices, since he also gave a natural virtue to nature, in the same way it can be said that the natural virtue too was enough for action. Nor will it be necessary that God, after having bestowed virtue upon nature, go on to work something more in nature's operation. But if the action of God is not sufficient, he must again do something else there; and if that is not enough, something else again, and so on in <u>infinitum</u>. This is impossible. Therefore we must take our stand on the first position and say that natural virtue suffices for natural action without any further operation of God therein.

Obj. 7. The two objections, 3 and 7, are as follows:
3) . . . si Deus operatur in qualibet operatione naturae, aut una et eadem operatione operatur Deus, et natura, aut diversis. Sed non una et eadem: unitas enim operationis attestatur unitati naturae; unde quia in Christo sunt duae naturae, sunt etiam ibi duae operationes: creaturae autem et Dei constat non esse unam naturam. Similiter nec est possibile quod sint operationes diversae; nam diversae operationes non videntur ad idem factum terminari; cum motus et operationes penes terminos distinguantur. Ergo nulla modo est possibile quod Deus in natura operetur. 7) . . . Si Deus in natura operante operatur, oportet, quod operando aliquid rei naturali tribuat; nam agens, agendo, aliquid actu facit. Aut ergo illud sufficit ad hoc quod natura possit per se operari, aut non. Si sufficit, cum etiam virtutem naturalem Deus naturae tribuerit, eadem ratione, potest dici quod et virtus naturalis sufficiebat ad agendum: nec oportebit quod Deus, postquam virtutem naturae contulit, ulterius ad eius operationem aliquid operetur. Si

51

*autem non sufficit, oportet quod ibi aliquid aliud iterum
faciat; et si illud non sufficit, iterum aliud, et sic in
infinitum: quod est impossibile. Nam unus effectus non potes
dependere ab actionibus infinitis: quia cum infinita non sit
pertransire, numquam compleretur. Ergo standum est in primo,
discendo quod virtus naturalis sufficit ad actionem naturale
sine hoc quod Deus in ea ulterius operetur. Cf. Summa Theol.
1a q. 105, a. 5.*

To the first of these objections St. Thomas answers

> it must be said that in the operation by which God operates by
> moving nature, nature does not operate: but the very operation
> of nature is also the operation of the divine virtue, just as the
> operation of an instrument is through the virtue of the principle
> agent. Nor is there any hindrance in that nature and God operate
> in the same effect, by reason of the order there is between God
> and nature.

Ad 3um.

Second,

> the natural virtue which was given to natural things in their
> creation is in them as a sort of form having a being fixed and
> firm in nature. But that which is done by God in a natural thing,
> by which it actually acts, is as a mere intention, having a sort
> of incomplete being, as colors are in the air and the virtue of
> art in the instrument of the artist. Just as, then, its edge could
> have been given to the axe so as to be in it a permanent form--
> but the power of acting as an instrument of art (vis artis) could
> not have been given it as a sort of permanent form unless it had
> intellect--so its own virtue could have been conferred on a
> natural thing as a form remaining in itself, but not the power
> by which, as the instrument of the first cause, it acts so as to
> produce being--unless it were given it to be the universal prin-
> ciple of being; nor, again, could a natural virtue have been
> endowed so as to move itself or conserve itself in being. Whence,
> as it is clear that an instrument of art could not have conferred
> on it that it operate without the motion of the artist, so a natural
> instrument could not have conferred on it that it operate without
> the divine operation.

*Ad 7um. 1. c. Ad tertium dicendum, quod in operatione qua
Deus operatur movendo naturam, non operatur natura; sed
ipsa naturae operatio est etiam operatio virtutis divinae;
sicut operatio instrumenti est per virtutem agentis principalis. Nec impeditur quin natura et Deus ad idem
operentur, propter ordinem qui est inter Deum et naturam
. . . Ad septimum dicendum, quod virtus naturalis quae
est rebus naturalibus in sua institutione collata, inest
eis ut quaedam forma habens esse ratum et firmum in natura.
Sed id quod a Deo fit in re naturali, quo actualiter agat,
est ut intentio sola, habens esse quoddam incompletum, per
modum quo colores sunt in aere, et virtus artis in instrumento artificis. Sicut ergo securi per artem dari potuit
acumen, ut esset forma in ea permanens, non autem dari ei
potuit quod vis artis esset in ea quasi quaedam forma
permanens, nisi haberet intellectum; ita rei naturali potuit
conferri virtus propria, ut forma in ipsa permanens, non
autem vis qua agit ad esse ut instrumentum primae causae;
nisi daretur ei quod esset universale principium essendi;
nec iterum virtuti naturali conferri potuit ut moveret seipsam, nec ut conservaret se in esse: unde sicut patet quod
instrumento artificis conferri non potuit quod operaretur
absque [motu?] artis; ita rei naturali conferri non potuit
quod operaretur absque operatione divina.*

The reasoning in these two answers to the two objections which
St. Thomas puts to himself is based on the <u>respondeo</u>.

It must simply be admitted that God operates in the operations
of nature and the will . . . But it must not be so understood
that God operates in every natural thing as though the natural
things did nothing . . . How this can be, in a way, understood,
must be shown . . . Another thing can be called the cause of
the action of something in many senses . . . because 1) it
contributes to it the virtue of acting . . . and keeps its virtue
in being . . . In this way can God be called the cause of action
inasmuch as he causes and conserves a natural virtue in being
. . . But, 2) since nothing moves or acts through itself, except it be moving and not moved . . . one thing is said to be
the cause of another thing's action inasmuch as it moves it to
act; this is not to be understood as a bestowal or conservation
of active power but as an application of the power to act . . .
It is thus, then, that God is the cause of the action of anything:
inasmuch as he gives the virtue to act, inasmuch as he conserves it, and inasmuch as it is by his virtue that every other

virtue acts. And when we add to this that God is his own virtue, and that he is within everything, not as a part of its essence but as holding a thing in being, it will follow that he immediately operates in whatsoever operates, without exclusion of the operations of the will and nature.

1. c.: [I shall quote the passage more fully than it has been translated.] Respondeo dicendum, quod simpliciter concedendum est Deum operari in natura et voluntate operantibus. Sed quidam hoc non intelligentes in errorem inciderunt: attribuentes Deo hoc modo omnem naturae operationem quod res penitus naturalis nihil ageret per virtutem propriam . . . Non ergo sic est intelligendum quod Deus in omni re naturali operetur, quasi res naturalis nihil operetur; sed quia in ipsa natura vel voluntate operante Deus operatur: quod quidem qualiter intelligi possit, ostendendum est. Sciendum namque est, quod actionis alicuius rei res alia potest dici causa multipliciter. Uno modo quia tribuit ei virtutem operandi . . . et hoc modo Deus agit omnes actiones naturae . . . non solum sicut generans virtutem tribuit gravi et levi, et eam ulterius non conservat, sed sicut continue tenens virtutem in esse . . . Ut sic possit dici Deus causa actionis inquantum causat et conservat naturalem in esse . . . Sed quia nulla res per seipsam movet vel agit nisi sit movens non motum; tertio modo [I have called this the second way] dicitur una res esse causa actionis alterius inquantum movet eam ad agendum; in quo non intelligitur collatio aut conservatio virtutis activae, sed applicatio virtutis ad agendum; sicut homo est causa incisionis cultelli ex hoc ipso quod applicat acumen cultelli ad incidendum movendo ipsum . . . Sic ergo Deus est causa actionis cuiuslibet inquantum dat virtutem agendi, et inquantum conservat eam, et in quantum applicat actioni, et in quantum eius virtute omnis alia virtus agit. Et cum conjunxerimus his, quod Deus sit sua virtus, et quod sit intra rem quamlibet non sicut pars essentiae, sed sicut tenens rem in esse, sequetur quod ipse in quolibet operante immediate operetur, non exclusa operatione voluntatis et naturae.

The importance of the passages quoted for the understanding of the theory of St. Thomas can scarcely be overestimated. This should appear from two sorts of commentaries which may be made --one textual, one general. From the text it would seem to be clear that the <u>motus</u>, the instrument of divine causality, is something

made by God in the creature by which it actually acts--id quod a
Deo fit in re naturali quo actualiter agat--

Ad 7um.

like the movement impressed by the artist upon his instrument.
Clearly, too, this motus is not the operation of the creature:
"in the operation by which God operates by moving nature, nature
does not operate."

Ad 3um.

Nor is this motus the bestowal or conservation of the nature of
the second cause. It is the applicatio virtutis ad agendum.

Resp. in corp.

That is, God, applicanda virtute ad agendum, first actualizes
creaturely activity by, second, making the creature actually to
act. (The first and second indicate ontological, not temporal,
phases of creaturely activity.) To put it in another way: an act is
specified (that is, it is of this or that kind) and individualized
(that is, it is this or that act.) The specific determination of an
act comes from the specific nature of the agent moved by God--
movet unumquodque secundum modum uniuscuiusque. The in-
dividual determination of activity comes from the divine applicatio
ad agendum, for this applicatio is id quod a Deo fit in re naturali
quo actualiter agat. In short, creatures really act because God
makes their acts to exist without thereby hindering those acts
from being their acts.

*1. c., resp. in corp. In qualibet autem re naturali
invenimus quod est ens, et quod est res naturalis, et
quod est talis vel talis naturae. Quorum primum est commune omnibus entibus; secundum omnibus rebus naturalibus;
tertium in una specie; et quartum, si addamus accidentia,
est proprium huic individuo. Hoc ergo individuum agendo
non potest constituere aliud in simili specie nisi prout
est instrumentum illius causae, quae respicit totam
speciem et ulterius totum esse naturae inferioris. Et
propter hoc nihil agit ad speciem in istis inferioribus
nisi per virtutem corporis coelestis, nec aliquid agit
ad esse nisi per virtutem Dei. Ipsum enim esse est com-
munissimus effectus primus et intimior omnibus aliis effectibus; et ideo soli Deo competit secundum virtutem*

propriam talis effectus . . . Si [sic?] ergo Deus est causa omnis actionis, prout quodlibet agens est instrumentum divinae virtutis ad agendum. Sic ergo si consideremus supposita agentia, quodlibet agens particulare est immediatum ad suum effectum. Si autem consideremus virtutem qua fit actio, sic virtus superioris causae erit immediatior effectui quam virtus inferioris . . . Sic ergo oportet virtutem divinam adesse cuilibet rei agenti . . .

The second comment, a general one, is this. If St. Thomas feels able to maintain at once the causality of creatures and the divine causality of their causality (in operatione qua Deus operatur movendo naturam, non operatur natura; sed ipsa natura operatio est etiam operatio virtutis divinae), this is because for him there are natures, real principles of operation. Such is his presupposition throughout the whole article of the De Potentia.

7 of q. 3.

Besides the response just quoted (ad 3um), the following may be noted: tam Deus quam natura immediate operatur;

Ad 4um.

de ratione virtutis inferioris est quod sit aliquo modo operationis principium in suo ordine, i.e., ut agat ut instrumentum superioris virtutis, etc.

Ad 5um.

The point is that the causality of creatures is real because they are real principles of operation, although the actualization of creaturely causality comes from God. And as for the natural order of activity, so, mutatis mutandis, for the supernatural. St. Thomas knew at least as well as Luther that man without grace cannot do a supernatural act. "Can anyone without grace merit eternal life?" "Can man merit for himself the first grace?" "Can he merit it for another?" "Can he merit reparation after a fall?" "Perserverance?"

Summa Theol., 1a 2ae, q. 114, aa. 2, 5, 6, 7, 9.

To all these questions the answer is always No. But to the question
"Can man merit God?" the answer is Yes. And the reason is <u>prout</u>
<u>id</u> <u>tanquam</u> <u>mercedem</u> <u>consequitur</u> <u>homo</u> <u>per</u> <u>suam</u> <u>operationem</u>,
<u>ad</u> <u>quod</u> <u>ei</u> <u>Deus</u> <u>operandi</u> <u>virtutem</u> <u>deputavit</u>.

1. c., a. 1.

The presupposition of all these positions is that just as beneath
the divine causality of natural activity there are natures, so
beneath the divine causality of supernatural activity there are
natures--natures deprived, it is true, of grace, but not depraved.

> <u>id</u> <u>homo</u> <u>consequatur</u> <u>a</u> <u>Deo</u> <u>per</u> <u>suam</u> <u>operationem</u>, <u>quasi</u>
> <u>mercedem</u>, <u>ad</u> <u>quod</u> <u>Deus</u> <u>ei</u> <u>virtutem</u> <u>operandi</u> <u>deputavit</u>; sicut
> <u>enim</u> <u>naturales</u> <u>hoc</u> <u>consequuntur</u> <u>per</u> <u>proprios</u> <u>motus</u> <u>et</u> <u>opera</u>-
> <u>tiones</u>, <u>ad</u> <u>quod</u> <u>a</u> <u>Deo</u> <u>sunt</u> <u>ordinatae</u>: <u>differenter</u> <u>tamen</u>; <u>quia</u>
> <u>creatura</u> <u>rationalis</u> <u>seipsam</u> <u>movet</u> <u>ad</u> <u>agendum</u> <u>per</u> <u>liberum</u>
> <u>arbitrium</u>. . .

*1. c., a. 1, resp. ad fin., and cf. . . . homo, in quantum
propria voluntate facit illud quod debet, meretur . . . ad 1um.
Cf. Et. Gilson, Moyen Age et Naturalisme in Archives d'histoire
doctrinale et litteraire du Moyen Age, T. VII, Vrin, 1933,
pp. 16, 17.*

In sum, although man cannot either in the natural or supernatural
order act without God, yet with God it is truly man who acts <u>per</u>
<u>virtutem</u> <u>Dei</u>.

And this holds true, as the last text indicated, also of free
choice. The nature of the <u>motio</u>, or <u>applicatio</u>, of free second
causes is such that, thanks to it, these causes do also move
themselves. "And just as from natural causes God, by moving
them, does not take away from them their natural activity; so
by moving voluntary causes he does not take away from them
their voluntary activity. Rather, it is this which he makes in
them. For he operates in each according to its property."

*<u>Summa</u> <u>Theol</u>., 1a q. 83, a. 1: Et sicut naturalibus causis,
movendo eas, non aufert [Deus] quin earum actus sint
naturales; ita, movendo causas voluntarias, non aufert
quin actiones earum sint voluntariae, sed potius hoc in
eis facit: operatur enim in unoquoque secundum eius pro-
prietatem. Cf. <u>Summa</u> <u>Theol</u>., 1a q. 105, a. 4: Per hoc quod
[voluntas] movetur ab alio, non excluditur quin moveatur ex se.*

St. Thomas sees no contradiction in the <u>moveri</u> <u>ab</u> <u>alio</u> and <u>moveri</u> <u>ex se</u>. "To move voluntarily is to move of oneself, i.e., from an intrinsic principle; but that intrinsic principle can be from other extrinsic principle; and so, to move oneself is not repugnant to being moved by another."

> *<u>Summa</u> <u>Theol</u>., 1a q. 105, a. 4, ad 2um: moveri voluntarie est moveri ex se, i.e., a principio intrinseco; sed illud principium intrinsecum potest esse ab alio principio extrinseco; et sic moveri ex se non repugnat ei quod movetur ab alio.*

But the question remains, How are free causes moved? In the will St. Thomas distinguishes two kinds of acts: the <u>velle</u> <u>bonum</u> <u>universale</u> and the <u>velle</u> <u>hoc</u> <u>vel</u> <u>illud</u> <u>bonum</u>. That <u>God</u> moves the will to the desire of the universal good is beyond question: <u>Deus</u> <u>movet</u> <u>voluntatem</u> <u>hominis</u>, <u>sicut</u> <u>universalis</u> <u>motor</u>, <u>ad</u> <u>universale</u> <u>objectum</u> <u>voluntatis</u>, <u>quod</u> est <u>bonum</u>; <u>et</u> <u>sine</u> <u>hac</u> <u>universali</u> <u>motione</u> <u>homo</u> <u>non</u> <u>potest</u> <u>aliquid</u> <u>velle</u>.

> *<u>Summa</u> <u>Theol</u>., 1a 2ae q. 9, a. 6, ad 3um.*

Does God also move the will to this or that act?

The eighty-ninth chapter of the third book <u>Contra</u> Gentiles is written expressly against those who denied that God makes us to wish this or that.

> *1. c.: Quidam vero, non intelligentes qualiter motum voluntatis Deus in nobis causare possit absque praejudicio libertatis voluntatis, conati sunt has auctoritates male exponere, ut sc., dicerent quod Deus causat in nobis velle et perficere in quantum dat nobis virtutem agendi, non autem sic quod faciat nos velle hoc vel illud, sicut Origenes exponit (περι αρχ ων 1.111, c. 1, P.G., 11; 270) . . . Unde [ex Isa. XXVI, 12: <u>omnia</u> <u>opera</u> <u>nostra</u> <u>operatus</u> <u>es</u> <u>nobis</u>, <u>Domine</u>] non solum virtutem volendi a Deo habemus, sed etiam operationem. Praeterea, Hoc ipsum quod Salomon dicit: <u>quocumque</u> <u>voluerit</u>, <u>inclinavit</u> <u>illud</u> (Prov. XXI, 1.) ostendit non solum divinam causalitatem ad potentiam voluntatis extendi, sed etiam ad actum ipsius . . . homo non potest virtute voluntatis sibi data uti, nisi in quantum agit in virtute Dei. Illud autem in cuius virtute agens agit est causa, non solum virtutis, sed etiam actus . . . Deus igitur est causa nobis, non solum voluntati sed etiam volendi.*

And if we seek a test case illustrative of the firmness with which
St. Thomas held to his doctrine that God moves the will to this or
that act, there is the instance of sin. "Since the act of sin is a
kind of movement of free choice, it must be said that the act of
sin, in so far as it is an act, is from God."

*De Malo, q. 3, q. 2, resp.: cum actus peccati sit quidam
motus liberi arbitrii, necesse est dicere quod actus
peccati, inquantum est actus, sit a Deo. Cf. Summa Theol.,
1a 2ae q. 79, a. 2.*

It is evident, then, that St. Thomas believes free acts to proceed
from the first mover.

As to how the free act so proceeds, it is clear that the will,
acting freely, moves itself. "The will, by the fact that it wills the
end, moves itself to will what leads to the end."

*Summa Theol., 1a 2ae q. 9, a. 3: voluntas per hoc quod
vult finem movet seipsam ad volendum ea quae sunt ad
finem.*

God's part in this will movement is thus described: "the will is
said to have the dominion of its act, not by the exclusion of the
first cause, but because the first cause does not so act in the will
that it, of necessity, determines the will ad unum as it does determine nature; and therefore the determination of the act is left
in the power of reason and the will."

*De Potentia, q. 3, a. 7, ad 13um: voluntas dicitur habere
dominium sui actus, non per exclusionem causae primae, sed
quia causa prima non ita agit in voluntate ut eam de necessitate ad unum determinet, sicut determinat naturam; et ideo
determinatio actus relinquitur in potestate rationis et
voluntatis.*

The following text too bears upon the same point. "Because the will
is an active principle not determined ad unum, but indifferent to
many things, God so moves it that he does not of necessity determine it ad unum; but its motion remains contingent and not
necessary, except in those ends to which it moves naturally."

*Summa Theol., 1a 2ae q. 10, a. 4, resp.: quia igitur voluntas
est activum principium non determinatum ad unum, sed indifferenter se habens ad multa; sic Deus ipsam movet, quod
non ex necessitate ad unum determinat, sed remanet motus*

eius contingens, et non necessarius, nisi in his ad quae
naturaliter movetur.

Again,

> God moves the will of man, as the universal mover, to the
> universal object of the will, which is the good: and without
> this universal motion a man cannot will anything. But man,
> through reason, determines himself to will this or that, which
> is a true or apparent good. Yet sometimes God specially moves
> some to will something which is good, determinately; as with
> those whom he moves by grace.

> *Summa Theol., 1a 2ae q. 9, a. 6, ad 3um: Deus movet vol-*
> *untatem hominis, sicut universalis motor, ad universale*
> *objectum voluntatis, quod est bonum; et sine hac universali*
> *motione homo non potest aliquid velle; sed homo per rationem*
> *determinat se ad volendum hoc vel illud quod est vere bonum,*
> *vel apparens bonum. Sed tamen interdum specialiter Deus*
> *movet aliquod ad aliquid determinate volendum quod est*
> *bonum, sicut in his quos movet per gratiam . . . Cf. In 2*
> *Sent., D. 39, q. 1: Ipsa potentia voluntatis, quantum in*
> *se est, indifferens est ad plura, sed quod determinate*
> *exeat in hunc actum vel in illum, non est ei ab alio*
> *determinante, sed ab ipsa voluntate.*

St. Thomas' answer, then, to the problem of how the divine
causality effects the free act may be summarized in the following
points. First, God <u>does</u> cause the act. Second, God's causality
determines the will to desire the good in general. Third, man,
through his reason, determines himself to will this or that.

> *On the first point see Contra Gent. 3, 89, supra p. 58,*
> *n. 3. On the second point see 1a 2ae q. 9, a. 6, ad 3um,*
> *supra pp. 58; 60, n. 1. On the third point see 1a 2ae*
> *q. 9. a. 6, ad 3um, supra p. 60, n. 1.*

The second and third points would seem to be an explanation of
the first: man, moved by God to will the good in general, determines himself to this or that good (<u>homo per rationem</u>
<u>determinat se ad volendum hoc vel illud</u> . . . <u>bonum</u>), and thus
it is that God moves a man to choose this or that good.

That the statements of St. Thomas are variously interpreted
is simply a matter of fact. This much is clear: the motion by God

of natural agents is not their motion--"in the operation by which God operates by moving nature, nature does not operate" (vid. p. 53, n.)--yet the "very operation of nature is also the operation of the divine virtue" (ibid.). Further, the motion by God of a natural thing is "that by which it actually acts" (ibid.). As for the application of these notions to the actions of free agents, it is also clear that they are moved by God to the good in general (velle bonum universale) naturally, and to the good in particular (velle hoc vel illud bonum), not as nature is determined (non sicut determinat naturam [vid. p. 59, n. 3]), but so as to have in themselves the power of determining their act--et ideo determinatio actus relinquitur in potestate rationis et voluntatis (ibid.).

Cf. "man, through reason, determines himself to will this or that," Summa Theol., 1a 2ae q. 9, a. 6, ad 3um.

The minimal valid interpretation of the theory would seem to be this. Just as God is the real cause of real natural causes, so (that is, just as truly) is he the real cause of free causes: "sicut naturalibus causis, movendo eas, non aufert quin actus earum sint naturales; ita, movendo causas voluntarias, non aufert quin actiones earum sint voluntariae, sed potius hoc in eis facit."

Summa Theol., 1a q. 83, a. 1.

It is an assertion, in either case, of the reality of two causalities: the divine on the one hand, and on the other the human or natural. The difficult and the different interpretations arise when we try to determine what the influence is under which the will passes from the velle bonum to the velle hoc bonum. Is the expression Deus non ita agit in voluntate ut eam de necessitate ad unum determinet, sicut determinat naturam.

De Potentia q. 3, a. 7, ad 13um, vid. p. 59, n. 3.

to be understood thus: God determines the will ad unum, though not as he does determine nature, that is, by necessity? Or thus: God, since he does not determine the will ad unum as he does determine nature, does not determine the will at all? To put it in another way, is only a natural determination ad unum necessitating? Or is every determination ad unum natural and therefore necessitating? At any rate I have stated what seems to me to be the least one cay say: God really causes the real causality of creatures, whether they be natural or free.

This leads us to St. Thomas' answer to the heart of the present problem. Thus far we have examined his theory of the nature of the relation between divine prescience and causality with the free, human act. There remains his reconciliation between divine causality and the liberty of choice.

And first as to the causality of God's prescience, scientia Dei est causa rerum. In answer to this objection--"from a necessary cause proceeds a necessary effect"--

Summa Theol., *1a q. 14, a. 23, 1 et ad 1um.*

St. Thomas answers: "though the supreme cause be necessary, nevertheless an effect can be contingent by reason of a proximate cause . . . in like manner the things known by God are contingent by reason of proximate causes, though the knowledge of God, which is the first cause, is necessary." The same doctrine is found in the Contra Gentiles:

> if therefore the proximate cause be contingent, its effect must be contingent, even though the remote cause be necessary . . . And the knowledge of God, though it is the cause of things known by it, is nevertheless their remote cause. Hence contingency is not repugnant to the necessity of what is known, since it is contingent that there be immediate contingent causes.

> *Contra Gentiles, 1, 67: Effectus non potest esse necessarius cuius causa est contingens. Contingit autem effectum esse, remota causa, Effectus autem ultimi causa est et proxima et remota. Si igitur proxima fuerit contingens, eius effectum contingentem oportet esse, etiam si causa remota necessaria sit; . . . Scientia autem Dei, etsi sit causa rerum scitarum per ipsam, est tamen causa remota earum. Igitur necessitati scitorum contingentia non repugnat, quum contingat causas intermedias contingentes esse. Cf. De Veritate, q. 2, a. 14, ad 5um.*

But the knowledge of God is the cause of things, adjuncta voluntate. And to reconcile this with human liberty is the pith of the problem. The reconciliation is this: "the efficacy of the divine will demands that not only that be which God wishes, but also that it be in the way God wishes it to be . . . Hence the efficacy of the divine will does not destroy contingency."

Contra Gent., 1. 85: *Vult enim Deus omnia quae requiruntur ad rem quam vult . . . Sed aliquibus rebus, secundum modum naturae, competit quod sint contingentes, non necessariae. Igitur vult aliquas res esse contingentes. Efficacia autem divinae voluntatis exigit ut non solum sit quod Deus vult, sed etiam ut hoc modo sit sicut Deus vult esse illud . . . Igitur efficacia divinae voluntatis contingentiam non tollit.*

Two more formulae bring out the same principle: "The divine will is the strongest agent. Hence its effect must in all ways be as-similated to it, so that not only is that done which God wishes . . . but it is done in the manner God wishes it to be done, neces-sarily or contingently." "From the very fact that nothing resists the will of God, it follows that not only are done the things which God wishes done, but that those things are done contingently or neces-sarily which he so wishes done."

De Veritate, q. 23, a. 5, resp. ad fin.; Summa Theol., 1a q. 19, a. 8, ad 2um. Cf., 1. c., in corp., cum aliqua causa efficax . . . ad complementum universi.

Clearly, the accord between divine causality and the contingence of second causes is made by St. Thomas upon the principle that God's causality effects not only the being of the effect but also the manner of that being, namely, its contingency or necessity. It is, in fact, precisely because of the efficacity of the will of God that free acts occur:

The divine will not only extends itself to the doing of something, through the thing which it moves, but also to the doing of it in that manner which suits the nature itself (of the thing which it moves); and so, it would be more repugnant to the divine motion if the will moved from necessity, which is not according to its nature, than if it moved freely, as is suited to its nature.

Summa Theol., 1a 2ae q. 10, a. 4, ad 1um: voluntas divina non solum se extendit ut aliquid fiat per rem quam movet, sed ut etiam eo modo fiat quo congruit naturae ipsius. Et ideo magis repugnaret divinae motioni, si voluntas ex necessitate moveretur, quod suae naturae non competit, quam si moveretur libere, prout competit suae naturae. Cf. Summa Theol., 1a q. 83, a. 1, ad 3um: . . . non aufert [Deus] quin actiones earum sint voluntariae, sed potius hoc in eis facit.

63

His point should be carefully noted: The absurdity (of God's moving an agent to act freely) is not that the will should be free under God's motion. Rather, the absurdity is the other way about--namely, that the will should not be free under God's motion--that is the absurdity. Truly, the appeal of St. Thomas to the infinitely efficacious will of God as the guarantee of human liberty would seem to be an appeal to the strongest guarantee of the freedom of choice which one can offer.

And as a response to those who might still insist that what is efficaciously moved is moved with necessity, St. Thomas says: si Deus movet voluntatem ad aliquid, incompossibile est huic positioni quod voluntas ad illud non moveretur; non tamen est impossible simpliciter. Unde non sequitur quod voluntas a Deo ex necessitate moveatur.

Summa Theol., *1a 2ae q. 10, a. 4, ad 3um.*

His reason is

> though the nonexistence of the effect of the divine will cannot stand together with the divine will [that there be an effect], nevertheless the potency of there being an effect can stand together with the divine will [that there be an effect]: for these [two] are not incompossible: "God wills that man to be saved"; and, "that man can be dammed"; but these two are incompossible: "God wills that man to be saved"; and, "that man is damned."

De Veritate, *q. 23, a. 5, ad 3um.*

The effect willed by God can not-be, precisely because the divine will attains in its effect this or that particular manner of being --namely, the necessary, the contingent (purely), or the free.

Cf. Summa Theol., *1a q. 22, a. 4.*

To summarize how the discussion of the theory of St. Thomas upon the relation between human choice and its antecedents: Antecedents to choice are human or divine. As to the divine antecedents, first, before man chooses God knows that he will choose. How does he know this? In the divine causality, sic Deus cognoscendo suam essentiam, alia cognoscit, sicut per cognitionem causae cognoscuntur effectus. Omnia igitur Deus cognoscit,

<u>suam</u> essentiam <u>cognoscendo</u>, ad <u>quae</u> <u>sua</u> <u>causalitas</u> <u>extenditur</u>.
<u>Extenditur</u> <u>autem</u> <u>ad</u> <u>operationes</u> <u>intellectus</u> <u>et</u> <u>voluntatis</u>.

Contra Gent., *1, 68. Cf. supra, p. 47, n. 3; p. 48, n. 2.*

Next, upon the supposition of some human choice, there is some
<u>cause</u> for that choice. In what sense? In that <u>sic</u> <u>Deus</u> <u>ipsam</u>
[<u>voluntatem</u>] <u>movet</u> <u>quod</u> <u>non</u> <u>ex</u> <u>necessitate</u> <u>ad</u> <u>unum</u> <u>determinat</u>,
<u>sed</u> <u>remanet</u> <u>motus</u> <u>eius</u> <u>contingens</u>, <u>et</u> <u>non</u> <u>necessarius</u>, <u>nisi</u> <u>in</u>
<u>his</u> <u>ad</u> <u>quae</u> naturaliter <u>movetur</u>.

Summa Theol., *1a 2ae q. 10, a. 4, resp.*

That is, God determines the will necessarily--because naturally
(<u>motus</u> <u>eius</u> <u>remanet</u> . . . <u>non</u> <u>necessarius</u>, <u>nisi</u> <u>in</u> <u>his</u> <u>ad</u> <u>quae</u>
<u>naturaliter</u> <u>movetur</u>)--to will the good; and he moves the will to
desire this or that good <u>non</u> <u>ex</u> <u>necessitate</u>, as he does determine
but freely.

Cf. De Potentia, q. 3, a. 7, ad 13um.

Third, how can the certain divine knowledge of what a man will
freely do, and the efficacious divine will that a man do what he
will do, be reconciled with human liberty? As to the certain divine
knowledge, "the things known by God are contingent by reason of
proximate causes, though the knowledge of God, which is the first
cause, is necessary." As to the efficacious will, "the efficacy of
the divine will demands that not only that be which God wishes,
but also that it be in the way God wishes it to be"; that is, necessarily or contingently.

Summa Theol., *1a q. 14, a. 13, 1 et ad 1um; Cont. Gent.,*
1. 85; De Veritate, q. 23, a. 5, resp. ad fin.

That there may, or may not, be something desiderated in this
theory, is not my concern. My interest is simply to have shown
what the theory is, in order that we may later appreciate better
the contrast to it which Molina's offers.

From St. Thomas' theory there emerge two points. The free
human act, first, is caused by God and, second, is foreseen,
or rather seen, by him as present in his eternity. God sees what
will happen as happening; and what happens he makes to happen,
either necessarily or freely.

Summa Theol., 1a q. 22, a. 4, resp.: *providentia divina quibusdam rebus necessitatem imponit, non autem omnibus . . . quibusdam effectibus praeparavit causas necessarias, ut necessario evenirent; quibusdam vero causas contingentes, ut evenirent contingenter, secundum conditionem proximarum causarum. Contra Gent., 1, 66: Quidquid igitur per totum temporis decursum agitur divinus intellectus in tota sua aeternitate intuetur quasi praesens.*

From these two points there emerges a third: The free act, considered in its human cause is imprevisible. For if the free act can be seen by God as being present, and only as being present, it is seen extra suas causas. Note that this is not to say that the free act is imprevisible in its divine cause. It is thus that God knows it, since he makes it free. But it is unknown in its human cause.

A contingent being can be considered in two ways. First, in itself, i.e., as it actually is; and thus it is not future but present. Nor is it contingent ad utrumlibet, but determined ad unum. As such it can be known with certainty, as, e.g., when I see Socrates sitting. Next, a contingent being can be considered in its cause. So considered it is future, and, as contingent, is not yet determined ad unum; because a contingent cause is related to opposite effects. Considered thus, a contingent being is not known with certainty to any knowledge. Whence whosoever knows a contingent effect merely in its cause has only conjectural knowledge about it. Now, God knows all contingents not only as they are in their causes, but also inasmuch as each one is in itself. And though they occur successively, yet God does not know them successively as they exist (as we know them), but all together. The reason is: his knowledge is measured by eternity, as is his being. And eternity, since it exists all together, embraces all time. Whence every-thing in time is eternally present to God, not merely inasmuch as he has present within himself the idea of everything, as some say, but because his vision stretches from eternity to all things as they are in their "presentiality." Whence it is manifest that contingent beings are infallibly known by God inasmuch as they are subject to his vision according to their "presentiality." They are future contingents in relation to their proximate causes.

Summa Theol., 1a q. 14, a. 13, resp.: *vid. p. 46, sq., n.*

A free act, then, cannot be known in its own cause with certainty, beforehand, by anyone.

Obviously, a contingent event depending upon some other condition or cause which may, or may not, be posited can be known with certainty by one who knows that condition. But the question here is of choice, which depends ex hypothesi upon no condition not under the domination of the will.

If the free act is thus absolutely imprevisible in its own cause, the question arises, What sort of liberty is implied thereby? This is the third point in St. Thomas' theory of the relation between choice and its antecedents, the notion of human liberty. Here, of course, the antecedents in question are human. And the problem amounts to this: what are the human conditions of liberty? The subject demands a special chapter.

4 ST. THOMAS' THEORY OF FREE CHOICE

W̲e have seen that according to St. Thomas the free act is exempt from necessity, as far as its divine antecedents are concerned, first because God non eum determinat ex necessitate ad unum sicut determinat naturam.

Vid. supra p. 61.

Second, strictly speaking, God does not foresee such an act; rather he sees it as present to his eternity. Last, if it be objected that God cannot cause what is exempt from necessity, St. Thomas' answer is that an infinite cause is, so to say, "quite up to it" precisely because such a cause is infinite. St. Thomas' conviction throughout is that the divine antecedents really cause the activity of real, free causes; that is, there are free natures.

Now, if the free act is not previsible in its own free and infinite cause--because there it is not determined ad unum, and only such a being (namely, one determined ad unum) can be cognized as so determined (otherwise the cognition would be of the determined in the undetermined)--the essence of liberty or of free choice demands--since choice is always determined (that is, it is always of this or that)--that the determination of choice be within the power of the chooser.

*De Veritate, q. 22, a. 6, resp. 2°: est voluntas in-
determinata respectu actus; quia circa objectum
determinatum potest uti actu suo cum voluerit, vel non
uti: potest enim exire in actum volendi respectu cuiuslibet, et non exire . . .*

Conceivably, the determination of choice by the chooser might be
a solely intellectual determination, or a solely voluntary determination, or a determination which is an admixture of both the
voluntary and the intellectual. But if the determination of choice
be solely intellectual, you cannot explain why a man might have
chosen otherwise--though you may explain, it is true, why he
chooses this or that. That is to say, if the determination of choice
be solely intellectual, you will have intellectual determinism.
Thus the act will not be free. On the other hand, if the determination of choice be solely voluntary, then, though issuing
spontaneously from the chooser, choice will have no reason in
it for not being necessitated. That is to say, if choice be purely
spontaneous, its immunity from necessity, if any, may be asserted; and though the assertion may or may not be true, it certainly cannot be true from the reason alledged, namely, that
choice is purely spontaneous. To put it shortly: if the reason for
choosing this or that is an exhaustive reason, such a reason explains not only why one chooses but also why one could not have
chosen otherwise; if there be no reason for choosing this or that,
why then, maybe one might have chosen otherwise and maybe not.
If choice be purely spontaneous, we simply do not know from the
nature of choice whether it be exempt from necessity or not. It is
essential to liberty then--if one wishes to maintain choice's exemption from necessity upon philosophical grounds--that the
determination of the free act ad unum be at once voluntary and
intellectual. Intellectual, in order that the reason for man's
choosing this render some account also of why his choosing this
was not necessitated; voluntary, in order that the reason for his
choice of this be his own reason. This position is no doubt deli-
cately subtle, but it seemed demanded by the exigencies of the
situation as seen by St. Thomas Aquinas. To repeat those exigencies: First, given the existence of liberty, God sees the
free act as present in his own eternity. Second, he does not see
the free act in its own cause. Third, if purely intellectual, the
free act cannot be spontaneous, since the intellect is determined
by its object. Fourth, if purely spontaneous, the free act may
or may not be immune from necessity, but the assertion that it is
so immune renders no account of the reason why it is.

St. Thomas will attempt to keep choice clear from the necessity arising from human antecedents, not indeed by denying their
causality (any more than he denied the divine causality of choice)
but by showing that, though real causes, these antecedents do
not necessitate.

Before examining St. Thomas' theory of liberty, insofar as it
touches the present question--that is, insofar as it is a theory of
intellectualist-voluntarism--it might be well, in order not to lose
the main thread of the thesis, to indicate right now the general
position of Molina. Molina encountered, as we have seen, the Reformers' objection: antecedents to choice which of themselves
determine choice are irreconcilable with the immunity of choice
from necessity but are not irreconcilable with the immunity of
choice from coercion. Now, there are such antecedents. Choice,
therefore, is not immune from necessity, but it is immune from
coercion. Molina denied the minor. That there were antecedents
to choice infallibly connected with it he of course admitted--
cor regis in manu Domini (Prov. 21, 1). But that these antecedents
of themselves determined choice he denied. Liberty was, according to Molina, immunity both from coercion and from necessity. In this contention he was quite in agreement with his own
theology. But, he thought, choice cannot be free from coercion
and necessity if the antecedents to choice of themselves determine
it. Free choice must therefore be cleared of the determinism of
antecedents. The starting point of his theory to effect this (I am
now only indicating what the theory is; later I shall support what
is here said with Molina's texts)

Vid. infra cc. 8, 9, 10.

is a certain sort of previsibility of free choice by the infinite
intellect of God. God knows not only what a man can do and will
do but also what a man would do in whatsoever circumstances a
man might be placed. Knowing what a man would do under given
circumstances, God posits the circumstances. A man, therefore, is free in the circumstances under which he chooses,
because God has foreseen that a man would freely choose under
those circumstances. Yet man's choice is anteceded by the
infallible knowledge and will of God, because God has posited
the circumstances under which he foresaw what a man would
freely do. If human choice be thus previsible and thus efficaciously willed by God, the question arises, Why is choice
immune from necessity? (Admittedly it is immune from coercion.)

70

Concretely, why is the velle hoc not being determined by circumstances not under the control of the chooser? Because of the intellectual prerequisites of choice? Molina denies this. Positis omnibus ad agendum requisitis agens liberum potest agere hoc vel illud.

Vid. supra, p. 2.

Then why? Because, answers Molina, the Council of Trent says so, and experience confirms it. Thus we see that the reasons he gives are theological and psychological. If Luther's theology landed Luther into a denial of choice from necessity, Molina's theology landed Molina into asserting the absence of necessity in choice. If one cares to consider Luther a bad theologian, Molina was at least a good one.

But to return to the theory of liberty of St. Thomas Aquinas. His theory has been well summarized as follows:

> The will follows--it does not precede--the intellect; it necessarily tends to what is presented to it as the good which fully satisfies its appetite; however, amid the many proposed goods, which are proposed to its appetite by a judgment to revision, it chooses freely; hence, election follows the ultimate practical judgment; but that the judgment be ultimate, is due to the will.

These theses are from the approbation of the Sacra Studiorum Congregatio in the Acta Apostolicae Sedis, Jul. 14, Ann. VI, vol. VI, Romae, Typ. Pol., p. 386: Intellectum sequitur non praecedit voluntas, quae necessario appetit id quod sibi praesentatur tamquam bonum ex omni parte explens appetitum, sed inter plura bona, quae judicio mutabili appetenda proponuntur, libere eligit. Sequitur proinde electio judicium practicum ultimum; at, quod sit ultimum, voluntas efficit (th. XXI). St. Thomas' theory of intellection is of course presupposed in his discussion of the will. A brief statement of that theory is had in theses XVIII, XIX, XX, op. cit., pp. 385-86--th. XVIII) Intellectuality is a necessary consequent of immateriality. In fact the further anything is removed from matter, the more intellectual it is. And though the adequate object of intellection is being itself, the proper object of the human intellect in its present state is the quiddity abstracted from its material conditions (XIX). Whence, we derive knowledge from sensible things. And since what is sensible is not actually intelligibile, there must be admitted, besides formal intel-

*ligence, an active power in the soul whose function it is
to abstract what is intelligible from the phantasms (XX).
It is through these abstracted species that we know directly
universals. Singulars we know by sense and by conversion to
the phantasms. Spiritual objects we know through analogy.
Cf. for th. XVIII, Summa Theol., 1a q. 14, a. 1; q. 74, a. 7;
q. 89, aa. 1, 2; Cont. Gent., 1, 66, 59, 72 et 4, 11; for th.
XIX, Summa Theol., 1a q. 79, aa. 6, 7; Cont. Gent., 2, 76;
for th. XX, Summa Theol., 1a qq. 85, 86, 87, 88.*

Here we have the essential points of Aquinas' doctrine: the relations
of the will and intellect, the will's necessary fixation upon the universal good, its independence of particular goods, the relation
between its election and the ultimate practical judgment.

The principle dominating the whole of this thesis is the first:
the will follows the intellect. To the understanding of this principle the following passage supplies the key.

It is necessary to assign an appetitive power to the soul. To
make this evident, we must observe that some inclination follows every form: for example, fire, by its form, is inclined
to rise, and to generate its like. Now, the form is found to
have a more perfect existence in those things which share in
knowledge than in those things which lack knowledge. For in
those which lack knowledge, the form is found to determine each
things only to its own being, i.e., to its nature. Therefore this
natural form is followed by a natural inclination, which is called
natural appetite. But in those things which have knowledge, each
one is determined to its own natural being by its natural form,
in such a manner that it is nevertheless receptive of the species
of other things: e.g., sense receives the species of all things
sensible, and the intellect of all things intelligible, so that the
soul of man is, in a way, all things by sense and intellect: and
thereby, those things that have knowledge, in a way, approach
to a likeness of God, in whom all things preexist, as Dionysius
says (Div. Nom. V). Therefore, as forms exist in those things
that have knowledge in a higher manner and above the manner
of natural forms; so must there be in them an inclination sur-
passing the natural inclination, which is called natural appetite.
And this superior inclination belongs to the appetitive power of
the soul, through which the animal is able to desire what it ap-
prehends, and not only that to which it is inclined by its natural
form. And so it is necessary to assign an appetitive power to
the soul.

Summa Theol., 1a q. 80, a. 1: *Ad cuius evidentiam considerandum est quod quamlibet formam sequitur aliqua inclinatio; sicut ignis ex sua forma inclinatur ad superiorem locum, et ad hoc quod generet sibi simile. Forma autem in his quae cognitionem participant altiori modo invenitur quam in his quae cognitione carent. In his enim quae cognitione carent invenitur tantummodo forma ad unum esse proprium determinans unumquodque, quod etiam naturale uniuscuiusque est. Hanc igitur formam naturalam sequitur naturalis inclinatio quae appetitus naturalis vocatur. In habentibus autem cognitionem sic determinatur unumquodque ad proprium esse naturale per formam naturalem, quod tamen est receptivum specierum aliarum rerum, sicut sensus recipit species omnium sensibilium, et intellectus omnium intelligibilium. Et sic anima hominis fit omnia quodammodo secundum sensum et intellectum, in quo cognitionem habentia ad Dei similitudinem quodammodo appropinquant, in quo omnia praeexistunt, sicut Dionysius dicit, de div. nom., c.v, col. 815, t. 1. Sicut igitur formae altiori modo existunt in habentibus cognitionem supra modum formarum naturalium, ita oportet quod in eis sit inclinatio supra modum inclinationis naturalis quae dicitur appetitus naturalis. Et haec superior inclinatio pertinet ad vim animae appetitivam, per quam animal appetere potest ea quae apprenhendit, non solum ea ad quae inclinatur ex forma naturali. Sic igitur necesse est ponere aliquam potentiam animae appetitivam. For Dionysius, see P.G., 3: 815, sqq.*

The point to be noted in the foregoing passage is this: one acts according to what one is (omne agens agit secundum quod est). Now knowing beings are not only what they are, by their physical or natural forms; they are also what they know, by their knowledge. Hence beings which know, will act not only according to the form which specifies their kind but also according to the form which specifies their knowledge. You may kick a stone as often as you please; its action, such as it is, will be merely according to what-it-is, the natural form; a stone has no knowledge. But the second time you kick, or try to, kick an animal, it will flee you; an animal acts according to its knowledge. Action therefore is consequent upon form, what-a-thing-is. If the form be natural-- that is, simply specifying the kind of being in question--the action consequent upon that form will be natural and the result of natural appetite. Such, for example, is the appetite of the fire which rises and generates its kind. But if to the natural form there accede cognitive forms, which specify knowledge, the action and the appetite from which the action issues will be either animal or rational. Animal appetite, issuing from sense cognition, St. Thomas sub-

divides into concupiscible and irascible. In beings which have intellectual knowledge we find intellectual or rational appetite,
which is called the will.

> *Cont*. *Gent*., *1, 47: Inest omnibus appetitus boni, quum
> bonum sit quod omnia appetunt, ut philosophi tradunt,
> Ethic. 1, c. 1. Huiusmodi autem appetitus, in his quidem
> quae cognitione carent, dicitur naturalis appetitus,
> sicut dicitur quod lapis appetit esse deorsum: in his
> autem quae cognitionem sensitivem habent, dicitur ap-
> petitus animalis, qui dividitur in concupiscibilem et
> irascibilem; in his vero quae intelligunt, dicitur ap-
> petitus intellectualis seu rationalis, qui est voluntas.
> For the Ethics vid. 1094, a. 3, Bekker. St. Thomas'
> Philosophi is his way of translating Aristotle's "It
> has been well said."*

The will, therefore, may be described as involving a tendency toward a good apprehended by the intellect. The will follows; it does
not precede the intellect.

> *Summa Theol., 1a 2ae q. 8, a. 1, resp.: cum omnis in-
> clinatio consequatur aliquam formam . . . appetitus . . .
> intellectivus, seu rationalis, qui dicitur voluntas, se-
> quitur formam apprehensam. Sicut igitur id in quod tendit
> appetitus naturalis est bonum existens in re, ita id in
> quod tendit appetitus animalis, vel voluntarius, est bonum
> apprehensum.*

It is thus clear that it would be a gross mistake to think that
St. Thomas holds that the will grasps blindly at its objects, much
as one might pick up blindly any stone to fling at an annoying object. Obviously a man might do that, but such an act would either
not issue from the kind of appetite of which Aquinas is speaking--
namely, rational appetite--or else, if it did issue, would be in
consequence of the form presented to the will by the intellect,
any-stone-will-do. We hit an object or try to with the stone which,
all things considered, seems best likely to attain our purpose.
And if any stone will do, then it is upon that intellectual form,
any-stone-will-do, that the choice of our will depends. To the
understanding, then, is due the determination of what a rational
agent does. "It is an understood good which moves the will."

> *Summa Theol., 1a q. 82, a. 3, ad 2um: bonum enim intel-
> lectum movet voluntatem.*

74

By way of parenthesis, before we examine how such a theory professes to escape intellectual determinism, it might be well to ask St. Thomas why a known good moves the will. What is the reason for appetite? Why is there any action at all? Why is an intellectual form dynamic? The answer is that action is in view of an end.

Contra Gent., *3, 2; 1a q. 44; Summa Theol.*, *1a 2ae q. 1 a. 2.*

If it were not, there would be no action; for an agent to which a determinate effect is indifferent does not tend to produce this determinate effect rather than any other--that is, such an agent does not act at all. But, in fact, there are actions, and therefore action is in view of an end.

Contra Gent., *3, 2: Si agens non tenderet ad aliquem ef-fectum determinatum, omnes effectus essent ei indifferentes. Quod autem indifferenter se habet ad multa, non magis unum eorum operatur quam aliud; unde a contingente ad utrumque non sequitur aliquis effectus, nisi per aliquid quod deter-minetur ad unum. Impossibile igitur esset quod ageret. Omne igitur agens tendit ad aliquem determinatum effectum, quod dicitur finis eius.*

Moreover, to act for an end implies that this end is suitable for the agent; else why act? The good and the end are thus convertible terms.

Contra Gent., *3, 3.*

To the question, then, Why do we act at all? the answer is Because we desire some good. Only the good can be the object of desire.

Summa Theol., *1a 2ae q. 8, a. 1, resp.: voluntas est ap-petitus quidam rationalis; omnis autem appetitus non est nisi boni. Cuius ratio est, quia appetitus nihil aliud est quam quaedam inclinatio appetitus in aliquid. Nihil autem inclinatur nisi in aliquid simile et conveniens. Cum igitur omnis res, inquantum est ens et substantia, sit quoddam bonum, necesse est ut omnis inclinatio sit in bonum.*

The same answer holds essentially for any sort of action, animal or natural, with the only difference being that if the action be natural, it is purely physical, not a conscious, tendency to a good; if the action be animal, it is a sense-conscious tendency to a sensible good.

Contra Gent., 3, 3.

Obviously there is no answer to the question, Why do we desire the good? It is like the question, Why is a thing what it is? To desire the good is of the very nature of the will.

And now to take up the question of intellectual determinism. St. Thomas' principle, that the will follows the intellect, would seem to lead to it. For, as he has explained, a free act must have some intellectual grounds for it, some sufficient reason to explain it. Without this sufficient reason, it may be objected, you cannot explain the act; with it you cannot explain the act otherwise. In short, since a free act is impossible without a reason, the reason why one chooses is also the reason why one cannot choose otherwise: thus, the act is not free.

We are thus led to the second and third points of Aquinas' theory of choice: the fixation of the will upon the good, its independence of all goods.

We have seen that rational activity has as its basis the dependence of the will upon the intellect: the will tends to the good as the good is presented to it by the understanding. But so to tend shows that the object of the will is the good: to will a good, one must first be able to will the good. As we have seen, everything acts naturally in accordance with the form which specifies what the thing is. Now, it is of the nature of the will to will the good.

Summa Theol., 1a 2ae q. 10, a. 1, resp.: natura multipliciter dicitur. Quandoque enim dicitur principium intrinsecum in rebus mobilibus; et talis natura est vel materia vel forma materialis . . . Alio modo dicitur natura quaelibet substantia vel quodlibet ens; et secundum hoc illud dicitur esse naturale rei quod convenit ei secundum suam substantiam, et hoc est quod per se inest rei. In omnibus autem ea quae non per se insunt reducuntur in aliquid quod per se inest sicut principium. Et ideo necesse est quod hoc modo accipiendo naturam, semper principium in his quae conveniunt rei, sit naturale. Et hoc manifeste apparet in intellectu; nam principia intellectualis cognitionis sunt naturaliter nota. Similiter

etiam principium motuum voluntariorum oportet esse ali-
quid naturaliter volitum. Hoc autem est bonum in com-
muni, in quod voluntas naturaliter tendit . . .

This means that the ratio volendi is in every instance of desire
the good, just as the ratio videndi is for the eye color. Of course
it is not the good as such which the will desires (nor is it color
as such which the eye sees). We see colored objects and desire
good things. But as color is the reason that we see colored objects, so the good is the reason that we desire good objects.
True, we often desire what is not good for us. But the point is
that, whether the good we desire be real or apparent, we do not
desire it because we think it bad. Evil (can anyone doubt it?) is
often thought to be the best way out. Although, then, the good
in itself is not the object of desire, it is always the reason for
desiring any object.

De Veritate, q. 22, a. 5, resp.: Natura autem et voluntas
hoc modo ordinata sunt, ut ipsa voluntas quaedam natura
sit; quia omne quod in rebus invenitur quaedam natura
dicitur. Et ideo in voluntate oportet invenire non solum
id quod voluntatis est, sed etiam quod naturae est. Hoc
autem est cuiuslibet naturae creatae, ut a Deo sit ordinata
in bonum, naturaliter appetens illud. Unde et voluntati
ipsi inest naturalis quidam appetitus sibi convenientis
boni; et praeter hoc habet appetere aliquid secundum pro-
priam determinationem, non ex necessitate; quod ei competit
in quantum voluntas est. Sicut autem est ordo naturae ad
voluntatem, ita se habet ordo eorum quae naturaliter vult
voluntas, ad ea respectu quorum a se ipsa determinatur,
non ex natura. Et ideo, sicut natura est voluntatis funda-
mentum, ita appetibile quod naturaliter appetitur, est
aliorum appetibilium principium et fundamentum. In appetibil-
ibus autem finis est fundamentum et principium eorum quae sunt
ad finem; cum quae sunt propter finem, non appetantur nisi
ratione finis.

Is this reason ever peremptory? Is there ever any instance of
some good object so concreting the reason for desiring it that
we must necessarily will that object? In our experience, never.
God, of course, would be such an object if we saw him; and when we
do there will be no question of what we shall do.

Summa Theol., 1a q. 82, a. 1; 1a 2ae q. 10, a. 1; De
Veritate, q. 22, a. 5.

But the incarnate goods with which we are confronted are such that we can accept or refuse them. The reason: the only supposition upon which we should have to embrace a given good would be that such a good so completely fulfilled the reason for desiring it that there would be no reason for not desiring it. The middle term of our practical syllogism, the ratio volendi, would have to cover the minor term, the desired object, de jure. For example in the syllogism--the good (M) is to be desired (P); this (S) is good (M); therefore this (S) is to be desired (P)--M would have to be exhausted by S. Obviously, the condition on which such a de jure identification of the good (M) with a good (S) could be made is the absolute goodness of the minor term (S). In fact, the minor term never measures up to the middle. This good is never, in our experience, the good; this good is always relative, defective. We do indeed accept the minor, this good; we do, in fact, substitute the values of M for S; but we do not have to. And the reason is that we see the difference. Thus, "Since the form conceived by the intelligence is universal [the ratio volendi, the good as such], under which many things can be comprised" and "our acts are related to singulars, none of which exhausts the possibility of the universal, the inclination of the will remains indeterminately related to many things; just so, an architect conceives in general the idea of a house, under which are comprised various forms of houses; his will can be inclined to make a round one, or a square one, or one of some other figure."

De Malo, q. 6, a. 1, resp.: forma intellecta est universalis sub qua multa possunt comprehendi; unde cum actus sint in singularibus, in quibus nullum est quod adaequet potentiam universalis, remanet inclinatio voluntatis indeterminate se habens ad multa: sicut si artifex concipiat formam domus in universali sub qua comprehenduntur diversae figurae domus, potest voluntas eius inclinari ad hoc quod faciat domum quadratam vel rotundam, vel alterius figurae.

It is precisely the sort of judgment by which we see the difference (between a good and the good), that is at the source of free choice. To bring this out St. Thomas compares free activity with other kinds. Fire, for example, rises, generates its kind; stones fall, and so forth. No judgment here. Animals act with judgment, but they are not free. The lamb flees the wolf, but this action is from natural instinct or from instinct together with the experience of having been chased. Man, however, compares;

78

he decides what he ought to do or not to do; and he does this not
because of a natural form or a cognitive form necessitating a
determinate action in a given case but because he deliberates,
weighs, hews his path amidst contingent affairs, now this way,
now that. Whence, since action is something contingent, since
further, the kind of action in our experience is also contingent
(concretely: since to act is good and also not good, since to do
this is good, and to do that is also good) since lastly, man
can know all this, it follows that precisely because man can
know it, he is free. A rational animal has free choice.

*Summa Theol., 1a q. 83, a. 1, resp.: quaedam agunt absque
judicio, sicut lapis movetur deorsum, et similiter omnia
cognitione carentia. Quaedam agunt judicio, sed non
libero, sicut animalia bruta; judicat enim ovis videns
lupum, eum esse fugiendum, naturali judicio, et non libero:
quia non ex collatione, sed ex naturali instinctu hoc
judicat, et simile est de quolibet judicio brutorum
animalium. Sed homo agit judicio, quia per vim cognos-
citivam judicat aliquid esse fugiendum vel prosequendum.
Sed quia judicium istud non est ex naturali instinctu in
particulari operabili, sed ex collatione quadam rationis;
ideo agit libero judicio, potens in diversa ferri. Ratio
enim circa contingentia habet viam ad opposita, ut patet
in dialecticis syllogismis, et rhetoricis persuasionibus.
Particularia autem operabilia sunt quaedam contingentia;
et ideo circa ea judicium rationis ad diversa se habet,
et non est determinatum ad unum. Et pro tanto necesse
est quod homo sit liberi arbitrii ex hoc ipso quod rationalis est.*

To resume, the will follows the good presented by the intellect,

*Summa Theol., 1a, q. 82, a. 3, ad 2um: bonum intellectum
movet voluntatem.*

unable to elect what is not a good,

*Ibid., a. 2, ad 1um, voluntas in nihil potest tendere,
nisi sub ratione boni.*

it is able nevertheless not to elect a good, or to elect a different
good; and this it can do because reason, which presents the good,
is collativa plurium.

Ibid., ad 3um.

But, it is insisted, if the will follows the judgment, then--although one may see that there are alternatives--nevertheless there is only one alternative which, ex hypothesi, can be chosen. If so, the reason for this choice, supposing the will follows this reason for the choice, is also the reason which makes any other choice impossible. Thus the will is not free.

St. Thomas' answer is that the judgment presenting a good which one is to accept, or reject, is brought about by an influence not wholly intellectual. We do indeed choose what we have finally decided is the best, but this only means--since "best" here is just a relative, contingent best--that our will has made it the best. We judge a thing best because we wish to judge it best. It might seem, says St. Thomas, that what is moved (the will) cannot move its mover (the intellect). But there are two meanings to the word move. The idea of "jostling a constable" might move me to such a venture. And it is thus that the intellect moves the will, by presenting, namely, a good which determines the will to a certain kind of action. Should I actually jostle a constable, however, I should indeed move him but this time only in the sense that I effectively communicate to him movement. In this second way--that is, by effectively communicating movement--does the will move the intellect as well as all the other powers of the soul. The will, which can desire any good, necessarily affects the powers whose goods are particular. Sight, for example, tends to color, hearing to sound, the intellect to the true, and so forth; but the will, not being limited to any particular object, must act on all the other powers of the soul and in particular upon the understanding.

Summa Theol., q. 83, a. 4, : 2 . . . movens non movetur a moto, nisi forte per accidens. Sed intellectus movet voluntatem; quia appetibile apprehensum per intellectum est movens non motum; appetitus autem movens motum. Ergo intellectus non movetur a voluntate . . . Respondeo dicendum quod aliquid dicitur movere dupliciter. Uno modo per modum finis, sicut dicitur quod finis movet efficientem; et hoc modo intellectus movet voluntatem, quia bonum apprehensum est objectum voluntatis et movet ipsam ut finis. Alio modo dicitur aliquid movere per modum agentis, sicut alterans movet alteratum, et impellens movet impulsum; et hoc modo voluntas movet intellectum et omnes animae vires . . . Cuius ratio est quia in omnibus potentiis ordinatis illa potentia quae respicit finem universalem movet potentias quae respiciunt fines particulares . . . Objectum autem voluntatis est bonum et finis in communi. Quaelibet autem potentia comparatur ad

aliquod bonum proprium sibi conveniens, sicut visus
ad perceptionem coloris, et intellectus ad cognitionem
veri. Et ideo voluntas per modum agentis movet omnes
animae potentias ad suos actus, praeter vires naturales
vegetativae partis, quae nostro arbitrio non subduntur
. . . Ad 2um dicendum, quod intellectus alio modo movet
intellectum quam voluntas intellectum.

We understand because we will to; we imagine because we will
to; and so on.

<u>*Cont*</u>. <u>*Gent*</u>., *1, 71, ad "in virtutibus."*

It is this reciprocal relation of the intellect and the will, each
acting and being acted upon in different orders of causality, that
is the very core of St. Thomas' explantion of free choice. The
good, the object of the will, is also presented to the intellect in
the guise of a particular truth: "that this is good is true." The
true, the object of the intellect, is also sought by the will in the
guise of a particular good: "that this is true is good." (That this
tendency of the will is put in the form of a judgment by me should
not mislead the reader. Really, the will <u>tends</u> to a true thing
inasmuch as it is a good thing.)

<u>*Summa Theol*</u>., *1a q. 82, a. 4, ad 2um: Ex his apparet ratio*
quare hae potentiae suis actibus invicem se includunt;
quia intellectus intelligit voluntatem velle, et voluntas
vult intellectum intelligere. Et simili ratione bonum
continetur sub vero, inquantum est quoddam verum intellectum;
et verum continetur sub bono, in quantum est quoddam bonum
desideratum. Cf. <u>*De Malo*</u>*, q. 6, a. 1, resp.: Unde et ipsum*
bonum, in quantum est quaedam forma apprehensibilis, con-
tinetur sub vero quasi quoddam verum et ipsum verum, in-
quantum est finis intellectualis operationis, continetur
sub bono ut quoddam particulare bonum.

Whence, the good is a particular kind of truth, and the true is a
particular kind of good.

Vid. <u>*Summa Theol*</u>., *1a q. 82, a. 4.*

The accomplishment of our acts is brought about by our will; the
specification of them is given by our intellect. In sum, since truth
and being are the objects of the intellect, and this object is the
first principle of formal causality; since, further, the good is

81

the object of the will, and this object is the first principle of final causality; since, lastly, the good is a particular kind of truth, and the true is a particular kind of good; it follows, first, that the intellect moves the will as a formal cause (specifying what is done) and final cause--since it presents to the will its object, the good--it follows, second, that the will moves the intellect as an efficient cause (that is, by causing the accomplishment of the act of the intellect) and final cause--since the good is at the same time what the agent realizes and what determines him to act.

Summa Theol., 1a 2ae q. 9, a. 1, ad 3um; 1a q. 82, a. 4; *Cont. Gent.*, 1, 72.

If insistence can make the importance of this aspect of St. Thomas' theory more apparent, insistence there must be. Man is not such that he chooses what he thinks he should not choose. What man chooses is what he thinks best, and what he thinks best in the field of action is what he wishes to think best.

The question here is of course about contingent propositions, not about necessary ones; about practical propositions, not about speculative ones nor even about speculative propositions in the practical order, (for example, that we should honor our parents). Rather, "Shall I hic et nunc, honor or dishonor my parents?" is the question, and its resolution, whether that resolution be morally bad or morally good, is not the point, is dependent ultimately upon my choice. Cf. De Anima, 3. 1. 6.

The origin, then, of our choices can be traced either [both] to the understanding or [and] to the will. It depends upon your point of view. If you ask, Why does Peter do this and not that? the answer is that Peter wishes to see it this way. The intellect is the first principle specifying choice; the will is the first principle which causes the accomplishment of choice. And since the true is a particular kind of good and the good a particular kind of truth, a man thinks it best to choose the way he does because he so wishes, and he so wishes because he thinks it best so to wish.

De Malo, q. 6, a. 1, resp.: Si autem consideremus objecta voluntatis et intellectus, inveniemus quod objectum intellectus est primum principium in genere causae formalis, est enim eius objectum ens et verum; sed objectum voluntatis est primum principium in genere causae finalis, eius ob-

jectum est bonum, sub quo comprehenduntur omnes fines,
sicut sub vero comprehenduntur omnes formae apprehensae.
Unde et ipsum bonum, in quantum est quaedam forma ap-
prehensibilis, continetur sub vero quasi quoddam verum;
et ipsum verum, in quantum est finis intellectualis
operationis, continetur sub bono ut quoddam particulare
bonum. Si ergo consideremus motum potentiarum ex parte
objecti specificantis actum, primum principium motionis
est ex intellectu; hoc enim modo bonum intellectum movet
etiam ipsam voluntatem. Si autem consideremus motus
potentiarum animae ex parte exercitii actus, sic
principium motionis est ex voluntate. Cf. Summa Theol.,
q. 9, a. 1 ad 3um; 1a q. 82, a. 4; Cont. Gent., 1.
72.

We have now the answer to the difficulty: without a reason a
free act is impossible; with a reason an act cannot be free. The
answer is that a free act has a reason, but this reason, though
determining, is itself determined by a voluntary influence.
"Election follows the ultimate practical judgment, but that the
judgment be ultimate is due to the will."

Vid. supra, p. 71.

And if it be urged, What, then, determines the will? the answer
is once more The intellect determines the will by presenting the
good in the guise of a particular truth ("that this is good is true").
So after all, it is the intellect which determines choice. Certainly, but in the sense explained and with the restriction that the
judgment ("that this is good is true") is affected quite as much by
the will's desiring the particular good that this be true--intelligo
quia volo.

De Malo, q. 6, a. 1, resp.

So after all, it is the will which determines the judgment. Again,
Yes, but with the restriction that the will's desire of a particular
good is influenced quite as much by the presentation, by the
intellect, of the truth of that good. But you must say one or the
other! Either the intellect determines the will, or the will determines the intellect! St. Thomas did not think that he should or
could say one or the other. Choice for him is a "sort of" judgment
--"sort of" because choice is essentially an act of the will which
wishes, not of the reason which judges. But though choice is es-

sentially an act of the will, St. Thomas includes in that act the judgment, the voluntary choice of which is the conclusion of a deliberation.

The following texts are pertinent. De Veritate, q. 24, a. 1, ad 20um: cum electio sit quoddam judicium de agendis . . . Summa Theol., 1a q. 83, a. 3, 2 et ad 2um; a. 15, resp.: electio habet in se aliquid voluntatis et aliquid rationis. Utrum autem sit actus proprie voluntatis, vel rationis Philosophus videtur relinquere sub dubio in VI Ethic., c. 2, non procul a fin., ubi dicit, quod electio vel est appetitus intellectivi, idest appetitus in ordine ad intellectum, vel intellectus appetitivi, idest appetitus in ordine ad intellectum. Primum autem verius est, sc., quod sit actus voluntatis in ordine ad rationem. Quod enim sit directe actus voluntatis, patet . . . primo ex ratione objecti: quia . . . objectum electionis . . . pertinet ad rationem boni, quod est objectum voluntatis . . . Secundo ex ratione ipsius actus. Electio enim est ultima acceptio qua aliquid accipitur ad prosequendum; quod quidem non est rationis, sed voluntatis; nam quantumcumque ratio unum alteri praefert, nondum est unum alteri praeacceptatum ad operandum, quousque voluntas inclinetur in unum magis quam in aliud; non enim de necessitate voluntas sequitur rationem Est tamen electio actus voluntatis non absolute, sed in ordine ad rationem; eo quod in electione apparet id quod est proprium rationis, sc., conferre unum alteri, vel praeferre. . . . practicae inquisitionis est duplex conclusio: una quae est in ratione, sc., sententia, quae est judicium de consiliatis; alia vero quae est in voluntate, et huismodi est electio: et dicitur conclusio per quandam similitudinem: quia sicut in speculativis ultimo statur in conclusione, ita in operativis ultimo statur in operatione.

An act which is a combination of the will and intellect, free choice is thus a willed judgment or a judged willing. Materially free choice is voluntary; formally it is rational. Just as one cannot define man by his form alone or by his matter alone but by both together--homo est animal rationalis--so free choice cannot be defined by either the will alone or the intellect alone, but by both together--electio est actus et voluntatis et rationis.

Summa Theol., 1a 2ae q. 13, a. 1, resp.: in nomine electionis importatur aliquid pertinens ad rationem, sive ad intellectum et aliquid pertinens ad voluntatem. Dicit enim Philosophus in VI Ethic., c. 2, quod "electio est appetitivus intellectus vel appetitus intellectivus." Quandocumque autem duo concurrunt ad aliquid unum constituendum, unum eorum est ut formale

84

*alterius. Unde Gregorius Nyss., lib. De natura homin., c.
33, dicit quod "electio neque est appetitus secundum
seipsam, neque consilium solum, sed ex his aliquod compositum." Sicut enim dicimus animal ex anima et corpore
compositum esse, neque vero corpus esse secundum seipsum,
neque animam solam, sed utrumque, ita et electionem. Est
autem considerandum in actibus animae, quod actus qui est
essentialiter unius potentiae vel habitus, recipit formam
et speciem a superiori potentia vel habitu, secundum quod
ordinatur inferius a superiori. Si enim aliquis actum
fortitudinis exerceat propter Dei amorem, actus quidem
ille materialiter est fortitudinis, formaliter vero
caritatis. Manifestum est autem quod ratio quodamodo
voluntatem praecedit, et ordinat eius, inquantum sc.,
voluntas in suum objectum tendit secundum ordinem
rationis, eo quod vis apprehensiva appetitivae suum
objectum repraesentat. Sic igitur ille actus quo voluntas
tendit in aliquid quod proponitur ut bonum, ex eo quod
per rationem est ordinatum ad finem, materialiter quidem
est voluntatis, formaliter autem rationis . . . In huiusmodi autem substantia actus materialiter se habet ad
ordinem qui imponitur a superiori potentia; et ideo electio
substantialiter non est actus rationis, sed voluntatis;
perficitur enim electio in motu quodam animae ad bonum quod
eligitur. Unde manifeste actus est appetitivae potentiae
. . . Ad 1um ergo dicendum, quod electio importat collationem
quamdam praecedentem, non quod essentialiter sit ipsa collatio
. . . Ad 2um dicendum, quod conclusio syllogismi, quae fit in
operabilibus, ad rationem pertinet, et dicitur sententia vel
judicium, quam sequitur electio; et ob hoc ipsa conclusio
pertinere videtur ad electionem tamquam ad consequens.* Gregory
of Nyssa here is rather Nemesius: vid. P.G., 40; 734.

It was suggested that this theory solves the difficulties raised by
intransigent intellectualism. The free act has a reason for it, but
this reason is determined by the will--intelligo quia volo. So too it
attempts to solve the difficulties raised by intransigent voluntarism.
The free act has will in it, but this will is determined by the in-
tellect--intellectus intelligit suum velle.

*Cf. Summa Theol., 1a 2ae q. 13, a. 6, resp.: homo non ex
necessitate eligit; et hoc ideo, quia quod possibile est
non esse, non necesse est esse. Huius ratio ex duplici
hominis potestate accipi potest. Potest enim homo velle
et non velle, agere et non agere; potest enim velle hoc
aut illud, et agere hoc aut illud: cuius ratio ex ipsa
virtute rationis accipitur. Quidquid enim ratio potest*

85

*apprehendere ut bonum, in hoc voluntas tendere potest.
Potest autem ratio apprehendere ut bonum, non solum
hoc quod est velle aut agere, sed hoc etiam quod est
non velle et non agere.*

But a closer examination of the acts leading up to and including
the free act may perhaps yield a clearer grasp of the fusion of
mind and will which is the very heart of the theory of free choice.
As we shall see, the interpenetration of mind and will in free
choice is but a special instance of a veritable cat's cradle of
their mutually reciprocal relations.

The will tends naturally to the good, its end. There is no
question, then, of deliberating about the end; it is given. Given
too is any and every end, considered as an end. No deliberation
concerns itself with any end.

*Summa Theol., 1a 2ae q. 14, a. 2, resp. et ad 1um: finis
in operabilibus habet rationem principii, eo quod rationes
eorum quae sunt ad finem ex fine sumuntur. Principium autem
non cadit sub quaestione; sed principia oportet supponere
in omni inquisitione. Unde cum consilium sit quaestio, de
fine non est consilium, sed solum de his quae sunt ad finem
. . . Ad 1um ergo dicendum quod id quod accipitur ut finis
est iam determinatum. Unde quamdiu habetur ut dubium, non
habetur ut finis; et ideo si de eo consilium habetur, non
erit consilium de fine, sed de eo quod est ad finem.*

Deliberation is about the means leading to the end. It follows--
since our acts are means leading to an end, and since too our acts
are singular, particular, and therefore not necessarily connected
with any end--that deliberation must precede our decision as to
what we shall do: act or not act, act thus or so.

*Of course, an act may be morally connected with some end,
but that is not the question. The question here is of a
logically necessary connection.*

Now, this deliberation, though it is the work of reason, is not--
and here we have the will invading reason for the first time--
without dependence upon the will. We deliberate about what we wish
to do; we wish to deliberate about what we wish to do, because we
will the end to which our action leads. Thus, deliberation is an
appetite in search of light.

Summa Theol., *1a 2ae q. 14, a. 1, ad 1um: actus rationis*
diligentis in his quae sunt ad finem, et actus voluntatis
secundum regimen rationis in ea tendentis ad se invicem
ordinantur. Unde et in actu voluntatis, qui est electio,
apparet aliquid rationis, sc., ordo; et in consilio, quod
est actus rationis, apparet aliquid voluntatis, sicut
materia, quia consilium est de his quae homo vult facere,
et etiam sicut motivum: quia ex hoc quod homo vult finem,
movetur ad consilium de his quae sunt ad finem. . . .
ita Demascenus [lib. 2 Orth. Fid., c. 22, vid. P.G., 94-
946.] dicit, "consilium est appetitus inquisitivus," ut
consilium aliquo modo pertinere ostendat et ad voluntatem,
circa quam et ex qua fit inquisitio, et ad rationem in-
quirentem.

Next comes the judgment, and in it too the same relation
between the will and intellect holds. The judgment, a conclusion
or one of the conclusions which terminate deliberation, involves
nearly all the phases, moments, relations, of that unique thing
we call the free act. Deliberation too is of course free in the
sense that I deliberate when and concerning that which I please.
But in deliberation a man does not definitely conclude anything
relating to the object about which he is deliberating. Obviously
he does, in deliberation, conclude that he will deliberate, and such
a judgment would be the conclusion of a deliberation about delib-
eration--and so far forth the very judgment which concerns us,
the definite decision about some particular good. It is this sort
of judgment, the one, namely, which establishes what we are to
do (not the preliminaries to it, deliberation), with which we are
concerned. Such a judgment is first of all the work of reason,
an intellectual determination therefore: ejusdem est syllogizare
et concludere. Syllogizare autem in operabilibus est rationis.
Cum igitur electio sit quasi conclusio in operabilibus, ut dicitur
in VII Ethic., cap. III, videtur quod sit actus rationis. As a
conclusion, therefore, of a syllogism which terminates discussion, the judgment about what one is to do is the work of
reason. But it is the work of reason which alights where it does
(this should be done), precisely because the will has brought it
down there: conclusio syllogismi, quae fit in operabilibus, ed
rationem pertinet, et dicitur sententia vel judicium, quam
sequitur electio; et ab hoc ipsa conclusio pertinere videtur ad
electionem tanquam ad consequens.

Summa Theol., *1a 2ae q. 13, a. 1. Obj. 2 et ad 2um.*

And the will has brought it to that point precisely because, on the one hand, of singulars there is no knowledge, which is to say that the intellect itself cannot determine for us what is for us intellectually inapprehensible, the singular action; on the other hand, we wish to and do conclude by willing the conclusion, the truth in the guise of a particular good.

De Veritate, q. 14, a. 1; Summa Theol., 2a 2ae q. 1, a. 4. Respondeo dicendum, quod fides importat assensum intellectu ad id quod creditur, Assentit autem intellectus alicui dupliciter: uno modo quia ad hoc movetur ab ipso objecto, quod est vel per seipsum cognitum, sicut patet in principii primis, quorum est intellectus; vel est per aliud cognitum, sicut patet de conclusionibus, quarum est scientia. Alio modo intellectus assentit alicui, non quia sufficienter moveatur ab objecto proprio, sed per quandam electionem voluntarie declinans in unam partem magis quam in aliam; et quidem hoc sit cum dubitatione et formidine alterius partis erit opinio; si autem sit cum certitudine absque tali formidine, erit fides. The doctrine here, though concerned with faith, is general.

The intellect does not will, nor does the will judge; but the intellect judges because moved thereto by the will, and the will wills because moved thereto by the intellect. The intellect does all it can to intellectualize a particular action, but there comes a point at which the will equivalently says "that will do," or, as Dr. Johnson, "there's an end on't."

If now we look upon the judgment as an accepted conclusion (above it was looked upon as a determined conclusion), it bears the relation of an antecedent to the consequent; and the consequent is the acceptance itself, or the election. The point is that the judgment which ends deliberation is at once determined and accepted. As determined it is the work of the intellect (mediante voluntate), as we have seen. As accepted it is the work of the will. But here in turn the intellect plays its part inasmuch as the will accepts, and can only accept, what has been judged preferable.

The pertinent texts are: p. 165, supra; Summa Theol., 1a q. 83, a. 3. resp., et ad 2um: . . . proprium liberii arbitrii esse dicimur, quod possumus unum recipere, alio recusato, quod est eligere; et ideo naturam liberi arbitrii ex electione considerare oportet. Ad electionem autem concurrit aliquid ex parte cognitivae virtutis, et aliquid ex parte appetitivae. Ex parte quidem cognitivae

requiritur consilium, per quod dijudicatur quid sit alteri
praeferendum. Ex parte autem appetitivae requiritur quod
appetendo acceptetur quod per consilium dijudicatur; et
ideo Aristoteles in VI Ethic., cap. II, sub dubio relinquit,
utrum principalius pertineat electio ad vim appetitivam,
vel ad vim cognitivam. Dicit enim quod electio vel est
"intellectus apppetitivus, vel appetitus intellectivus."
Sed in III Ethic., cap. III, in hoc magis declinat quod
sit appetitus intellectivus, nominans electionem "de-
siderium consiliabile." Et hujus ratio est, quia proprium
objectum electionis est illud quod est ad finem. Hoc
autem, inquantum hujusmodi, habet rationem boni quod
dicitur utile. Unde cum bonum, inquantum hujusmodi, sit
objectum appetitus, sequitur quod electio sit principaliter
actus appetitivae virtutis. Et sic liberum arbitrium est
appetitiva potentia . . . judicium est quasi conclusio et
determinatio consilii. Determinatur autem consilium primo
quidem per sententiam rationis, et secundo per accepta-
tionem appetitus. Unde Philosophus dicit in III Ethic.,
loco nunc cit., quod "ex consiliari judicantes desideramus
secundum consilium." Et hoc modo ipsa electio dicitur quod-
dam judicium, a quo nominatur liberum arbitrium. Cf.
Summa Theol., 1a 2ae q. 13. resp.

The conclusion of all this seems to be, the will is a rational
appetite; as such, choice is its act. And rational here is not to
be separated from appetite nor appetite from rational. The two
are to be conjugated in every act which is not the result of
either one's nature. The conjugation begins with deliberation,
grows into union in the judgment and is there an undivided unity
so intimate that one factor cannot act apart from the other, any
more than form can exist apart from matter, or potency apart
from act. Thus, all the just claims of intellectualism seem to
be conceded, operari sequitur esse: thus, too, is voluntarism
preserved, for the esse is of our own fabrication since it is the
esse cognitum in operabilibus.

5 ST. THOMAS UPON DIVINE AND HUMAN CAUSALITY OF CHOICE

The difficulties in reconciling its antecedents with free choice are admittedly great.

Cf. St. Augustine, Lib. de gratia Christi, XLVII, 52, P.L. 44; 383: Ista quaestio, ubi de voluntate et Dei gratia disputatur, ita est ad discernendum difficilis ut quando defenditur liberum arbitrium, negari Dei gratia videatur, quando qutem asseritur Dei gratia, liberum arbitrium putetur auferri.

But the Angelic Doctor's attempt to do so effected at least this much: to any difficulty which might be brought against liberty by reason either of the divine or human antecedents of choice his answers left untouched certain acquisitions which are the com - mon patrimony of Christian thought. Let us run through these difficulties and their answers. Is there not a contradiction between prescience and choice? There is none, if God does not know strictly beforehand what a man will choose.

Contra Gent., 1. 66: Quidquid igitur in quacumque parte temporis est, coexistit aeterno quasi praesens eidem, etsi respectus alterius partis temporis sit praeteritum

vel futurum. Aeterno autem non potest aliquid praesenti
aliter coexistere nisi toti, quia successionis duration-
em non habet. Quidquid igitur per totum decursum temporis
agitur, divinus intellectus in tota sua aeternitate in-
tuetur quasi praesens: nec tamen quod quadam temporis
parte agitur, semper fuit existens. Cf. Summa Theol., 1a
q. 14, a. 13, resp.

If divine prescience be certain, and if its certainty does not
destroy the contingence of future free acts, the constant reason
of St. Thomas for this is that future free acts, in virtue of the
simultaneous presence of time in eternity, are eternally realized,
eternally actual, under the eye of God. But God causes free acts!
Of course. How else could man be free, unless a divine cause of
liberty guaranteed it? The difficulty is not that man is free under
divine causality; the difficulty, if any, is how can man be free
without a divine cause of his freedom?

Contra Gent., 1. 85; De Veritate, q. 23, a. 5: Summa Theol.,
1a q. 19, a. 8: 1a 2ae q. 10, a. 4; 1a q. 83, a. 1, ad 3um.
Cf. pp. 117, 118.

According to St. Thomas, there is no contradiction between the
efficacity of divine causality and human liberty; rather the contradiction is between that efficacity and a necessity imposed upon
human action.

Summa Theol., 1a 2ae q. 10, a. 4, ad 3um; De Veritate,
q. 23, a. 5, ad 3um.

But how can the human antecedents of free choice stand together
with the immunity of choice from necessity? Choice implies a
determination (velle hoc) of which the chooser is the author. The
determination of the wish is from the intellect of the man choosing,
and the wish that the determination be such is from the man's will.
Not only, therefore, is man the author of his choice as a principle
of spontaneity, but he is under no necessity to make the choice
whose intellectual determination is from himself.

Summa Theol., 1a q. 83, a. 1.

If finally, a more close scrutiny of the relation between divine
antecedents and choice be demanded, St. Thomas answers that God
is the principal cause of choice, man its secondary cause. The re-

lation between the two is precisely this: God, since he causes the velle bonum, causes also the velle hoc bonum. The reason is that man's determinate desire of bonum (which is caused by God) is the reason that man can determine, through his reason, his desire of hoc bonum.

De Malo, q. 6, a. 1, ad 1um: dicendum quod actualitas illa [electio humana, quae non libera videretur ex eo quod "non est hominis via eius," Hierem, 10.23.] dupliciter potest intelligi . . . quantum ad exercutionem electionis: non enim est in potestate hominis ut expleat in effectu quod mente deliberat . . . alio modo potest intelligi quantum ad hoc quod etiam interior voluntas movetur ab aliquo superiori principio, quod est Deus: et secundum hoc Apostolus dicit quod non volentis, sc., velle, neque currantis, currere, sicut primi principii, sed miserentis est Dei. Summa Theol., 1a 2ae q. 9, a. 6, ad 3um: Deus movet voluntatem hominis sicut universalis motor ad universale obiectum voluntatis, quod est bonum. Et sine hac universali motione homo non potest aliquid velle. Sed homo per rationem determinat se ad volendum hoc vel illud, quod est vere bonum vel apparens bonum.

The fundamental points, therefore, of the theory are, on the side of the divine antecedents of choice, the infinitely efficacious causality of God; on the side of the human antecedents of choice, they are the mutual and reciprocal causality of the will and intellect in diverse orders of causality--

intellectus enim intelligit se et voluntatem . . . et similiter voluntas vult se velle et intellectum intelligere . . . sicut intellectus cum intelligit voluntatem velle, accipit in se ipso rationem volendi . . . et ipsa voluntas, cum fertur super potentias animae, fertur in eas quasdam quibus convenit motus et operatio . . .

De Veritate, q. 22, a. 12, resp., ad fin.

If, then, we consider free choice from the viewpoint of its accomplishment (quoad exercitium actus), it follows that the first movement of the will (velle bonum) is to be explained by the movement of God. For if one who has not chosen chooses, he must be moved by something; if one is moved by himself, he must have been moved thereto by deliberation; and if by deliberation, he must have chosen to deliberate, but this (delib-

92

eration preceded by choice and choice preceded by deliberation) cannot go on forever. After all, a man chooses. Therefore, <u>statur</u> <u>in</u> <u>appetitu</u> <u>naturali</u>.

> *De Veritate, q. 22, a. 12, 2 et ad 2um: Praeterea, si voluntas movet intellectum ad suum actum, tunc sequitur quod intellectus intelligat quia voluntas vult ipsum intelligere. Sed voluntas non vult aliquid nisi intellectum. Ergo prius intellectus intellexit ipsum intelligere quam voluntas illud vellet. Sed antequam intellectus hoc intelligeret, oportet ponere quod voluntas illud vellet, quia ponitur intellectus a voluntate moveri. Ergo est abire in infinitum; vel dicendum quod voluntas non movet intellectum. Ad secundum dicendum quod non est procedere in infinitum; statur enim in appetitu naturali, quo inclinatur intellectus in suum actum. Cf. Summa Theol., 1a 2ae q. 15, a. 3.*

But this divinely determined wish (<u>velle</u> <u>bonum</u>) does not introduce any necessity in our voluntarily determined choices. God moves everything conformably with its nature. By determining the will <u>velle</u> <u>bonum</u>, he has conferred upon it a movement which can be directed to different objects. There are many <u>bona</u>. So, if the will be viewed as the source of its choices, there are in it only the overhand grips of choice over deliberation, of deliberation over choice; but the origin of this movement is God, who moves the will indeterminately to <u>bona</u>, determinately to <u>bonum</u>. If now we look upon the specification of choice (<u>quoad</u> <u>specificationem</u> actus), there is likewise in this specification no necessity. For, though an act of free choice is specified by the <u>bonum</u> <u>apprehensum</u>, yet this <u>bonum</u> does not necessitate the intellect. The reason is that this <u>bonum</u> can under some aspects be a <u>minus</u> <u>bonum</u>, and we can see this. Moreover, our choices are singulars, and there is only one singular good under every aspect: God. Yet even God would only specify our choices necessarily (we could not wish the contrary to God--if we knew him); he could not force us to know him. We cannot but wish to be happy, if we think of it--but we need not think of it.

> *De Malo, q. 6. a. 1, resp.: Sic ergo ad ostendendum quod voluntas non ex necessitate movetur, oportet considerare motum voluntatis et quantum ad exercitium actus, et quantum ad determinationem actus, qui est ex objecto. Quantum ergo ad exercitium actus, primo quidem manifestum est quod voluntas movetur a seipsa; sicut enim movet alias potentias, ita et sepsam movet. Nec propter hoc sequitur quod voluntas*

secundum idem sit in potentia et in actu. Sicut enim homo
secundum intellectum in via inventionis movet seipsum ad
scientiam, inquantum ex uno noto in actu venit in aliquid
ignotum, quod erat solum in potentia notum; ita per hoc
quod homo aliquid vult in actu, movet se ad volendum ali-
quid aliud in actu, sicut per hoc quod vult sanitatem,
movet se ad volendum sumere potionem; ex hoc enim quod
vult sanitatem, incipit consiliari de his quae conferunt
ad sanitatem; et tandem determinato consilio vult accipere
potionem. Sic ergo voluntatem accipiendi potionem praecedit
consilium, quod quidem procedit ex voluntate volentis con-
siliari. Cum ergo voluntas se consilio moveat, consilium
autem est inquisitio quaedam non demonstrativa, sed ad
opposita viam habens, non ex necessitate voluntas seipsam
movet. Sed cum voluntas non semper voluerit consiliari,
necesse est quod ab aliquo moveatur ad hoc quod velit con-
siliari; et si quidem a seipsa, necesse est iterum quod
motum voluntatis praecedat consilium, et consilium prae-
cedat actus voluntatis; et cum hoc in infinitum pro-
cedere non possit, necesse est ponere quod quantum ad
primum motum voluntatis moveatur voluntas cujuscumque non
semper actu volentis ab aliquo exteriori, cujus instinctu
voluntas velle incipiat.

   Relinquitur ergo, sicut concludit Aristoteles in cap.
De bona fortuna, lib. VII Moral. ad Eudemum, cap. XVIII
[l. c. 1248a, Bekker], quod id quod primo movet voluntatem
et intellectum sit aliquid supra voluntatem et intellectum,
scilicet Deus; qui cum omnia moveat secundum rationem
molilium, ut levia sursum et gravia deorsum, etiam volun-
tatem movet secundum ejus conditionem, non ut ex necessitate,
sed ut indeterminate se habentem ad multa. Patet ergo quod
si consideretur motus voluntatis ex parte exercitii actus,
non movetur ex necessitate; si autem consideretur motus
voluntatis ex parte objecti determinantis actum voluntatis
ad hoc vel illud volendum, considerandum est quod objectum
movens voluntatem est bonum conveniens apprehensum; unde si
aliquod bonum proponatur quod apprehendatur in ratione boni,
non autem in ratione convenientis, non movebit voluntatem.
Cum autem consilia et electiones sint circa particularia
quorum est actus, requiritur ut id quod apprehenditur ut
bonum et conveniens, apprehendatur ut bonum et conveniens
in particulari, et non in universali tantum. Si ergo ap-
prehendatur aliquid ut bonum conveniens secundum omnia
particularia quae considerari possunt ex necessitate movebit
voluntatem; et propter hoc homo ex necessitate appetit
beatitudinem, quae, secundum Boetium, lib. III De consolat.,
prosa II, P.L., t. LXIII, col. 724, est "Status omnium bonorum
congregatione perfectus." Dico autem ex necessitate quantum ad
determinationem actus, quia non potest velle oppositum; non

*autem quantum ad exercitium actus, quia potest aliquis non
velle tunc cogitare de beatitudine; quia etiam ipsi actus
intellectus et voluntatis particulares sunt. Si autem sit
tale bonum quod non inveniatur esse bonum secundum omnia
particularia quae considerari possunt, non ex necessitate
movebit etiam quantum ad determinationem actus; poterit
enim aliquis velle ejus oppositum, etiam de eo cogitans,
quia forte est bonum vel conveniens secundum aliquod aliud
particulare consideratum; sicut quod est bonum sanitati
non est bonum delectationi, et sic de aliis. Et quod
voluntas feratur in id quod sibi offertur magis secundum
hanc particularem conditionem quam secundum aliam, potest
contingere tripliciter. Uno quidem modo inquantum una prae-
ponderat, et tunc movetur voluntas secundum rationem; puta,
cum homo praeeligit id quod est utile sanitati, eo quod est
utile voluntati. Alio vero modo inquantum cogitat de una
particulari circumstantia et non de alia; et hoc contingit
plerumque per aliquam occasionem exhibitam vel ab interiori
vel ab exteriori, ut ei talis cogitatio occurrat. Tertio
vero modo contingit ex dispositione hominis; quia, secundum
Philosophum, lib. III Ethic., cap. V., a med., [1. c. 1114b,
Bekker], qualis unusquisque est, talis finis videtur ei. Unde
aliter movetur ad aliquid voluntas irati et voluntas quieti,
quia non idem est conveniens utrique; sicut etiam aliter ac-
ceptatur cibus a sano et aegro. Si ergo dispositio, per quam
alicui videtur aliquid bonum et conveniens, fuerit naturalis
et non subjacens voluntati, ex necessitate naturali voluntas
praeeligit illud, sicut omnes homines naturaliter desiderant
esse, vivere et intelligere. Si autem sit talis dispositio
quae non sit naturalis, sed subjacens voluntati, puta, cum
aliquid disponitur per habitum vel passionem ad hoc quod sibi
videatur aliquid vel bonum vel malum in hoc particulari, non
ex necessitate movetur voluntas; quia poterit hanc dispositionem removere, ut sibi non videatur aliquid sic; ut scilicet
aliquid quietat in se iram, ut non judicet de aliquo tanquam
iratus. Facilius tamen removetur passio quam habitus. Sic ergo
quantum ad aliqua voluntas ex necessitate movetur ex parte
objecti, non autem quantum ad omnia; sed ex parte exercitii
actus, non ex necessitate movetur.*

In short, since, thanks to God, we like the good--since further
we see, thanks to God who gives us reason, alternatives among
goods--we can choose without necessity though moved thereto
by God.

Why did not Molina accept this position? I suggest, first, that
he really did not understand it. In fact, he says so. The cardinal
points of St. Thomas' theory are the divine causality of choice,

the divine prescience of choice, the theory of liberty implied in the relation between free choice and the one who knows and causes it, God. Let us see what Molina has to say about each point.

In the first part of the Summa Theologica the question is Does God operate in everything which operates?

Summa Theol., 1a, q. 105, a. 5.

St. Thomas adduces the opinion of those who think that God operates in the action of creatures. But this, he says, is impossible--for thus, subtraheretur ordo causae et causati a rebus creatis: quod pertinent ad impotentiam creantis--further, omnes res creatae viderentur esse frustra; cum res sint propter propriam operationem. (Notice here the supposition: there are natures which have propriam suam operationem. It seems to be the contradictory to Luther's: si non nos, sed solus Deus operatur salutem in nobis, nihil ante opus eius operamur salutare, velimus, nolimus; rursus, si Deus in nobis operatur, voluntas pergit amando bonum, sicut antea voluit et lubuit et amavit malum.

Vid. supra, p. 10.

Creatures, therefore, really act. But God acts in them. He is the fin cause of their activity, as the principle of the good; he applies to activity the form of the agent in such wise that the agent too acts.

Summa Theol., 1a q. 105, a. 5: principium actionis est finis qui movet agentem; secundo vero agens; tertio autem eius, qu ab agente applicatur ad agendum, quamvis et ipsum agens per formam suam agat. . .

It is the answer we have already seen:

Cf. supra, pp. 50-56.

divine causality effects creaturely causality. Nor is there any difficulty in that one operation be attributable to the creature and God, for una actio non procedit a duobus agentibus unius ordinis; rather, una et eadem actio procedit a primo et secundo agente.

Summa Theol., 1a q. 105, a. 5, 2 et ad 2um.

The point is that creaturely activity is caused by God applicando res ad operationem.

To this Molina says: non videam quidnam sit motus ille et applicatio in causis secundis.

L. Molina, Concordia, ed. cit., p. 152. Cf. De Concurso Generali, in Stegmüller, op. cit., p. 198, sqq.

His reason is that some creatures are quite up to their own activity: fire can burn, seed can generate, and so forth, without any further application by God of their power to act. Whence, "I find it difficult to understand the motion and application which St. Thomas demands in second causes."

L. Molina, De Concursu Generali, in Stegmüller, op. cit., p. 199: semen enim, quando operatur, non movetur a generante, cuius est instrumentum; fieri enim potest, ut generans iam non sit. Et calor ignis, quando calefacit, non movetur aut applicatur ad calefaciendum ab igne, in quo est et cuius est instrumentum, sed per se ipsum sine alia motione calefacit. Quare difficile est mihi intelligere motionem et applicationem, quam d. Thomas exigit in causis secundis. Cf. L. Molina, Concordia, ed. cit., pp. 152, 153.

Molina's difficulty here seems to lie rather in himself than in philosophy. With more metaphysics he might have seen that St. Thomas was asserting, not trying to explain how it was so, that God is the cause of everything which is: creatures are real causes of their acts, because God really causes their acts. Molina has another difficulty. If St. Thomas' answer be correct, then it must be said that God causes creaturely activity through the medium of creatures. If so, God does not effect their activity; rather he affects them.

De Concursu Generali, vid. Stegmüller, op. cit., p. 199: Secundum, quod mihi parit difficultatem, est, quod iuxta haec dicta d. Thomae Deus non concurrit immediate immediatione suppositi ad effectus causarum secundarum, sed solum mediate, mediantibus scil, causis secundis. Nam tam virtutes causarum secundarum, quas Deus confert et conservat, quam etiam motus et applicatio causarum secundarum sunt in ipsismet causis secundis. Quare si Deus per hoc tantum concurrit, non influit immediate immediatione suppositi. Cf. L. Molina, Concordia, p. 153.

It must be, then, that God effects creaturely activity without affecting creatures. Yet the cooperation of creatures is not superfluous. Their cooperation determines the divine causality, much as the sun's causality is determined by man in the production of his kind.

> *1. c., pp. 199, 191: Dicendum est igitur, Deum immediate immediatione suppositi concurrere cum causis secundis ad effectus earum, ita quod concursus Dei universalis nihil aliud est, quam influxus Dei immediatus in omnes effectus. Neque superfluit influxus et concursus causarum secundarum, quia Deus influit ut causa universalis influxu quodam indifferenti ad plures effectus: determinatur vero ab influxu causarum secundarum ad productionem huius vel illius effectus, ad modum quo influxus solis (qui etiam universalis est) determinatur ab influxu et concursu hominis ad producer hominem, et ab influxu et concursu equi ad producendum equu sol enim et homo generant hominem, ut habetur 2 phys., sol item et equus generant equum. Sicut ergo ad generationem equi non sufficit influxus solis sine influxu equi, neque influxus equi sine influxu solis, ita ad nullius effectus productionem sufficit influxus Dei per solum concursum universalem sine influxu causae secundae particularis, a que determinetur, neque influxus causae secundae particularis sine influxu Dei per concursum universalem, quo adiuvetur et quem statuit numquam de lege ordinari denegare. Quare ut, cessante causa secunda influere, cessat etiam Deus influere nullaque sequitur actio, eo quod influxus Dei per concursum universalem pendeat in suo esse ab influxu causae particular cooperantis, ita cessante Deo influere per concursum univers ut cessavit influere cum igne in fornace, cessat continuo i fluxus atque actio secundae causae, ut ibi cessavit influxue et actio ignis, quia pendet similiter in suo esse ab influxu Dei. Cf. L. Molina, Concordia, pp. 153-57.*

On this second difficulty of Molina we shall see more later. Suffice it for the present to observe that here again Molina was short of metaphysics. St. Thomas has already put Molina's difficulty: videtur quod Deus non operetur in omni operante. Nulla enim insufficientia est Deo attribuenda, si igitur Deus operatur in omni operante, sufficienter in quolibet operatur. Superfluum igitur esset quod agens creatum aliquid operaretur. His answer is Deus sufficienter operatur in rebus ad modum primi agentis; nec propter hoc superfluit operatio secundorum agentium.

> *Summa Theol., 1a, q. 105, a. 5. 1 et ad 1um.*

Clearly, for St. Thomas, God causes the activity of real causes. Molina, who cannot understand this, thinks that God and creatures work together, like two men towing a boat.

De Concursu Generali, vid. Stegmüller, op. cit., p. 200: Ex dictis intelliges, quod, si sit sermo de causa totali omnino ut comprehendit omnem requisitam, tam universalem quam particularem, Deus per concursum universalem et causae secondae efficiunt unam integram causam totalem et plures partiales respectu cuiusque effectus causarum secundarum, quarum neutra sine alia sufficit. Cum autem audis efficere plures partiales, intellige partialitate causae, non vero effectus; quia totus effectus est ab unaquaque earum, sed non totaliter, quia est concurrente et influente simul alia; ad modum quo, quando duo trahunt navim, totus motus est ab unoquoque trahentium, sed non totaliter, quia est influente et causante simul alio singulas partes eiusdem motus. Si vero sit sermo de causa totali non omnino sed in suo ordine, tunc Deus per concursum universalem est causa totalis in ordine causae universalissimae, quia nulla alia concurrit cum eo in eodem ordine, et causae secundae possunt etiam esse totales unaquaeque in suo ordine. Cf. L. Molina, Concordia, p. 157.

And generally speaking, in fact, the relation between subordinate and superior causes is such that they both together effect the result, but not by way of the superior cause affecting the subordinate one.

1. c., p. 200: Ex dictis quoque intelliges, non esse necesse quod, quando causae sunt ordinatae inter se, ita ut quae- dam sint universaliores et quaedam minus universales aut particulares, superior in isto ordine moveat inferiorem, quantumcumque sint essentialiter subordinatae et mutuo pendeant inter se in causando, sed omnes immediate influere in effectum.

A bizarre sort of metaphysics, this: though God is the cause of creatures' acts, still, he does not move them.

1. c. Cf. L. Molina, Concordia, ed. cit., p. 158.

As much as to say, a cause is not a cause.

The second point of St. Thomas' theory is the divine prescience of future contingents. Origen has objected [Super Epist. ad Rom., P.L., 4: 1126]: "Non propterea aliquid erit quia id scit Deus esse futurum: sed quia futurum est, ideo scitur a Deo, antequam fiat."

99

St. Thomas answered: "Origen spoke with the knowledge of God in mind which is not causal unless his will be joined thereto."

Summa Theol., *1a q. 14, a. 8, 1 et ad 1um.*

Whereupon Molina comments: "not therefore will things be because God foreknows them, but contrariwise . . . though, to tell the truth, St. Thomas seems to suggest the contrary."

L. Molina, Concordia, pp. 324, 325: Ex his facile intelligi potest, quamvis Deus nullam scientiam sumat a rebus, sed quicquid cognoscit, id in sua essentia et in determinatione liberae suae voluntatis cognoscat et comprehendat; attamen non quia cognoscit aliquid esse futurum, ideo illud futurum, sed e contrario, quia illud futurum est ex suis causis, ideo cognoscere illud esse futurum. Quia enim res primi generis ex sola libera voluntate Dei, tanquam ex immediata et tota causa, sunt futurae, ideo Deus per scientiam liberam, quae determinationem illam voluntatis consequitur in Deo, in ea ipsa determinatione voluntatis tanquam in causa quod sunt futurae, scit eas futuras, non vero e contrario, quia scit illas esse futuras, ideo sunt futurae quandoquidem prius, nostro intelligendi more cum fundamento in re, illae sunt futurae ex determinatione libera voluntatis divinae, quam id a Deo ex eadem ipsa determinatione sciatur. Quia etiam res secundi generis, partim ex libera voluntate Dei, qua causas secundas statuit immediate creare, et cum eisdem tanquam universalis causa concurrere, partim ex necessario influxu ipsarummet causarum secundarum ita sunt futurae, ut nulla alia causa ejusmodi effectus valeat impedire, utique (praeexistente scientia naturali qua praevidet ejusmodi res necessario esse futuras, ex hypothesi quod causas earum velit creare) praescivit, in determinatione voluntatis qua illas statuit creare, per scientiam liberam, quae ejusmodi determinationem consequitur, tales effectus absolute et sine hypothesi esse futuros, quia ex dictis causis erant futuri; non vero e contrario, quia scivit illos esse futuros, ideo futuri sunt ex eisdem causis. Denique quia res tertii generis, cooperantibus tum aliis causis secundis, tum etiam Deo partim ut causa particulari, ex libero arbitrio creato, aut dependenter ab illo, ita sunt futurae ut possint non esse, praevidente Deo per scientiam naturalem, et per illam mediam inter mere naturalem et liberam, illas pro libertate arbitrii esse futuras, ex hypothesi quod creare vellet homines et angelos in eo ordine rerum quo illos collocavit, in determinatione libera voluntatis qua illos ita creare constituit,

*scivit per scientiam liberam, quae determinationem illam
consequitur, res illas esse futuras, quia illae pro libertate arbitrii erant ita eventurae, non vero e contrario,
quia illas praescivit eventuras, ideo erunt vel fuerunt.*

    *Hoc vero, quod ultimo loco diximus, affirmant etiam
omnes illi doctores quos disputatione praecedente citavimus.
Dum enim asseverant, libero arbitrio hoc, vel ejus oppositum,
indifferenter pro innata sibi libertate in futurum eligente,
Deum effecturum ut non aliud ipse ex aeternitate praescivit,
manifeste docent, non ideo res esse futuras, quia Deus id
praescit, sed e contrario. In eadem sententia videntur esse
caeteri doctores scholastici, quamvis, ut verum fatear, contrarium innuere videatur D. Thomas, supra art. 8 in respon-
sione ad primum, dum exponit, atque in contrarium sensum
reducere conatur, testimonium Origenis mox referrendum, quo
idem aperte docet.*

St. Thomas did indeed. We have heard him explaining

Vid. supra, pp. 41-46.

that God knows future contingents as present to his eternity.

Summa Theol., 1a q. 14, a. 13; cf. q. 22, a. 4.

Molina remarks, haec sententia mihi numquam placuit. And the
reason for his discontent is, mainly, that he does not see what
the presence of all being to the eternity of God has got to do with
it. This would seem to be his real reason: he truly does not see
the point. But he adduces his counter arguments: God would not then
know the free futuribles (namely, choices which could, but will not,
be), for these have no esse existentiae in eternity. Yet God must
know them if he be omniscient. Further, God knows that he can
create before he knows that he will create, and he must decide to
create before he knows what will be. Either, therefore, future
contingents existed before God knew them--and thus divine providence is destroyed--or else they are known consequently upon
God's voluntary determination of them--and thus not in their
esse existentiae.

*L. Molina, De Scientia Dei, in Stegmüller, op. cit., pp.
226, 227, 228: Licet propositio, d. Thomae in sensu a
Caietano, Capreolo et Ferrariensi explicato ita facile
defendatur, opinio tamen d. Thomae hoc loco, quatenus
asserit futura contingentia neque a Deo optimo maximo
cognosci certo in suis atque ex suis causis, sed cognosci*

certo quatenus in sua aeternitate sunt extra suas causas in suo esse existentiae, numquam mihi placuit; neque video quantum conferat propositio illa in sensu explicato ad hanc sententiam statuendam.

Moveor autem primo, quia ex scripturis sacris aperte constat, Deum optimum maximum habere certam cognitionem aliquorum futurorum contingentium quae pendent ex libero arbitrio humano, et quae neque sunt neque fuerunt neque erunt et subinde non sunt in suo esse existentiae in aeternitate. Ergo ut Deus cognoscat futura contingentia non est necessaria existentia eorum in aeternitate, sed satis sunt causae ex quibus sunt futura. Consequentia patet; et antecedens probatur: Quia Deus scit futuram fuisse in Tyriis et Sidoniis paenitentiam in cinere et cilicio, ex suppositione quod in Tyro et Sidone factae fuissent virtutes quae factae sunt Corozaim et Betsaidae, – ut patet ex illo Matth. 11: "Si in Tyro et Sidone factae essent virtutes, quae factae sunt in vobis, olim in cilicio et cinere paenitentiam egissent, – et tamen poenitentia illa in cinere et cilio" [sic] data illa suppositione erat futuram contingens, pendens ex libertate arbitrii illorum hominum, quae neque fuit neque erit.

Secundo: Quia ridiculum est indignumque perfectione et eminentia scientias divinae, asserere Deum ignorare, quid ego pro libertate mei arbitrii essem facturus, si mihi concessisset maius auxilium quam de facto statuit concedere, et si prolongasset mihi vitam plus quam statuit prolongare, aut permisisset graviores tentationes quam statuit permittere. Cum ergo quae tunc essent futura, sint futura contingentia, fit ut ad certam scientiam futurorum contingentium in Deo non necessaria sit existentia rerum in aeternitate, sed sat sit cognitio causarum a quibus sunt futura.

Tertio: Quamquam Deus ab aeterno simul duratione cognoverit se posse creare aut non creare mundum et statuerit creare ac sciverit mundum tali tempore esse futurum, prius tamen est scire per scientiam naturalem se posse creare et non creare, quam statuere creare (est enim illud praerequisitum ad hoc secundum); et prius est statuere creare quam scire mundum tali tempore esse futurum, oritur enim hoc secundum ex illo et non contra. Peto ergo: vel prius fuit, saltem modo prioritatis proxime explicato, futura contingentia quae pendent ex libero arbitrio hominis esse in aeternitate secundum suum esse existentiae, quam Deus cognosceret illa esse futura quasi quid praerequisitum ad talem cognitionem, vel prius cognovit esse futura ex suppositione, si statueret producere causas, ex quibus essent futura. Si detur hoc secundum: ergo antequam sint in esse existentiae cognoscuntur futura ex suppositione determinationis voluntatis divinae ad producendum causas; et subinde in ipsa deter-

*minatione voluntatis divinae, quae antecedit esse existent-
iae causarum et a fortiori effectuum, cognoscentur certo et
infallibiliter futura. Non ergo est necessarium esse existentiae eorum ut a Deo cognoscantur futura. - Quod si detur
primum, quod scil. effectus a suis causis prius oriantur
in esse existentiae, quam a Deo saltem modo explicato ex
suppositione determinationis suae voluntatis praecognoscantur
futuri, non video quomodo in Deo salvetur providentia, per-
missio peccatorum, quae praevidet alium pro sua libertate
esse facturum et non impedit, ac praedestinatio. Neque credo
aliquem sanae mentis admissurum effectus ita egredi in aeternitate a suis causis, quasi Deus, prius saltem natura quam
egrediantur, non videat quomodo sint egressuri, sed solum in
ipso egressu videat quales egrediantur, quasi cognitio divina
pendeat ab egressu. Cf. L. Molina, Concordia, pp. 288-91.*

Molina goes on and on. His point, which we shall see more fully
later, is this: if God knows what a man would do because he knows
what a man can do, there is no providence; on the other hand, if
God knows what a man would do because God knows what he himself will do, there is no liberty. Midway, therefore, between God's
knowledge of what can be and his knowledge of what will be there
lies the scientia media: God's knowledge of what would be, if he
should decide to create.

*L. Molina, De Scientia Dei, in Stegmüller, op. cit., pp.
238-40: dicendum est, Deum ex comprehensione et omnimoda
penetratione per suam scientiam naturalem omnium causarum
in sua essentia, etiam liberarum, ad quam partem pro sua
libertate cum his aut illis circumstantiis se essent determinaturae, ex suppositione tamen seu sub conditione: si
creentur hoc aut illo modo, cum his aut illis circumstantiis
etc., una cum determinatione libera suae voluntatis, qua
statuit creare mundum eo modo quo creavit et cum circumstantiis quae de facto cernuntur, praecognovisse certo et
infallibiliter omnia futura contingentia, manente de facto
libero arbitrio in causis agentibus per intellectum et
voluntatem.
      Ad huius rei intelligentiam sciendum est, Deum in sua
aeternitate ante determinationem liberam suae voluntatis ad
aliquid creandum aut producendum ex intuitu suae essentiae et
potentiae cognovisse per scientiam naturalem omnia quae
poterat facere, sc. se posse creare hunc mundum et infinitos
alios; posse creare hunc in tali vel tali parte temporis
aut in quacumque alia; posse in eo creare angelos, aut non hos
sed infinitos alios; posse creare in hoc mundo homines quos
statuit creare, aut non hos sed alios; posse ita disponere hoc*

*universum ut essent hae aut illae occasiones et circum-
stantiae, aut non hae sed aliae; posse se hominibus et
angelis conferre tantum aut tantum gratiae atque
auxilii, aut non tantum sed plus aut minus; posse
unicuique permittere has aut illas tentationes aut occasiones, tribuereque unicuique hominum talem vel talem
complexionem, aut non hanc sed aliam; et ita de infinitis
aliis ordinibus et combinationibus rerum aut circumstantiarum, quas sua omnipotentia poterat facere in hoc
universo.*

*Sciendum est praeterea, in eadem sua aeternitate ante
determinationem suae voluntatis eadem scientia naturali
ex omnimodo comprehensione et penetratione rerum atque
causarum vidisse, quid esset futurum, si hunc ordinem aut
illum eligeret producere, quid unusquisque angelorum suo
libero arbitrio relictus facturus esset pro sua libertate
cum tanto aut tanto auxilio et cum his aut illis occasionibus aut circumstantiis, quid unusquisque hominum
cum tanto aut tanto auxilio et cum his aut illis occasionibus,
tentationibus aut circumstantiis pro sua libertate esset
facturus, cum tamen si vellet posset oppositum existentibus
eisdem circumstantiis, tentationibus aut occasionibus,
Hactenus ergo optimus nulli adimens libertatem arbitrii sua
scientia naturali cognoscit in sua essentia atque potentia
omnia contingentia futura, non in esse futuri absolute sed
sub conditione, si per determinationem liberam suae voluntatis
statuit creare hunc aut illum ordinem rerum, cognoscitque
non solum ea, quae de facto sunt, fuerunt aut erunt, sed
etiam infinita illa, quae essent, si alium ordinem statueret
aut si in hoc ordine statueret alias circumstantias; scit
enim futuram fuisse paenitentiam Tyriorum et Sidoniorum
in cinere et cilicio ex suppositione si statuisset, ut in
Tyro et Sidone fierent virtutes et miracula, quae Coronzaim
et Betsaidae facta sunt.*

*Accedente ergo libera determinatione suae voluntatis,
qua ab aeterno statuit et elegit creare ordinem eorum
quae de facto creavit cum circumstantiis quae de facto sunt,
ab aeterno libere scivit, omnia contingentia futura in
esse futuri absolute, nulli adimens libertatem arbitrii,
sed ipsum relinquens potentem ut de facto possit facere
oppositum. Si tamen ipse de facto esset pro sua libertate
facturus oppositum, ut potest, Deus id praescivisset, et
non id quod de facto modo scit; unde praescientia aut
electio voluntatis divinae nulli necessitatem imponit aut
adimit libertatem. Cf. L. Molina, Concordia, pp. 302,
317; L. Molina, Epitome de Praedestinatione, in Stegmüller,
op. cit., pp. 336, sqq.*

The theory has subtlety but not the bracing subtlety of the thought of St. Thomas. St. Thomas had said simply, God causes every-thing--the necessary, the accidental, the free.

Cf. supra, pp. 46-48.

For such are the natures of things--namely, to be either neces-sary, accidental, or free--and God is the author of natures. And if it be asked, How can God know the future free act? it seems to be a sufficient answer to remind us that he knows it as present. But futuribles do not exist! The answer is fundamentally the same! He knows the futuribles too, for these also are natures of which he is the author. That free futurables merely would exist is also conditioned by the divine causality, and thus their esse is as present to him as is the esse of anything which is. God knows what will be and what would be, because for him both what will be and what would be are: the first are things which will exist; the second, things which would exist.

Summa Theol., 1a 2ae q. 10, a. 4: Respondeo dicendum, quod, sicut Dionysius dicit IV cap. De div. nom., 33, col. 734, t. 1, ad Providentiam divinam non pertinet naturam rerum corrumpere, sed servare. Unde omnia movet secundum eorum conditionem; ita quod ex causis necessariis per motionem divinam consequuntur effectus ex necessitate; ex causis autem contingentibus sequuntur effectus contingenter.
Quia igitur voluntas est activum principium non deter-minatum ad unum, sed indifferenter se habens ad multa; sic Deus ipsam movet, quod non ex necessitate ad unum determinat, sed remanet motus ejus contingens, et non necessarius, nisi in his ad quae naturaliter movetur.
Ad primum ergo dicendum, quod voluntas divina non solum se extendit ut aliquid fiat per rem quam movet, sed ut etiam eo modo fiat quo congruit naturae ipsius. Et ideo magis repugnaret divinae motioni, si voluntas ex necessitate moveretur, quod suae naturae non competit, quam si moveretur libere, prout competit suae naturae. On God's knowledge of future free acts cf. pp. 48-49 supra, and Summa Theol., 1a q. 22, a. 4.

But both, metaphysically, are. Molina could not see what the "presentiality" of all things in their divine cause had to do with it. "Presentiality" has this to do with it: it witnessed to St. Thomas' conviction that God is the source of all being, that all being is as immediate to his knowledge as to his causality, and

105

it is immediate to his knowledge because immediate to his causality. But Molina, unable to see this, attempted to wedge between St. Thomas' scientia visionis and scientia simplicis intelligentiae

Cf. supra, p. 43 sqq.

--which for St. Thomas were adequate divisions of divine knowledge-- his scientia media quae antecedit liberam determinationem divinae voluntatis.

L. Molina, De Scientia Dei, in Stegmüller, op. cit., p. 239: Ad huius rei intelligentiam sciendum est, Deum in sua aeternitate ante determinationem liberam suae voluntatis ad aliquid creandum aut producendum ex intuitu suae essentiae et potentiae cognovisse per scientiam naturalem omnia quae poterat facere . . . Sciendum est praeterea, in eadem sua aeternitate ante determinationem suae voluntatis eadem scientia naturali ex omnimoda comprehensione et penetratione rerum atque causarum vidisse, quid esset futurum, si hunc ordinem aut illum eligeret producere, quid unusquisque angelorum suo libero arbitrio relictus facturus esset pro sua libertate cum tanto aut tanto auxilio et cum his aut illis occasionibus aut circumstantiis, quid unusquisque hominum tanto aut tanto auxilio et cum his aut illis occasionibus, tentationibus aut circumstantiis pro sua libertate esset facturus, cum tamen si vellet posset oppositum existentibus eisdem circumstantiis, tentationibus aut occasionibus. Cf. L. Molina, Concordia, pp. 302, 317.

Metaphysics did not demand this. A sort of divine psychology, if you will, did demand that God know the futuribles, but to postulate further that he knows them without causing them seems to turn theodicy into a divine psychology.

L. Molina, De Scientia Dei, in Stegmüller, op. cit., p. 204: "Utrum in Deo sit scientia futurorum contingentium." In partem negativam arguitur primo: A causa necessaria provenit effectus necessarius. Scientia Dei est causa rerum. Cum ergo sit necessaria, fit ut nihil scitum a Deo sit contingenter futurum, sed omne sit necessarium. p. 248: Superest respondeamus ad argumenta initio totius disputationis proposita. Ad primum ergo neganda est imprimis minor, si sit sermo de scientia futurorum contingentium in esse futuri, de qua est sermo hoc loco. Hanc enim ostendimus art. 8 non esse causam rerum. Haec namque est post determinationem liberam voluntatis divinae; scientia vero quae est causa rerum est quae

dictat modum operandi, et antecedit determinationem
voluntatis divinae determinaturque ad operandum per
actum voluntatis supervenientem--Deinde: Si in minori
sit sermo de scientia, quae antecedit actum voluntatis,
et qua Deus naturaliter cognoscit modum faciendi res
mandandique eas executioni, distinguenda est maior. Si
enim sit sermo de causae totali sufficiente sola ad ef-
fectum et non impedibili, vera est. Scientia autem
divina non est totalis causa rerum, sed indiget concursu
libero voluntatis divinae, quo determinetur ad operandum;
ratione cuius concursus effectus non provenit necessario
sed libere, ita ut possit non provenire--Praeterea: In
ordine ad effectus, quos Deus statuit non producere per
se ipsum solum, sed mediantibus causis secundis, indiget
ulterius concursu etiam causarum secundarum, ratione
cuius, vel quia liber est, vel quia, si sit naturalis,
impedibilis est ratione aliarum causarum concurrentium,
effectus evenire possunt contingenter.

Molina thus seems to describe what happens in the divine order
without ascribing any reason for its happening. God knows the
futuribles, because there they are, and there God is, and what
more could one ask?

Just so, Molina's theory of liberty seems in contrast to the
theory of St. Thomas to be a psychology. By a psychology of
liberty in contrast to a metaphysic is meant here a description
of what happens in the free act. By a philosophy or metaphysic
of liberty is meant the explanation of what happens in the free act.
The first is a knowledge through experience, the second, knowledge
per causas. Molina will state what occurs in the free act, and this
statement he confuses with the explanation of what occurs.

Whether or no his confusion here is also caused by his inability
to understand St. Thomas I do not know. Certainly he did not understand St. Thomas upon divine prescience and causality. I rather
think that upon liberty too he missed the point. One who "never
thought much" of an able theologian's theory would be likely to
miss the point.

The point is what is the relation of intellection to choice?
Molina saw quite clearly that intellection was necessary for
voluntary action. There had to be, he knew, a judgment of
reason preceding choice, in order that choice be rational.

L. Molina, Censura contra Dominicum Bannes, in Stegmüller,
op. cit., p. 490: nam voluntas, quando caret intellectione,
non habet sufficiens principium volendi, quoniam intellectus

ad volitionem est prorsus necessaria [necessarius?].
Quoniam vero non ita operatur [agens liberum] nisi
praevio arbitrio, judicioque rationis, inde est, quod,
quatenus ita praeexigit judicium rationis, liberum ap-
pelletur arbitrium. Cf. L. Molina, Concordia, p. 10,
ad calc.

But the question is Why? Are the intellectual antecedents of the
free act the radix libertatis, the cause of liberty? If so, they
are the explanation of choice. For choice is, as anything, explained per causas. If not, they are what they are, but they are
not causes, and in default of a cause of freedom you have only
an assertion, not an explanation of freedom. Molina did not think
that intellectual antecedents of choice caused it. This is apparent, first, from his definition of freedom: he allows that judgment
must precede choice, but for him the relation between choice and
judgment is that of something post hoc, not propter hoc.

Cf. p. 2, n., supra, esp., quo fit ut liberum . . .
arbitrium non sit aliud, quam voluntas . . .

Second, and by way of confirmation of the above interpretation,
Molina rejects St. Thomas' theory of intellectual imperium in
choice. St. Thomas' point is this: although the usage of an executive power succeeds the election of, or the choosing to use that
power (for example, a man decides to sit; he sits after his
decision to sit), nevertheless the usage of reason by the will in
order to determine the will's election, precedes that election.

Summa Theol., 1a 2ae q. 16, a. 4, resp., ad fin: unde
manifestum est quod usus [secundum quod voluntas utitur
potentia executiva] sequitur electionem. Sed quia voluntas
etiam quodammodo rationem movet, et utitur ea; potest
intelligi usus eius quod est ad finem, secundum quod est
in consideratione rationis referentis ipsum in finem. Et
hoc modo usus praecedit electionem.

It is the already-discussed theory of the mutual and reciprocal
causality of the will and intellect in diverse orders of causality
--the intellect determines the choice (quis intelligo me velle)--
which determines the intellect (quia volo intelligere). Of this
theory Molina says, haec tamen sententia numquam mihi
placuit.

108

For . . . unless I am mistaken, we have shown that the act
of commanding [this, in St. Thomas' theory, is intellectual
determination] . . . , in order that one may dominate one's
own will or members or executive faculty, or the election of
means or their usage to attain an end, is not necessary. But
it is enough that there be a judgment by which the intellect
knows the means, the suitability of each to the end, or their
relatively greater expediency, in order that the will, without
further command from the intellect [clearly, Molina knew,
even if he did not understand, what he was rejecting here],
may elect what it pleases . . .

Concordia L. Molina, p. 429, 430: Haec tamen sententia
mihi numquam placuit. In primis enim, ut prima secundae
loco citato satis, ni fallor, ostendimus, necessarius
non est imperandi actus a prudentia monastica elicitus,
ut quis, vel propriae voluntati, vel membris, facultative
suae executrici, imperet, sive electionem medii, sive
usum illius ad finem comparandum; sed satis est judicium,
quo intellectus cognoscit media, aptitudinemque singulorum
ad finem, quaeve eorum magis expediant, ut voluntas, sine
alio imperio intellectus, eligat quod maluerit, moveatque
membra facultatemve executricem ad operationem; eodemque
modo satis est ex arte cognoscere qualis modus tenendus
sit in quaque re fabricanda, ut voluntas absque alio imperio
intellectus moveat membra, caeteraque instrumenta ad con-
ficiendum artefactum.

The opposition between the two is important enough for further
insistence. More texts will serve to emphasize the difference
between St. Thomas' concept of the relation between choice and
its intellectual antecedents and Molina's. The question is still
about the imperium: utrum imperare sit actus rationis vel
voluntatis? The imperium in question is id quo quis sibi imperat.
St. Thomas answers: to command belongs essentially to the
reason, although of course an act of the will is the presupposition
of this imperium, in virtue of which act of the will reason itself,
per imperium, moves in regard to the exercise of the act. The
subtlety of this answer demands that St. Thomas' reasons be
quoted in full.

The act of the reason and of the will can be brought to bear
on one another, in so far as the reason reasons about willing,
and the will wills to reason. The result is that the act of the
reason precedes the act of the will, and conversely. And

109

since the power of the preceding act continues in the act which follows, it sometimes happens that there is an act of the will insofar as it retains in itself something of the act of the reason, as was said concerning usage and election; and conversely, that there is an act of the reason inasmuch as it retains in itself something of an act of the will. Now, command is essentially indeed an act of reason . . . in two ways. First, absolutely . . . as when one says to another: this is what you should do . . . and . . . as when it is said to someone: do this. Now the first mover among the powers of the soul to the doing of an act, is the will.

Summa. Theol., 1a 2ae, q. 9, a. 1.

Since, therefore, the second mover does not move, except in virtue of the first mover, it follows that the very fact that the reason moves by commanding is dependent upon the power of the will. Consequently it follows that to command is an act of the reason, presupposing an act of the will, in virtue of which the reason by its command moves to the exercise of the act . . . The root of liberty is the will as the subject thereof; but it is the reason as its cause. For the will can tend freely toward various objects, precisely because the reason can have various conceptions of the good. Whence philosophers define free choice as being a free judgment arising from reason, as though reason is the cause of liberty.

Summa Theol., 1a 2ae q. 17, a. 1, resp. et ad 2um. The subject of election mentioned in the passage, is in Summa Theol., 1a 2ae q. 13, a. 1, resp. et ad 2um: in nomine electionis importatur aliquid pertinens ad rationem, sive ad intellectum, ad aliquid pertinens ad voluntatem . . . sicut enim dicimus animal ex anima et corpore compositum esse, neque vero corpus esse secundum seipsum, neque animam solam, sed utrumque, ita et electionem. Est autem considerandum . . . quod actus qui est essentialiter unius potentiae vel habitus, recipit formam et speciem a superiori potentia vel habitu . . . Si enim aliquis actum fortitudinis exerceat propter Dei amorem, actus quidem ille materialiter est fortitudinis, formaliter vero charitatis. Manifestum est autem quod ratio quoddammodo voluntatem praecedit et ordinat actum eius, inquantum sc. voluntas in suum objectum tendit secundum ordinem rationis, eo quod vis apprehensiva appetitivae suum objectum repraesentat. Sic igitur ille actus quo voluntas tendit in aliquid quod proponitur ut

110

bonum, ex eo quod per rationem est ordinatum ad finem, materialiter quidem est voluntatis, formaliter autem rationis . . . Et electio substantialiter non est actus rationis sed voluntatis . . . Ad 2um. Conclusio syllogismi, quae fit in operabilibus, ad rationem pertinet, et dicitur sententia vel judicium, quam sequitur electio; et ob hoc ipsa conclusio pertinere videtur ad electionem tamquam ad consequens.

It is the theory of the mutual, reciprocal, and diverse causality of will and intellect over again.

Molina denies the theory. Answering the question, Why are the free acts of children not imputable? he says that children do not as yet know enough to distinguish between moral good and evil, though they have sufficient knowledge to act freely. He then goes on: "Anyhow, I think freedom is in the will, not in the intellect. Nor," he continues,

> is intellectual deliberation as necessary as many think, still less is the command of the intellect, by which it governs the will, necessary. It is enough that the intellect see some good in the object in order to will it, or some evil in order to reject it . . . Accordingly, with the same intellectual dis- position and knowledge . . . the will can, by its innate liberty, will, or not will, or do neither . . . To refrain freely from acting by not willing, when we can will, or by not being un- willing, when we can be unwilling, are quite different, e.g., freely to will to restrain an act by eliciting an act of the will whereby we will to check an act in reference to some object. To do the latter, i.e., to elicit an act in order to refrain from choosing some object, one must have some knowledge of the good of not acting. To do the former, i.e., not to will, there is no need that the good of not acting be known--since there will be no act. But it is enough, when the good is presented, that such a good does not necessitate the act, for by that very fact the will is able not to act, and hence freely to check its act.

So for evil. However tangled Molina's thought be, this at least emerges: not only is choice not caused by present knowledge ("with the same intellectual disposition and knowledge, the will can by its innate liberty will or not will, or do neither"), but, seemingly, some choice--for example, the choice not to will--is not caused by any knowledge: ad illud primum [libere continere

111

actum <u>non</u> volendo] necesse <u>non</u> est representari intellectui <u>sub</u>
<u>boni</u> ratione continere actum.

*L. Molina, <u>Concordia</u>, pp. 12, 13: Caeterum arbitror
libertatem esse in voluntate, et non in intellectu, atque ad libertatem volendi, aut nolendi, vel continendi
actum non volendo, quando velle possumus, et non nolendo,
quando possumus nolle, non esse necessariam tantam
deliberationem ex parte intellectus, quantam multi
necessariam esse existimant, et multo minus imperium
intellectus, quo voluntati imperet, ut velit, aut nolit,
vel contineat actum: sed ad volendum satis esse notitiam
bonitatis alicujus, quae in objecto eluceat, vel delecta-
bilis, vel utilis, aut honestae; ea vero bonitas si tanta
non sit, et tam persipcue cognita, quae voluntati necessitatem inferat, ut nulla est talis praeter Deum clare
visum, integrum est voluntati non elicere actum; tametsi
regulariter illum eliceat, si magna sit, nihilque adsit,
quod ab eo eliciendo retrahat: similiter existente notitia
alicujus mali, integrum eidem voluntati est nolle ac
respuere objectum; nec tamen necessitatur ad nolendum,
sed potest non elicere nolitionem continendo actum; licet,
quando objectum est vehemens, regulariter nolitionem
eliciet, nisi adsit, quod aliunde moveat ad illam non
eliciendam, aut etiam ad contristativum amplectendum
propter bonum cum eo conjunctum. Itaque existente eadem
dispositione ac notitia ex parte intellectus, qualis explicata est, potest voluntas sua innata libertate velle,
aut nolle, vel neutrum elicere actum, ut ex iis, quae
prima secundae q. IX., fuse docuimus, et ex parte in hac
prima parte, dum nobis de peccato angelorum est sermo
exposuimus, atque ex propria cujusque nostrum experientia
constat.--Illud obiter circa eandem interrogationem ad-
monuerim: longe diversa esse libere continere actum non
volendo, quando velle possumus, aut non nolendo, quando
nolle possumus, ut libere velle continere actum, eliciendo
voluntatis actum, quo continere actum circa aliquod objectum volumus. Atque ad hoc quidem secundum necesse est
praecedat in intellectu notitia alicujus bonitatis, quae
eluceat in eo, quod actus contineatur: quandoquidem debet
id esse volitum actu voluntatis: volitio autem in nullam
rem tendere potest nisi sub ratione boni. Ad illud vero
primum necesse non est repraesentari intellectui sub boni
ratione continere actum; quippe cum voluntas circa id
nullam elicere debeat actum: sed satis est, quando repraesentatur aliquod objectum sub ratione boni, potestque
voluntas illud velle, non esse tantam bonitatem illius
evidenter cognitam, quae voluntati ad eum actum eliciendum*

112

necessitatem inferat: eo enim ipso in potestate volunta-
tis est non elicere eum actum, ac proinde libere eum
continere. Satis similiter est, quando voluntati ob-
jectum aliquod repraesentatur sub ratione mali, potest-
que voluntas illud nolle, non necessitari ad illud
nolendum: eo enim ipso in potestate ipsius est, non
elicere eum nolendi actum, ac proinde libere illum con-
tinere.

Anyhow, choice for Molina is clearly not caused by intellection. Later we shall see Molina opposing Banes upon the same point.

But his opposition, and the reason for it, to St. Thomas seem fairly clear. Unable to understand St. Thomas' applicatio virtutis ad agendum--non video, he writes, quid sit ista applicatio. Failing to see what the "presentiality" of future contingents to God's eternity had to do with the question, and, anyhow, holding that opinion lightly, haec tamen sententia numquam mihi placuit, Molina was necessarily unable to understand St. Thomas' concept of the relations between the will and intellect, the very core of St. Thomas' theory of liberty. For, the relation between divine prescient causality and choice is analogously the same as the relation between the will and intellect: God knows, because he causes, the free act (or God causes, because he knows the free act); man knows, because he causes, his choice (or, man causes, because he knows, his choice). If Molina missed the significance of this two-way relation between will and intellect (the one's act causing and being caused by the other), it is small wonder that for him the radix libertatis, reason, though preserved, no longer functions as a cause of choice. Yet though his intellectual antecedents of choice do not cause it, Molina did describe what seems to occur in choice; we choose without being necessitated. This I have called a psychology of liberty, an assertion of a fact, or what seems to be a fact, without any explanation for it. Theologically Molina was right. The dogma which Molina was defending did demand that choice be exempt from necessity. But to reassert that dogma without, if possible, giving a reason for it (recall that the reason is reason) is not exactly to evince a philosophy of free choice.

6 MOLINA AND BANES

I have suggested that Molina did not accept St. Thomas because he did not understand him. I suggest, secondly, that the reason that Molina did not accept St. Thomas' position stemmed from the version of it proposed by Dominic Banes.

The reader will by this time allow that repetitions of the slippery ideas involved in this subject are pardonable. One can scarcely seize the points in question once for all. The most one can do is to take a fresh grip each time.

That God knows what will be, including the free acts of man, in his own causality, is the constant assertion of St. Thomas. This implies that the reason for God's certainty about what a man will freely do, and the reason for the efficacy of God's causality of what man freely does, is the divine causality itself. The question is How is God's causality, which is efficacious and of whose efficacy God is certain, related to human freedom? St. Thomas' answer, as we have seen, was this: God's knowledge of future free acts is certain because those acts are present to his eternity; God's causality effects the liberty of free acts because it reaches not only to their being but also to their manner of being; namely, contingent or necessary being. In short, God knows what will freely be because he sees what will be, actually realized, and that it be freely realized is the effect of his infinite causality.

Summa Theol., 1a q. 22, a. 4. Cf. pp. 84 sqq. supra.

The human liberty implied in these relations is, on the side of the accomplishment of the act of choice, a series of overhand grips of choice over deliberation over choice, over deliberation, and so forth until statur in appetitu naturali. This desire of the good is indeterminate with respect to good, for there are many bona. On the side of the specification of choice, liberty (that is, the absence of necessity in choice) is maintained by reason of the fact that there is a scale of goods; the good can be more or less good. And we can see this. The fact that we can leaves choice free.

Cf. pp. 92-95, supra, and *Summa Theol.*, 1a q. 83, a. 1, resp.: et pro tanto necesse est quod homo sit liberi arbitrii ex hoc ipso quod rationalis est. Cf. p. 79 supra.

Dominic Banes proposed the following version of the above position, a version contained in a number of propositions which Molina singles out for censure. After stating these propositions together with Molina's reasons for rejecting them, I shall indicate whatever discrepancy there seems to be between Molina and Banes and between both and St. Thomas. Since not all Banes' propositions censured by Molina concern this subject I shall number them to suit convenience.

Banes says--Molina is quoting him--

1 Some think that the collation of efficacious grace is not the adequate cause of conversion to God. Their reason is that grace is not the only cause, since free choice cooperates together with grace. This solution is highly satisfactory to certain theologians, but it cannot satisfy us . . . The reason is: the very concurrence of free choice is an effect necessarily consequent, by the necessity of the consequence, upon efficacious grace.

In Stegmüller, op. cit., p. 480: Aliqui existimant, collationem divini auxilii efficacis non esse causam adaequatam conversionis in Deum, quia non est causa sola, eo

*quod simul concurrit liberum arbitrium cum divino auxilio.
Et haec solutio quibusdam theologis valde placet, nobis
tamen placere non potest.--Quia ipsamet concurrentia
liberi arbitrii effectus est necessario consequens necessitate consequentiae ex divino auxilio efficaci. Dominicus
Banes, scholastica commentaria in I. partem, q. 23, a. 3,
dub. 3, post concl. 10 ad 6 arg., ed. Douai, 1614, p. 280.*

This assertion, Molina thinks, differs in little or nothing from
Calvin's. For an adequate and sole cause excludes every other
cause, since its working is the effect of God alone. Now, the
Council of Trent states that by gratia excitans et adiuvans men
are disposed to convert themselves by assenting to and cooperating
with the same grace, and that man himself, receiving the inspi-
ration, acts; and he so acts that he can reject grace. And in the
canon are condemned those who say that free choice, moved by
God, cooperates in no wise by assenting to God's gratia excitans,
by which stimulus a man prepares and disposes himself to conversion, and that it [free choice] cannot dissent if it wishes.

*L. Molina, Censura contra Dominicum Bannes in Stegmüller,
op. cit., pp. 480-82; cf. op. cit., pp. 433-34. For Calvin's
texts see p. 27, n., supra, p. 31, n., supra. The passage
from the Council of Trent is in Denziger-Bannwart, Enchiridion Symbolorum, nn. 797, 814: Declarat praeterea
ipsius justificationis exordium in adultis a Dei per Christum
Jesum praeveniente gratia sumendum esse: hoc est, ab ejus
vocatione, qua nullis eorum existentibus meritis vocantur;
ut, qui per peccata a Deo aversi erant, per ejus excitantem
atque adjuvantem gratiam ad convertendum se ad suam ipsorum
justificationem, eidem gratia libere assentiendo et cooperando
disponantur; ita ut tangente Deo cor hominis per Spiritus
Sancti illuminationem, neque homo ipse nihil omnino agat,
inspirationem illam recipiens, quippe qui illam et abjicere
potest, neque tamen sine gratia Dei movere se ad justitiam
coram illo libera sua voluntate possit. Unde in sacris litte-
cum dicitur: Convertimini ad me, et ego convertar ad vos;
libertatis nostrae admonemur; cum respondemus: Converte nos
Domine ad te, et convertemur; Dei nos gratia praeveniri
confitemur.--Can. 4. Si quis dixerit, liberum hominis arbitr
a Deo motum et excitatum nihil cooperari assentiendo Deo excitanti atque vocanti, quo ad obtinendam justificationis
gratiam se disponat ac praeparet, neque posse dissentire, si
velit, sed veluti inanime quoddam nihil omnino agere, mere-
que passive se habere; A. S.*

2 Just as grace with Banes is the adequate cause of conversion, so its denial is the adequate cause of nonconversion, inasmuch as its denial is a pure negation of being. "There is no need to fear," writes Banes, "the concession that, just as divine help is the efficacious cause of grace and conversion to God, so the denial of efficacious help is the cause of nonconversion to God." Since, then, Molina contends, Banes had said in the preceding proposition that efficacious grace was the sole and adequate cause of conversion, therefore its denial is, according to him, the sole and adequate cause of nonconversion.

D. Bannes, op. cit., q. 23, a. 3, dub. 3 ad 6, p. 280 a E, in Stegmüller, op. cit., p. 485: Nihil verendum est concedere, quod sicut divinum auxilium est causa efficax gratia et conversionis in Deum, ita negatio auxilii efficacis causa est non-conversionis in Deum. For Molina's text, vid. Stegmüller, ibid.

This proposition Molina regards as at least erroneous and favorable to heresy. For if it be true, damnation is to be ascribed rather to God, who denies help, than to man, who cannot be converted without help. Nor will Molina admit that Banes' qualification--a man's nonconversion is a privation (by which is implied that God is not the cause of the privation but only of the denial of grace)--saves the opinion from error. For first, after Banes had affirmed that the denial of grace was the cause of nonconversion, he straightway added: "thus God is said, by denying that efficacious help, to blind and harden; from this negation there straightway follows, by the necessity of the consequence, that one is not converted." Whence Banes thinks, Molina urges, that by the denial of grace God is the cause of excaecatio and induratio. Plainly, this must refer not to a negation but to a privation of help. Second, it is contradictory to assert that God is the cause of negation of a form (grace) in a subject which by its nature can receive that form and yet say that God is not the cause of the privation of that form.

D. Bannes, op. cit., p. 280 a E F, p. 280 a F, in Stegmüller, op. cit., pp. 486, 487: Quatenus non-conversio est privatio.--Hoc modo dicitur Deus excaecare et indurare, negando illud auxilium efficax; ex qua negatione statim sequetur necessitate consequentiae, quod aliquis non convertatur. For Molina's text vid. Stegmüller, ibid.

3 The third proposition of Banes which Molina selects for censure is this: perfect providence comprises not only the plan of suitable means to an end but also the plan of certainly efficacious means. Molina regards this as suspect and Calvinistic. His reason is that, if it be true, man could not then freely dissent to the predetermined and predefined plan of God. That Banes meant precisely that, Molina will later try to show. Meanwhile he adduces from Banes in support of his own interpretation this: "there antecedes our free operation the certain and immutable counsel of the divine will, i.e., the infallible predefinition of divine providence, which predefines every free operation which is good, and even every operation insofar as it is good."

> *D. Banes, op. cit., q. 22, a. 1, concl. 1, pp. 260 b F, in Stegmüller, op. cit., pp. 487, 488: Si providentia consideretur secundum rationem simpliciter perfectae providentiae, includit intrinsece non solum rationem certae efficaciae mediorum ad assequendum finem; quia alias imperfecta est providentia et inefficax, et omnia media frustra sunt apposita. Ex quo sequitur, quod cum divina providentia sit perfectissima, ad illam pertinet intrinsece, ut sit ratio assecutionis finis.--Primum est, antecedit operationem nostram liberam divinae voluntatis certum et immutabile consilium, sive divinae providentiae infallibilis praedefinitio, quae omnem bonam operationem liberam praedefinivit, immo et omnem operationem, in quantum bona est. Cf. Stegmüller, op. cit., pp. 418, 413, 424; for Molina's texts, vid., Stegmüller, ibid. For Calvin's texts, whose meaning Molina identifies with Banes', vid. p. 29, n., supra.*

4 Banes' fourth proposition is this: "God has from eternity decided by his absolute or consequent will not to give to all men [namely, to those who in fact are not going to receive it] the aids to the supernatural life."

> *D. Banes, op. cit., q. 23, a. 3, dub. 3, concl. 10, p. 278 a C, in Stegmüller, op. cit., p. 489: Deus ab aeterno statuit voluntate vel absoluta vel consequenti non dare omnibus supernaturalia auxilia, videlicet eis, qui revera non erant recepturi. Cf. Stegmüller, op. cit. p. 426.*

God's absolute will, Banes explains, is that which semper expletur.

> *D. Banes, 1. c., p. 278 a A, in Stegmüller, op. cit., p. 426*

This, Molina thinks, is to make salvation impossible for some. For some men would then lack the help without which, and because God denied it to them, they could not be saved.

L. Molina, Censura contra D. Bannes, in Stegmüller, op. cit., pp. 489-92.

5 Banes' fifth proposition touches directly the subject of liberty.

It must be noted that we place indifference in the object judged; and it is not necessary that we understand that there is indifference in the intellect itself or in its act . . . as often as the act of the will arises from the aforesaid root of the judgment, it will always be free. Whence, whatever precedes, accompanies, or supervenes upon the act of the will, if it does not destroy that judgment concerning the means to the end, will not destroy the liberty of the operation: for, since the definition of a free act is thus verified, the act must necessarily be free.

D. Banes, op. cit., q. 19, a. 10, sol. 1, ad 5, p. 255 a D, 255 a C, in Stegmüller, p. 492: Observandum est quod indifferentiam collocamus in ipso obiecto indicato; non autem opus est, ut in ipso intellectu vel in actu ipsius indifferentiam esse intelligamus. Quotiescumque actus voluntatis oritur ex praedicta radice iudicii, semper erit liber. Unde quidquid antecesserit vel comitabitur vel supervenerit ad actum voluntatis, si non tollat iudicium illud medii respectu finis, non destruit libertatem operationis, qua stante definitione actus liberi necesse est actum esse liberum.

The continuation of this text from Banes

Op. cit., p. 255 b A.

is necessary to the understanding of Molina's objection to it.

And now, to come a bit closer to more difficult points. There antecedes our free operation the eternal and immutable counsel of the divine will, viz., the infallible predefinition of divine providence, which predefines every free operation which is good, and even every operation insofar as it is good and is concerned with the good. Yet because God himself does not, by his providence and immutable counsel, bind or destroy our judgment--by which we judge that the means are indif-

119

ferent, adaptable, and to be adapted to the end, he likewise does not destroy the liberty of our operation, but efficaciously causes, cherishes and protects it.

D. Banes, op. cit., 1. c.: Nunc ergo ad difficiliora paulatim accede. Antecedit quidem operationem nostram liberam divinae voluntatis aeternum et immutabile consilium sive divinae providentiae infallibilis praedefinitio, quae omnem bonam operationem liberam praedefinivit, immo et omnem operationem, in quantum bona est et circa bonum exercetur. At vero quia ipse Deus sua providentia et immutabili consilio non ligat neque destruit iudicium nostrum, quo iudicamus indifferentiam medii et ordinabilitatem eius, et ordinandum esse ad finem, non etiam nostrae operationis libertatem destruit, sed potius illam efficaciter efficit, fovet atque conservat.

This proposition Molina regards as favorable to heresy. Calvin and Luther, he contends, admitted implicitly that choice contained an intellectual judgment about means indifferent to an end. Either, then, Trent was wrong in condemning them, or Banes' account of liberty is wrong. Further, the admission that a determination to choice does not impede liberty is all the Reformers need to shout victory. And the freedom to choose utrumlibet, which Trent and Scripture affirm, is not reconcilable with a Bannesian determination ad unum. In short, Banes and the heretics differ only in their expressions: the same act which Banes calls free they say is necessitated.

L. Molina, Censura contra D. Bannes, in Stegmüller, op. cit., pp. 492-98.

6 Banes' sixth proposition is an endeavor to extricate himself from the conclusion which Molina was to draw; namely, that Banes' account of free choice differs only in words from the account proposed by the Reformers. "Man's free choice, moved and excited by God, cannot in sensu composito dissent." Trent had defined that man's free choice, moved and excited by God, could dissent if it chose. Banes' interpretation of this was that free choice can in sensu diviso dissent, but not in sensu composito.

D. Banes, op. cit., ed. Roma., 1584, col. 419 C, in
Stegmüller, op. cit., p. 498: Liberum hominis arbitrium
a Deo motum et excitatum non potest dissentire in sensu
composito. For Banes' interpretation of Trent (in
Denziger-Bannwart, Enchiridion Symbolorum, n. 814, vid.
p. 116, n., supra; see D. Bannes, de fide spe et caritate,
ed. Rom., 1586, col. 398, B D, col. 399 A, in Stegmüller,
op. cit., p. 499: Tunc enim [etiam si sermo sit de
motione Dei efficaci] simpliciter et absolute loquendo
verificatur quod homo habet potestatem dissentiendi si
velit . . . Quid ergo mirantur isti, si dicamus, quod
impossibile est in sensu composito, quod Deo sic excitanti
et vocanti homo velit resistere et dissentire; see also
D. Bannes, schol. comment. in lum partem, ed. Rom., 1584,
col. 467 A, 438 F, 439 A, in Stegmüller, op. cit., p. 499:
Implicat contradictionem, quod simul stante auxilio Dei
efficaci homo non consentiat Deo vocanti et praeparanti.
Impossibile est, quod Deus proponat istum hominem prae-
parare ad gratiam. hic et nunc, et quod iste homo non
praeparetur.--Efficaciter Deus movet voluntatem nostram;
neque effectus divinae voluntatis impediri potest a
voluntate nostra, sed necesse est necessitate consequentiae
et suppositionis, quod voluntas nostra sequatur efficacem
Dei directionem et concursum--ad illud vero Tridentini:
Si Concilium loquitur de auxilio efficaci, quo homo
iustificatur, dicendum est, quod liberum arbitrium
simpliciter, in sensu diviso, potest dissentire, si
velit, non autem in sensu composito.

I understand, says Molina, this sensus compositus and divisus
thus: if the will be considered before (sensu diviso) it is determined by God, it is determinable in utramvis partem; if it be
considered after it is determined (sensu composito) by God, it
is not able not to choose. This places liberty not in man but in
God, Calvin's position.

L. Molina, Summa Haeresium Maior, in Stegmüller, op. cit.
p. 403; for Calvin see ch. 2 supra.

Moreover, Trent means that man dissentire potest, si velit, when
he is actually moved by God (liberum arbitrium motum et excitatum a Deo), and this excludes the Bannesian sensus compositus.

Later followers of Banes admitted that the will, in sensu
composito cum divina motione, could dissent if it chose,
but that its power was not ad non-actum (if the divine

*determination was ad actum); nor was it ad actum (if the
divine determination was ad non-actum); its power was
that simply of acting or not acting. Cf. e.g., Billuart,
De Deo, D. 6, a. 4, no. 2; Tract. de act. hum. D. 2, a. 1,
no. 4, Mondovii, 1903.*

From the array of councils, Fathers, and scholastics which
Molina opposes to Banes' sensus divisus and compositus, it is
significant to note Molina's selection and interpretation of St.
Thomas. "Since, then, " wrote St. Thomas, "the will is an active
principle, not determined ad unum, but indifferent to many things,
God so moves it that it is not from necessity determined ad unum,
but its motion remains contingent." Therefore, concludes Molina,
if when the motion of God is posited the will is not determined
ad unum, the will can, according to St. Thomas, dissent if it
chooses.

*For Molina's text vid. Stegmüller, op. cit., pp. 508,
509. St. Thomas' texts are in the Summa Theol., 1a 2ae
q. 10, a. 4; 1a q. 41, a. 2; De Potentia, q. 3, a. 7, ad
13um.*

7 Banes' seventh proposition Molina regards as the radix et
origo errorum quos docent haeretici. Molina states it as follows.
No second cause can operate except it be efficaciously determined
by the first cause; and no second cause can escape from the
determination of the first cause.

*Molina takes this proposition from D. Bannes, scholastica
Commentaria in 1am partem, q. 14, a. 13, dub. ult., col.
326 C, 325, 313, ed. Rom., 1584, vid. Stegmüller, op. cit.,
pp. 511, 512; Si concursus primae causae non esset efficax
ad determinandum omnes causas secundas, nulla causa secunda
operaretur suum effectum, quia nulla secunda causa potest
operari, nisi sit efficaciter a prima determinata. —
Ista necessitas sumitur ex efficacissima primae causae
virtute, quae ita determinat omnes causas secundas ad suos
effectus producendos, quod nulla causa secunda potest exire
ab eius determinatione. Cf. Roma, Bib. Vitt. Eman., cod.
2807 Ges. 678, in Stegmüller, op. cit., pp. 512, 523;
Futura contingentia certo et infallibiliter cognoscuntur a
Deo determinatione suae voluntatis, qua absolute et ante
praevisionem operum praedeterminavit quoad substantiam et
singulas circumstantias particulares omnes actus liberos
supernaturales et naturales, etc.*

From this position of Banes, Molina complains, the heretics have deduced their conclusions: the denial of liberty, because the will is so determined ad unum by God's concursus that illi motioni refragari non possit; the assertion that God is the sole cause of good works and of sin. Thence too follows Banes' conclusion: that the will is not indifferent sensu composito cum motione divina. Hence Banes' displeasure at the assertion that God is not the sole and adequate cause of conversion. Hence, last, Banes' contention that the will is determined ad entitatem peccati by God. The two sets of conclusions and their principle are, Molina thinks, identical. But he insists upon the destruction of liberty which the proposition seems to effect; for the will must act, according to Banes, under the divine determination, and it cannot act without it. Nor can the will command the determination. If, then, liberty be the indifference to act or not to act, the divine determination which destroys indifference destroys liberty. As for the Bannesian distinction of the sensus compositus et sensu divisus, all that distinction shows is that necessity in sensu composito does not impede liberty if the composition between choice and its conditions be such that the conditions depend upon, or somehow involve, the free consent of the will. The reason: the necessity arising from this sort of conditioning of a free act supposes the free act. Such, for example, is the necessity by which a thing will be, if God knows it will be, for God's knowledge that a thing will be supposes that the will is going to choose freely. Whence it is not enough that the necessity which does not destroy liberty be merely in sensu composito (with the conditions of the free act) and ex suppositione (namely, from the supposition of the conditions of the free act). There is further required that the conditions of choice somehow involve choice itself. If conditions of choice somehow involve choice itself, it is then correct to say that in sensu composito with these conditions choice is necessary but free; but not otherwise. In short, in sensu composito with a supposition which does not depend on the will, choice is necessary with a necessity of the consequent. And it is the latter position that is Banes' though he denies it, for he asserts that the supposition (divine determination) is not dependent on the will. This too was Luther's and Calvin's position.

For Molina's text vid. Stegmüller, op. cit., pp. 512-17.

Under the circumstances Molina felt it necessary to show that St. Thomas was on his side. The proposition is this: St. Thomas agrees that under the divine motion the will can dissent and hence that the will, under divine motion, is not determined ad unum, for he writes, says Molina, Deus movet voluntatem sicut universalis motor, et sine hac universali motione homo non potest aliquid velle. Sed homo per rationem determinat se ad volendum hoc vel illud, quod est vere bonum vel apparens bonum.

> *Vid. Stegmuller, op. cit., p. 521; Summa Theol., 1a 2ae q. 9, a. 6 ad 13um; q. 10, a. 4.*

Hence he thought that a man determines himself and is not antecedently predetermined by God. More clearly:

> Deus operatur in omnibus ita tamen quod in unoquoque secundum eius conditionem. Unde in rebus naturalibus operatur sicut ministrans virtutem agendi et sicut determinans naturam ad talem actionem. In libero autem hoc modo agit, ut virtutem agendi sibi ministret et ipso operante liberum arbitrium agat; sed tamen determinatio actionis in potestate liberi arbitrii constituitur. Unde remanet sibi dominium sui actus, etc.

> *2 Dist. 25, q. 1, a. 1 ad 3um.*

Further, the general principles of St. Thomas are opposed to Bannesian predetermination. Had he admitted Banes' contention, St. Thomas would never have toiled to explain how God knew infallibly future free acts; nor would he have appealed to the difficult explanation according to which future free acts coexist in the eternity of God.

> *Summa Theol., 1a q. 14, a. 13.*

Compared with St. Thomas', Banes' explanation was easy: God knows future free acts in their predetermining cause. Nor would St. Thomas have distinguished the antecedent from the consequent will of God, had he admitted Bannesian predetermination.

> *Summa Theol., 1a q. 19, ad. 6, ad 1um.*

The antecedent will of God, which may not be fulfilled because it is not related to all the circumstances of its effects, cannot stand with an efficacious determination à la Banes, with which an effect is necessarily connected. Again, after distinguishing the acts of the will into first acts and those following thereon [first act, velle bonum; the following, velle hoc vel illud bonum], St. Thomas, had he admitted Bannesian determinations, would not have said that our first act was moved by God and that the will, in the following acts, moved itself.

Summa Theol., 1a 2ae q. 9, aa. 3 et 4; q. 111, a. 2; q. 109, a. 2 ad 1um.

For in Banes' supposition the will is moved to all acts, the first and the rest. And it does not determine itself; it is always predetermined by God. Moreover, St. Thomas would not have said that the same effect is produced both by God and the inferior agent, and by both immediately.

Contra Gentiles 3, 70.

In that case the medium would have been that predetermination by which God rather acts in the inferior cause than is in the effect. Nor would St. Thomas have taught that secondary agents determine the action of the first agent.

1. c., 3, 66, ratione 5.

Secondary agents, he writes, are quasi particular and determinative of the action of the first agent. Lastly, St. Thomas, in order to explain the certainty of predestination, would not have had recourse to the adminicula a Deo parata praedestinatis by reason of which those predestined will infallibly consent.

De Veritate, q. 6, a. 3.

If he had thought that God's certainty of the salvation of those predestined lay in efficacious predetermination, he would have appealed to that and not to the adminicula a Deo praeparata praedestinatis.

Vid. Stegmüller, op. cit., pp. 521-23.

8 Banes' last proposition and Molina's reason for rejecting it contain nothing that is not already implied. "God efficaciously

predetermines the will to the acts of sin according to their entity or matter."

D. Banes, op. cit., col. 326 C, in Stegmüller, op. cit.,
pp. 523, 524: Futura contingentia etc. certo et infallibiliter cognoscuntur a Deo in determinatione suae voluntatis,
qua absolute et ante provisionem operum praedeterminavit
quoad substantiam et singulas circumstantias particulares
omnes actus liberos supernaturales et naturales, immo et
peccata quoad eorum materiale. Cf. 325 E, 382 C, 406 A.

7 DIFFERENCES AMONG ST. THOMAS, BANES, AND MOLINA

$\mathbf{T}$he discrepancy between Banes and Molina lies in two fields: the field of the relation between divine antecedents and choice and that of the relation between human antecedents and choice. Each of the two fields is commanded by a central position which each man adopts. To the question, Is the divine causality of the free human choice a physically predetermining causality of that act ad unum? Molina says No, and this is his central position. Banes says Yes, and this is his central position.

L. Molina, Summa Haeresium Maior, in Stegmüller, op. cit., pp. 431, 432: Nunc paucis accipe discrimen inter nos et autorem cum quo disputamus. Is autor censet, quoties arbitrium elicit actum credendi, sperandi, diligendi, paenitendi, aut quemcumque alium supernaturalem, a Deo praemoveri et determinari ad eum actum auxilio quodam ita ex parte Dei efficaci, ut in potestate arbitrii non relinquatur non elicere tunc eum actum, tametsi consentiat, eumque eliciat sua sponte minimeque coactum. Si vero auxilio alio inefficaci praemoveatur, non esse in potestate ipsius arbitrii elicere actum illum cum eo auxilio. Atque ita a sola efficacia divinae providentiae et divinae voluntatis censet pendere, quem actum supernaturalem *eliciamus aut non eliciamus. Idem sentit de actibus voluntatis creatae naturalibus non malis, immo et de malis sumptis materialiter, ut supra relatum est. Atque (ut nunc de solis actibus supernaturalibus dicamus) efficaciam ad hos actus ponere videtur in gratia praeveniente, qua praemoveri, determinari et adiuvari censet voluntatem creatam ad actum supernaturalem eliciendum, ita ut integrum illi non relinquatur eum tunc non elicere. Et quia arbitratur ita efficaciter determinari voluntatem per id auxilium ad influxum voluntati proprium in eum actum, tribuit gratiae influxum voluntatis in talem actum supernaturalem. Atque ita vult iustos etiam quoad illum influxum voluntatis proprium discerni a Deo a non justis, nihilque habere quod a Deo non acceperint per auxilium gratiae; in quibus sane nihil hic autor a Calvino et saltem Chemnitio differt.*

Whence Molina charges Banes with the error, as he saw it, of the Reformers: there are antecedents to choice which of them- selves effect choice. This was the Reformers' minor.

The fact is that Banes, conceding their minor, was denying the major of the Reformers: antecedents to choice which of themselves effect choice are incompatible with the immunity of choice from necessity. Some antecedents, Banes was saying, are <u>not</u> incompatible with the exemption of choice from necessity.

Banes' position was simply this: God knows free acts in his own causality; but God causes free acts by his predetermining causality, for of such sort is the divine causality; therefore God knows free acts in his predetermining causality. This reasoning implies, first, that the reason for God's certainty about free acts is the divine predetermining decree; second, that the reason for the efficacity of these decrees is the determination of choice ad <u>unum</u> which those decrees effect. As for liberty, that is ex- plained by the fact that the divine predetermining decree, though physically effecting an ad <u>unum</u> choice, leaves untouched never- theless the <u>potentia in utrumlibet</u>. For all this Banes' reason was that liberty grew out of its conditions. If and since the divine ante- cedents of choice are infinitely efficacious, the <u>infinite</u> efficacity of them effects the mode of freedom in the free act. If and since the human antecedents of choice are intellectual, the very intel- lectuality of them demands that freedom be a power of choosing ad <u>utrumlibet</u>. Given the indifference of the judgment, Banes maintains (not, of course, that the judgment itself is indifferent but rather in the sense that it is <u>by</u> the judgment that the indifference of the object or means is judged with respect to the will or choice) that, given the indifference of the judgment, the will must choose freely. If not freely, then, just as it is contradictory that the will choose what is not proposed by the intellect--namely, something unknown (ignoti nulla cupido)--so it is contradictory that the will choose otherwise than as the object is proposed-- namely, that it choose necessarily what is proposed indifferently. In either case you would and would not have a rational appetite. Analogously, just as the will is freely determined by the judgment, so it is freely determined by the natural and, if given, super- natural concourse of God.

The points involved are divine knowledge, divine cauality and human liberty. On divine knowledge see D. Banes, schol. comment. in I partem, ed. Douai, 1614, pp. 207aD, 207bA, 207bD, 208aD in Stegmüller, op. cit., pp. 402, 403, 404: Deus cognoscit futura contingentia in suis causis parti- cularibus, quatenus ipsae causae particulares subiciuntur determinationi et dispositioni diuinae scientiae et volun- tatis, quae est prima causa. Sed causae particulares futurorum contingentium, quatenus subiciuntur determina- tioni divinae scientiae et voluntatis, sunt determinatae et completae et non impeditae ad producendos suos effectus contingentes. Ergo Deus cognoscit futura contingentia prout sunt in causis determinatis et completis et non impeditis. Minor est certissima; et maior probatur: Nam Deus cognoscit omnes causas creatas per suam essentiam, prout est prima causa dans esse et virtutem et deter- minationem omnibus causis; ergo. Sed aduertendum est circa istam rationem, quod licet causae contingentes, prout subduntur determinationi primae causae, sint deter- minatae et completae ad operandum in sensu composito, tamen simpliciter et in sensu diuiso contingentes manent et indeterminatae et incompletae; et ex consequenti earum effectus simpliciter sunt appellandi futura contin- gentia.--Etiam si Deus non cognosceret futura contingentia tanquam praesentia in sua aeternitate sed solum in causis ipsorum, eius cognitio esset certa et infallibilis. Is- tam conclusionem sicut et praecedentem intelligo de omnibus futuris contingentibus, etiam de illis quae pendent ex sola libera voluntate. Itaque contingens in praesentia comprehendit liberum. Probatur, quia apertissime colligitur ex secunda parte conclusionis praecedentis. Nam cognitio quae habetur per causas determinatas et completas certa est et infallibilis; sed Deus cognoscit contingentia per causas determinatas et completas, ut diximus conclusione praecedente; ergo.--Idea complete et consummate sumpta

non solum est forma quae est principium cognoscendi, sed
etiam est principium operandi et per modum causae exemplaris. Ex quo sequitur, quod idea, prout est principium
operandi, intrinsece claudit liberam Dei voluntatem et
eius liberam determinationem; quia non potest esse principium operandi nisi voluntate adiuncta, et illorum dumtaxat effectuum, quos libera Dei voluntas decrevit ab
aeterno producendos esse in tempore. Itaque idea habet
quod sit repraesentatiua per modum causae exemplaris futurorum contingentium, quatenus repraesentat diuinam essentiam
prout est voluntas Dei, vel (ut proprius loquar) prout est
forma cognita ab intellectu diuino per modum voluntatis
Dei. Nam cognoscens Deus suam essentiam prout est voluntas,
cognoscit omnem determinationem et dispositionem ipsius
voluntatis diuinae circa creaturas producendas. Ex hoc
sequitur, quod idea quantum ad actualem existentiam
rerum non repraesentat naturaliter et necessario, simpliciter loquendo, sed tantum in sensu composito, supposita
libera diuinae voluntatis determinatione circa ipsos
effectus creatos. Ex dictis sequitur, quartam conclusionem d. Thomae in qua dicitur, quod cognitio futurorum contingentium quae habetur in eorum causis non potest esse
certa, debere intelligi de cognitione quae habetur in
causis prout sunt indeterminatae et incompletae; quae
cognitio omnino repugnat Deo, qui, ut diximus, cognoscit
futura in suis causis prout subsunt determinationi primae
causae. On divine causality see op. cit., p. 214bE, in
Stegmüller, op. cit., p. 404: Si consideretur scientia
Dei in quantum causa, etiam aliquam habet necessitatem.
Quae necessitas non consistit in hoc quod necessario
producat effectum, quoniam prima causa libere operatur
et non necessario; sed consistit in duobus: Primum in
immobilitate diuini intellectus et voluntatis, propter
quam, si semel se determinauit ad operandum, necessario
manet determinata ad operandum. Secundo in efficacia
primae causae, cui nulla inferior causa potest resistere
neque subtrahere se ab eius determinatione, iuxta illud
ad Rom. 9, 19: Voluntati eius quis resistet. Sed haec
necessitas, ut statim explicabitur, non inducit necessitatem simpliciter in actu. On God's causality and
liberty see op. cit., p. 215bC, in Stegmüller, op. cit.,
404, 405, 406: Deinceps oportet explicemus necessitatem,
quam habet in ordine ad eandem scientiam ut causa est.
Et ista necessitas sumitur ex efficacissima primae causae
virtute, quae ita determinat omnes causas secundas ad
suos effectus producendos, quod nulla causa secunda
potest exire ab eius determinatione. Pro quo aduerte,
quod concursus primae causae ita est efficax ad deter-

130

minandum causas secundas, quod simul est suauis conformans
se cum naturis secundarum causarum, ita ut cum causa
necessaria necessitatem efficiat et cum contingenti con-
tingentiam. Et huius rei est duplex causa. Prima quoniam
Deus est autor totius naturae et idcirco potest mouere
naturam quamlibet iuxta modum eius, ita quod simul salue-
tur efficacia primae causae et modus operandi proprius
causae secundae. Secunda causa est, quam d. Thomas as-
signat q. 19, a. 8, scilicet efficacia summa primae
causae, quae non solum potest producere effectum quem
intendit, quantum ad eius substantiam sed etiam quantum
ad omnem modum quo ipsa vult producere, videlicet neces-
sario aut contingenter. Itaque prima causa determinat
meam voluntatem ad legendum, non utcumque, sed ad libere
legendum. Ex hoc sequitur, quod tam necessarium est in
sensu composito, quod ego modo libere legam, quam quod
absolute legam, quoniam utrumque cadit sub determinatione
efficacissima primae causae determinantis meam voluntatem,
ut velim libere legere. Haec doctrina colligitur ex arti-
culo octauo citato ad 2 [1a q. 19].--Sed arguet quispiam:
Videtur manifesta implicatio, quod ego simul et libere
legam et necessario legam.--Ad hoc respondetur ex d.
Thoma in resp. ad 3 huius articuli, et clarius q. 6 de
veritate art. 3 ad 7 et 8, quod uni et eidem rei potest
simul competi uterque modus iste, scilicet necessitatis
et contingentiae, sed aliter. Nempe modus contingentiae
conuenit ei simpliciter, id est ab intrinseco et ex pro-
pria natura. Alter vero, scilicet modus necessitatis,
conuenit secundum quid, id est per respectum ad extrin-
secum. Et quidem nullum est inconueniens, quod aliquis
effectus sit contingens simpliciter et necessarius secundum
quid, sicut homo potest esse niger simpliciter et albus
secundum quid. Ita in praesentia dico, quod haec propositio:
antichristus erit, simpliciter loquendo contingens est,
quoniam iste effectus ex natura sua et ex proximis suis
causis habet intrinsecam contingentiam. Est autem neces-
saria illa propositio secundum quid, i.e. per respectum ad
dispositionem diuinae scientiae et determinationem diuinae
voluntatis, quae efficaciter, licet suauiter ut explicui,
determinat omnes causas secundas ad suos effectus. Ita-
que ille modus necessitatis, qui conuenit effectui per
ordinem ad primam causam, compatitur secum modum contin-
gentiae, qui conuenit effectui ab intrinseco et ex proximis
suis causis. Et quamuis non bene possimus a priori explicare,
quo pacto concursus primae causae efficax sit et necessarius
et simul conformetur cum natura causae contingentis et
liberae, id tamen a posteriori constat nobis esse certis-
simum. Quoniam si concursus primae causae non esset efficax

*ad determinandum omnes causas secundas, nulla secunda
causa operaretur suum effectum, quia nulla secunda
causa potest operari nisi sit efficaciter a prima
determinata. Si vero concursus primae causae taliter
esset efficax, quod non accomodaretur naturis causarum
inferiorum, concursus primae causae omnem libertatem
et contingentiam auferret a causis secundis. Quocirca
dicamus illud Sap. 8, 1: Deus attingit a fine usque ad
finem fortiter et disponit omnia suaviter. On liberty
see op. cit., p. 255: libertas actus voluntatis . . .
consurgit ex radice actus intellectus, videlicet ex tali
actu et iudicio intellectus. Proponit enim intellectus
voluntati objectum, quod de seipso indifferens est ad
assecutionem obiecti voluntatis, neque cum illo necessariam connexionem habet, et nihilominus indicat ordin-
abile esse ad finem voluntatis, vel ad assecutionem illius,
vel ad participandam aliquam bonitatem ex fine, et tunc
iudicat, ut ordinetur ad finem et tunc voluntas eligit,
et in tali electione formaliter est libera. Quae libertas
oritur tamquam ex radice ex praedicto intellectus iudicio
. . . Quod quidem iudicium practicum est et cum electione
voluntatis necessario coniunctum tanquam radix efficax,
inde originatur actualis libertas operantis per voluntatem . . . Quotiescumque actus voluntatis oritur ex
praedicta radice iudicii, semper erit liber. Unde . . .
quicquid antecesserit, vel comitabitur, vel supervenerit,
ad actum voluntatis, si non tollat iudicium illud circa
medium respectu finis, non destruit libertatem operationis
. . . Antecedit quidem operationem nostram liberam divinae
voluntatis aeternum et immutabile consilium sive divinae
providentiae infallibilis praedefinitio . . . At vero quia
. . . Deus non ligat neque destruit iudicium nostrum, quo
iudicamus indifferentiam medii et ordinabilitatem eius, et
ordinandum esse ad finem, non etiam nostrae operationis
libertatem destruit, sed potius illam efficaciter efficit,
fovet atque conservat.*

This position, as was said, denied the Reformers' major:
antecedents which of themselves effect choice necessitate choice.
The necessity of choice, Banes thought, is not consequent upon a
cause effective of choice, if that cause effect also the contingence
of choice. Such a cause is in the divine order God, in the human
order and analogously, the human intellect. Liberty, then, for
Banes means the power, which one who is predetermined possesses,
of choosing among alternatives. God's part is to determine the
act of choice, which act--because God's causality of it is effica-
cissima--itself issues unnecessitated from a free power to choose.

It did look strange, this theory: a predetermined act issuing from
a free faculty; the power of choosing otherwise, though the act
of that power is predetermined; the power to choose utramvis partem,
though the choice elected be predeterminately haec pars.

D. Banes, 1. c. p. 215 bC, in Stegmüller, op. cit., 405,
406. Cf. p. 129, n., p. 131 supra especially: Secunda
causa [sc., quod concursus primae causae cum causa necessaria necessitatem efficit et cum contingenti contingentiam]
. . . omnia suaviter.

Even Banes felt the difficulty.
The difficulty seems to arise from an emphasis which Banes
places upon the physical or voluntary aspect of divine causality.
That is to say, 1) Banes insists that it is the will of God, determining the future free act, which is the reason that God knows
that act; he insists 2) it is also the will of God which is the
reason that, between choice and its antecedents, there is an infallible connexion.

D. Banes, op. cit., p. 207 bD, in Stegmüller, op. cit.,
p. 404, 405. Cf. p. 129, n., sqq. supra, especially
pp. 130-31: Itaque idea . . . effectus creatos - itaque
prima causa . . . libere legere.

Of course the infinite efficacity of the divine will leaves untouched
the liberty of the human choice. The divine voluntary determination,
then, is the reason both for the divine prescience of free acts and
the divine efficacity of those acts.
Now this gives rise to three questions: 1) Is the divine voluntary
determination the explantion of divine prescience? 2) If so, how?
3) Is the divine voluntary determination the reason for the divine
efficacity of free acts?
Let us examine these three questions in order. And, in order
to bring out more precisely Molina's position, let us examine
them in the light of his, of Banes', and of St. Thomas' answers.
1) Is the divine voluntary determination the explanation of divine
prescience? We have just heard Banes assert that it is:

itaque idea [sc., futurorum contingentium] . . . repraesentat
divinam essentiam prout est voluntas Dei, vel (ut proprius
loquar) prout est forma cognita ab intellectu divino per modum
voluntatis Dei. Nam cognoscens Deus suam essentiam prout
est voluntas, cognoscit omnem determinationem et disposition-

em ipsius voluntatis divinae circa creaturas producendas.

1. c., p. 207 bD, in Stegmüller, op. cit., p. 404; cf. supra p. 130.

St. Thomas' answer is the same as Banes', but with a qualification, and the qualification brings into focus another element.
The reason, for St. Thomas, that God knows alia a se is of
course the divine causality. But in that causality there is his will
and intellect. In fact, there is his will because there is his intellect. There is will and intellect:

> cum virtus divina se extendat ad alia, eo quod ipsa est prima
> causa effectiva omnium entium, necesse est quod Deus alia a
> se cognoscat. Et hoc etiam evidentius fit si adjungatur quod
> ipsum esse causae agentis primae, sc., Deus, est eius in-
> telligere. Unde quicumque effectus praeexistunt in Deo sicut
> in causa prima, necesse est quod sint in ipso eius intelligere.

Summa Theol., 1a q. 14, a. 5; Cf. *Cont. Gent.*, 1, 49;
De Veritate, 2, a. 3.

In fact, divine causality is constituted by the divine will because
of the divine intellect:

> effectus procedunt a causa agente, secundum quod praeexistunt
> in ea; quia omne agens agit sibi simile. Praeexistunt autem
> effectus in causa secundum modum causae. Unde cum esse
> divinum sit ipsum eius intelligere, praeexistunt in eo effectus
> eius secundum modum intelligibilem; unde et per modum in-
> telligibilem procedunt ab eo, et sic, per consequens, per
> voluntatis. Nam inclinatio eius ad agendum quod intellectu
> conceptum est, pertinet ad voluntatem. Voluntas igitur Dei
> est causa rerum.

Summa Theol., 1a q. 19, a. 4, 3°.

This constitution of divine causality by divine will and intellect is
the reason that, when there is question of divine prescience of
contingent future events, St. Thomas always answers that such
events are known as present. The reason: they cannot be known
with certainty by anyone in their cause (for there they are undetermined, future), and if known as extra causas, then, in

134

order that they be still known as contingent, it must be that the
one who causes them causes them because he knows them as such.
The supposition is that contingency is consequent upon being,
and the certain knowledge of the future contingent will thence be
in the one who is the author of being. All this is condensed into
the formula, God knows the contingents prout sunt in sua praesentialitate. Being is contingent or necessary. God sees both.
He sees the contingent in its cause, but there the contingent is
uncertain. He sees it extra causas, but there it is not necessarily related to its own cause, since God sees and causes it as
it is; namely, as contingent. How, then, can God see what is not
necessary as certain or, vice versa, see what is certain as not
necessary? By seeing it, being its cause, as it is, in sua praesentialitate.

*Cf. p. 46, n., supra; and Summa Theol., 1a q. 22, a. 4,
ad 3um: necessarium et contingens proprie consequentur
ens, in quantum huiusmodi. Unde modus contingentiae et
necessitatis cadit sub provisione Dei, qui est universalis
provisor totius entis . . .*

Another way of putting the same thing is this: that a free act exist
depends upon the will of God joined to his intelligence. For, only
that can exist which is possible, and only that is possible which
can be and, therefore, can be known by God, the intellectual
author of being. If known by God as possible (that is, as not yet
existing) yet as something certain withal, this must be because
he sees it as caused; namely, as present to his eternity.

Now, by insisting upon the divine will as the explanation of
divine prescience to the exclusion--or to a greater exclusion than
St. Thomas would seem to allow--of the divine intellect, Banes
is able to write: etiamsi Deus non cognosceret futura contingentia
tamquam praesentia in sua aeternitate, sed solum in causis ipsorum, eius cognitio esset certa et infallibilis.

*D. Banes, op. cit., p. 207 bA, in Stegmüller, op. cit.,
p. 403.*

St. Thomas did not say that. True, God knows future contingents
in their divine cause, but their divine cause being God's intellect
and will, he knows them prouti sunt in sua praesentialitate. Hence
Banes seems to be forcing a note until out of the delicate Thomistic
harmony in the relation between divine prescience and free choice

there breaks this discordant question: if God causes free acts
before he knows them as present, how can this consort with
liberty? St. Thomas had said that God knows, but not beforehand,
what a free agent will do; and he knows this because he causes,
but not beforehand, the free act. Divine will and divine intelligence
seem to be the medium in St. Thomas in which God knows future
free acts, not the divine will alone. And, for the last time, the
reason for this is evinced by the conviction of St. Thomas that
God knows everything as present. If he knows things as present,
it is not solely in his will that such knowledge is had; the reason
is, per modum intelligibilem procedunt [effectus] ab eo, et sic,
per consequens, per modum voluntatis.

Summa Theol., 1a q. 1a, a. 4, 3°. See p. 9, supra.

Banes is willing to argue that it is solely in God's will that such
knowledge is had: futura contingentia . . . cognoscuntur a Deo
in determinatione suae voluntatis, qua absolute et ante provisionem
operum praedeterminavit . . . omnes actus . . .

Summa Theol., 1a q. 14, a. 13. See p. 126, n., supra.

If Banes seems to be forcing a note, Molina seems to strike
the wrong one. His answer to the question--Is the divine voluntary
determination the explanation of divine prescience?--is as follows.
Commenting on St. Thomas in the forty-ninth disputation of his
L. Molina, Concordia, op. cit., pp. 286-96, Molina first adduces
St. Thomas' thesis that future contingents are known by God as
present to his eternity. But St. Thomas, thinks Molina, did not
mean that their "presentiality" was the only ground for the divine
knowledge of future contingents.

*1. c., p. 288: Verum ut circa hanc rem totam dicam quod
sentio, in primis rationibus paulo ante adductis nihil
obstantibus, affirmare non ausim D. Thomam, quem in omnibus
patronum potius quam adversarium habere percupio, credidisse,
ex solo capite praesentiae rerum secundum esse existentiae
Deum cognoscere certo futura contingentia; quin potius,
ut credo, si ea de re consuleretur, contrariam sententiam
affirmaret.*

The further ground, according to Molina, is this: the infinite
knowledge of God comprehends not only what will be in consequence

of the divine decision to create but also, antecedently to that
decision, whatever would be.

*1. c., p. 289: Deus non ex eo solo capite, quod res
existant extra suas causas in aeternitate, cognoscit
certo futura contingentia; sed ex altitudine suae
scientiae, prius nostro modo intelligendi, cum fundamento tamen in re, quam quicquam statueret, comprehendit in seipso omnia, quae contingenter, aut mere
libere, per causas omnes secundas ex sua omnipotentia
possibiles essent futura, ex hypothesi, quod hos vel
illos rerum ordines, cum his vel illis circumstantiis
vellet statuere: eo autem ipso quod libera sua voluntate
fieri statuit eum ordinem rerum et causarum, quem
reipsa statuit, prius, non solum quam quicquam esset in
tempore, sed etiam nostro modo intelligendi cum fundamento in re, quam quicquam creatum existeret in duratione
aeternitatis; in se ipso atque in illo suo decreto comprehendit omnia, quae per causas secundas contingeret
aut libere reipsa erant, aut non futura.*

To support this contention Molina reasons first that God knew
what would have occurred had Tyre and Sidon done penance
(Matt. 11:21). And there are many other instances from Scripture
of God's knowledge of what might have been.

1. c., pp. 289, 290.

Second, it is unworthy to assert that God is ignorant of what might
have happened had a man been placed in circumstances other than
those which actually surround him.

*1. c., pp. 290, 291: Secundo, Deus per scientiam natural-
em se ipsum comprehendit, et in se ipso omnia quae in
ipso eminenter sunt, atque adeo liberum arbitrium cujus-
cunque creaturae quam per suam omnipotentiam potest condere: ergo ante ullam liberam determinationem suae voluntatis ex altitudine suae scientiae naturalis, qua infinite
superat singula quae in seipso eminenter continet, penetrat
quid liberum arbitrium cujusque creaturae, data hypothesi
quod velit illud creare in hoc vel in illo ordine rerum
cum his vel illis circumstantiis, aut auxiliis, pro sua
innata libertate sit facturum; cum tamen, si vellet, posset
continere actum, aut facere oppositum, et si esset id
facturum, ut libere potest, Deus id ipsum prospiceret non
vero, quod re ipsa ab eo faciendum esse prospicit: indignum
namque altitudine et perfectione divinae scientiae, imo et*

impium, minimeque cohaerens cum comprehensione liberi
arbitrii singularum creaturarum, esset asserere, Deum
ignorare quid ego pro libertate mei arbitrii essem
facturus, si me constituisset in alio ordine rerum,
vel si in hoc ipso, in quo me constituit, statuisset
conferre mihi majora aut minora auxilia, quam re ipsa
donare statuit, vel si concessisset mihi longiorem
vitam, aut graviores tentationes permisisset: fit
ergo, ut, etiam antequam quicquam libera sua voluntate
statueret, per scientiam naturalem cognoverit certo
futura omnia contingentia, non quidem absolute esse
aut non esse futura, sed ex hypothesi, si ipse hunc
aut illum ordinem rerum cum his aut illis circum-
stantiis statueret creare; ac proinde fit, ut eo ipso,
quod libere elegit eum ordinem rerum, quem re ipsa
elegit, in ipsamet electione et decreto suae voluntatis,
prius, nostro saltem modo intelligendi sum fundamento
in re, quam quicquam vel in tempore, vel in aeternitate
inde secundum esse reale existentiae emanaverit, cogno-
verit certo et absolute quaenam contingentia essent,
aut non essent futura: non ergo indiget Deus existentia
eorum in sua aeternitate, ut ea certo cognoscat. Coacti
sumus tangere radicem totam, unde credimus Deum certo
cognoscere futura omnia contingentia, atque unde non
obscure, ne fallimur, libertatem arbitrii et contingentiam
rerum cum divina praescientia disputatione penultima com-
ponemus.

Third, God's knowledge is not from things, but he knows all things
in himself. Hence the existence of things sive in tempore sive in
aeternitate has nothing to do with his certain knowledge of what
will, or will not, be.

> *1. c., p. 291: Tertio, Deus non accipit, cognitionem a*
> *rebus, sed id seipso atque ex se ipso cognoscit omnia:*
> *ergo existentia rerum, sive in tempore, sive in aeternitate,*
> *nihil confert, ut Deus certo sciat quid futurum aut non*
> *futurum sit.*

Fourth, if God be provident, he must know what will happen should
he decide to create, and he must know this before he decides to
create.

> *1. c., pp. 291, 292: Quarto, in Deo est providentia, et*
> *praedestinatio circa futura contingentia: ergo est prae-*
> *cognitio certa, qua praecognoscit, antequam quicquam*
> *existat, quid futurum, aut non futurum sit, ex hypothesi*

ac conditione, quod hoc vel illud auxilium aut medium
adhibeat, vel quod hoc aut alio modo res disponat. Sin
minus, quanam ratione praeordinavit, et disposuit res
per suam providentiam, effectus quidem bonos contingentes
per causas tam naturales, quam liberas intendendo, malos
autem permittendo, ut inde majora eliceret bona? Quo-
modo item fuit praedestinatio quarundam causarum libere
agentium ut ad effectus ac fines contingentes his vel
illis mediis pervenirent?

Whence, the proposition ex aeternitate omnia coexistunt Deo
helps in no way either to show the certainty of divine prescience
or to conciliate contingency with divine prescience.

1. c., pp. 292, 293.

If St. Thomas, following Boethius [5⁰ de Consolat.], meant
that God's knowledge of temporal things is an anticipatory knowledge of them, inasmuch as they exist and are known in eternity
before they are in time, Molina frankly confesses that he does
not understand and cannot admit this.

1. c., p. 293: Moveor ad hoc asserendum primo, quoniam
praeterquam quod ab existentia rerum creatarum nihil
omnino conferatur scientiae, quam de illis Deus habet,
nec ab illa pendeat, nec ullam perfectionem, ac proinde
neque certitudinem, ab ea recipiat, ut paulo ante ex-
plicatum est: existimandum non est, res, quae successive
fiunt in tempore, existere prius in aeternitate, quam
in tempore, ut ex anticipatione aliqua, quam, quoad
existentiam extra suas causas, habeant in aeternitate,
cognoscantur certo in aeternitate, dum adhuc futurae
sunt in tempore: quod tamen verum esse oportebat, ut ex
rerum existentia in aeternitate praecognosceret eas
Deus certo, antequam in tempore fierent. Quod si Boetius,
et D. Thomas, caeterique, qui ex illo capite affirmant
Deum cognoscere certo futura contingentia, hoc voluerunt,
ingenue fateor, me id non intelligere, neque ulla ratione
verum esse posse existimo. For Boethius see De. Conso-
latione Philosophine, a Fortescue, ed., Burns Oates,
1925, pr. V.

His main reason is that free choice would then cease to be possible. For then a man could not choose in time except as he had
chosen in eternity.

1. c., p. 294: *Quod autem libertas arbitrii nostri rerum-*
que contingentia omnino tollatur, si quis asserat, ex eo
quod aeternitas sit tota simul, prius res in ea, quam
in tempore, existere, ita ut omnia quae in tempore sunt
futura, jam in hoc temporis puncto, imo ex aeternitate
sint extra suas causas secundum veras existentias in
aeternitate, idque tanta firmitate ut ex ea radice Deus
certo cognoscat ea, quae in tempore sunt contingenter
futura, facile ostendi potest. Etenim neque liberum
arbitrium, neque caeterae causae efficere possent in
futurum, quin ipsae eaedem causae idem, eodemque modo,
eademque actione in tempore futuro efficerent, quod jam
antea in aeternitate effecerunt; vel si possent aliud
efficere, non tanta profecto firmitate esset jam modo
in aeternitate, quin possit non esse; atque adeo ex tali
rerum existentia in aeternitate provenire non posset
certitudo divinae scientiae circa ea, quae contingenter
in tempore evenient.

Peter's sin, for example, can not-be in time; therefore, it can
not-be in eternity.

Having rejected St. Thomas' theory of the divine prescience
of future contingents as present to the eternal vision of God on
the score that "presentiality" had nothing to do with the question,
Molina thus explains how God knows future free acts. Two sup-
positions command Molina's answer: divine providence and
human liberty. God knows what will be, yet any given future
choice, though it will be, could have been otherwise. Now, if
God knows what will be only because he knows what can be,
there is no providence (since the possible is not yet the future);
on the other hand, if God knows what will be, solely because he
wills it to be, there is no liberty (since the free act could not
then be otherwise than as God wills it). It must be, therefore,
that before God wills the future, he knows what would be under
any given hypothesis which he might effect. This block of futurible
being (what-would-be upon the hypothesis of divine choice) pre-
serves, Molina thinks, the infallibility of providence and the
exigencies of liberty. Thus, God knows what a man will choose,
without prejudicing man's freedom, for God has chosen the
future hypotheses under which he has foreseen man freely coming
to salvation or perdition. Thus, too, man will infallibly choose
whatever God has foreseen him choosing, for God elected the
hypotheses of man's free choice. Divine causality, then, explains
divine prescience of the future only in the sense that God causes

the hypotheses under which he had foreseen what a man could freely choose.

More textual support of Molina's position will be given in ch. 8. Meanwhile see L. Molina, Epitome de Praedestinatione, in Stegmüller, op. cit., pp. 336–55.

This answer clearly differs from that of Banes and St. Thomas. For Banes, the will of God explains his prescience. For St. Thomas, the will of God, et hoc evidentius si ei adjungatur intellectus, explains his prescience.

Vid. p. 134, supra.

That is to say, the intellectus divinus of St. Thomas is the provisor totius entis.

Vid. p. 134, supra.

God sees, because he causes, whatever can, would, or will be; and he causes all this because he sees all this; whereas the intellectus divinus of Banes is not in St. Thomas' sense the provisor totius entis. Before future contingents are seen by God, they are caused by him.

Vid. pp. 129–32, supra, especially 130: itaque idea . . . effectus creatos, and p. 126, n., supra.

Whereas, Molina's intellectus divinus sees future contingents before they are divinely caused.

Molina's intellectus divinus has against it this fundamental and, I believe, unanswerable difficulty. Let us put it as simply as possible. I see my hand. Why? Because I have placed it before my eyes. Further, I see my hand not only because I have placed it before my eyes but also because it is there. So here. God sees future free acts. Why? Not only because he causes them, but also because they are there. Now the difficulty against Molina is this: though it is true that my hand must be there for me to see it, nothing can, so to say, be there unless God have caused it. More abstractly, the essential status of futurible choice is just as dependent upon God as its existential status. And that dependence is for St. Thomas the dependence of a thing which is known because it is caused by the one who

141

knows it, God (or it is caused because it is known by the one who caused it, God). For Banes, recall, that dependence of the future free act upon God was that of a thing which before it is known is willed. But Molina's futurible free act is simply there before the vision of God. The difficulty is how it got there. Whence comes its essence? It is no answer to say that it must be there; otherwise there is either no liberty (if only God's will causes it) or no providence (if only God's intellect causes it). No answer, I say, because Molina's dilemma is valid only on his own supposition; namely, that there is no third possibility. The third possibility is the one advanced by St. Thomas: neither God's intellect alone nor God's will alone causes the future free act; both together do it. God is the <u>provisor totius entis</u> because he causes all being, or God causes all being because he sees it all.

The reader will no doubt have appreciated the fact that this is the strongest position of the three. Of course it does not attempt to give the last word of explanation. But perhaps this was higher wisdom than either Banes or Molina possessed. If every problem <u>abit in mysterium</u>, it is better to put the mystery of this problem in its proper place: God is infinitely efficacious, infinitely provident. He can, therefore, effect a free act, and he can know it. Better, I say, to put the mystery in its proper place than to bedeck a contradiction with a sacred word. Banes' mystery, and contradiction, is that God causes a free act before he knows it. Molina's mystery, and contradiction, is this: God knows a free act before he causes it. St. Thomas' mystery is this: God knows a free act because he causes it. The answer seems intellectually satisfying. After all, the cause in question is infinite.

A second question divides Molina from Banes and both, it seems, from St. Thomas. The question arises, How is the divine will the cause of divine prescience? or, to take the question concretely, How is the divine will the cause of the object of God's vision, the free act, the <u>velle hoc</u>? Is the ultimate efficient cause of the <u>velle hoc</u> a divinely caused determination received in the will before (that is, causally, not temporally <u>before)</u> it determines itself? Or is the velle hoc to be explained by a divinely caused determination to will the good (<u>velle bonum</u>), which a man proceeds to canalize by determining himself to will a particular good? If the first explanation be true, God is the immediate cause of the velle hoc. If the second explanation be true, the immediate cause of the <u>velle hoc</u> is man. Banes, insisting upon the immediacy of divine causality, seems to subtract the <u>velle hoc</u> from the power

142

of man. Molina, insisting upon the immediacy of the human cause of the velle hoc, seems to subtract the velle hoc from the causality of God.

For Banes' position see p. 129, n., supra: Deus cognoscit . . . non impeditis.--Etiam si Deus . . . conclusione praecedente. For Molina's position see p. 127, n., supra.

For Banes, actual human choice is known by God because it is caused by him before that choice is actual: Deus cognoscit futura contingentia in suis causis particularibus quatenus . . . subiciuntur determinationi . . . divinae scientiae et voluntatis. For Molina, actual human choice is known by God because in its futurible state, before God elected to posit the circumstances under which it would be actual, it was known as something which hypothetically would be the following: God thus causes the circumstances under which choice is actual, but the choice so circumstanced has simply moved from the sphere of its futurible being, where it was uncaused, into the sphere of its actual being.

L. Molina, Concordia, pp. 324, 325: Denique quia res tertii generis [quae, sc., a libero arbitrio emanant], cooperantibus tum aliis causis secundis, tum etiam Deo partim ut causa particulari, ex libero arbitrio creato, aut dependenter ab illo, ita sunt futurae ut possint non esse, praevidente Deo per scientiam naturalem, et per illam mediam inter mere naturalem et liberam, illas pro libertate arbitrii esse futuras, ex hypothesi quod creare vellet homines et angelos in eo ordine rerum quo illos collocavit, in determinatione libera voluntatis qua illos ita creare constituit, scivit per scientiam liberam, quae determinationem illam consequitur, res illas esse futuras, quia illae pro libertate arbitrii erant ita eventurae, non vero a contrario, quia illas praescivit eventuras, ideo erunt vel fuerunt. Cf. 1. c., p. 325: non ideo res esse futuras quia id Deus praescit, sed e contrario.

St. Thomas seems here also to stand midway between the two. After affirming that the divine will does not impose necessity upon everything that is willed, he examines the reasons alleged. Some have said, he explains, that the reason that God does not impose necessity upon everything willed is ex causis mediis. Therefore is an effect contingent, they said [the Arabs], because it is consequent upon the contingence of the proximate cause, not because it is consequent upon the necessity of the first cause. But this reason, St. Thomas goes on to say, is not sufficienter dictum. Note well, the reason is not false; it is insufficient. Oportet aliam principalem rationem assignare contingentiae in rebus, cui causa praeassignata subserviat. And this alia ratio principalis is the efficacity of the divine will. "Thus, we do not say that some divine effects are contingent only by reason of the contingence of proximate causes, but rather by reason of the dispositions of the divine will which provides such an order of things."

> *De Veritate, q. 23, a. 5. resp.: Sic non dicimus quod aliqui divinorum effectuum sunt contingentes solummodo propter contingentiam secundarum causarum, sed magis propter dispositionem divinae voluntatis quae talem ordinem rebus providit. Cf. Summa Theol., q. 19, a. 8.*

Clearly, the reason, in St. Thomas, for the contingence of effects is truly the contingence of second causes, though this is not the only or the principal reason. The exact thought of St. Thomas seems to be condensed into this formula: non igitur propterea effectus voliti a Deo eveniunt contingentes, quia causae proximae sunt contingentes, sed propterea quia Deus voluit eos contingenter evenire, contingentes causas ad eos praeparavit.

> *Summa Theol., 1. q. 19. a. 8, resp. Cf. Quodl. 11. a. 3; 12.3.*

Clearly the reason for the velle hoc (an effectus contingens willed by God) is not only that the cause of it is contingent but also, and mainly, because God, having willed contingent effects, wills that there be contingent causes which can produce them. The text must be reread before it dawns on one that St. Thomas means: 1) God causes the velle hoc 2) not solely because man causes it nor 3) because man does not cause it; but 4) because God wills the velle hoc, therefore are there contingent causes which will also will it. And when one has arrived at that understanding, one sees that after all that is what St. Thomas said.

> *Cf. Contra Gent. 3.72; Summa Theol., 1. q. 23, a. 6.*

Admitting now that God determines the velle hoc, not inasmuch as the contingent cause alone wills it but inasmuch as God wills that the contingent cause will it, the question arises, Does God determine the velle hoc because he determines the velle bonum, or does he determine the velle hoc by a determination different from the velle bonum, a determination, moreover, which causally antecedes and effects the velle hoc? If the first, then St. Thomas is not Banes' patron, though he is not Molina's either; if the second, St. Thomas is Banes' patron. And on this point I do not see how it can be doubted that God determines the velle hoc not by a determination different from the velle bonum and effective of itself of the velle hoc but rather by the determination of the velle bonum alone, which determination a man proceeds to limit by his reason to this or that good. Able to specify, limit, canalize, the divine determination to the good, man can choose this good only because God determines him to will the good. And acting thus, a man is not the cause of being; he is the cause of the limitation of being. The being in the velle hoc is the divine torrent of the velle bonum; the hoc is the rill canalized by the banks of reason. One text will suffice:

> Deus movet voluntatem hominis sicut universalis motor ad universale obiectum voluntatis, quod est bonum. Et sine hac universali motione homo non potest aliquid velle. Sed homo per rationem determinat se ad volendum hoc vel illud, quod est vere bonum vel apparens bonum.
>
> *Summa Theol.*, 1a 2ae q. 9, a. 6, ad 3um. Cf. 1. q. 22, a. 2, ad 4um; 1a 2ae q. 10, a. 4; *De Veritate*, q. 22, a. 4; *De Pot.* q. 3, a. 7, ad 13um.

From all this it will appear that Banes is on this point no more Thomistic than is Molina on other points. God, in Banes' opinion, is the immediate cause of the velle hoc by a determination caused by him and received in the will ad hoc, before the will determines itself. In St. Thomas, God is the cause of the velle hoc, but not immediately: God causes the velle hoc because he causes the velle bonum.

> *Cf. De Veritate, q. 2. a. 14: Unde inter scientiam Dei, quae est causa rei, et ipsam rem causatam, invenitur duplex medium: unum ex parte Dei, sc., divina voluntas, aliud ex parte ipsarum rerum, quantum ad quosdam effectus, sc., causae secundae, quibus mediantibus proveniunt res a scientia Dei. Omnis autem effectum non solum sequitur conditionem causae primae, sed etiam mediae.*

145

No doubt this is historically the strongest point against the Bannesian version of St. Thomas.

The third point of debate between Banes and Molina, and seem-ingly between both and St. Thomas, is as follows. With Banes the divine determination is not only the reason why God's causality of free acts is infallible. We have already seen the difficulty caused by assigning the divine determination as the reason for certain divine prescience. As to the second difficulty: "The whole organization of things involved in predestination" (ipso ordo praedestinationis), says St. Thomas,

> is infallibly certain: yet the proximate cause, free choice,
> is ordained to salvation not necessarily but contingently.
> This can be considered thus. We find that organization
> [ordinem] is compossible with respect to something, in two
> ways: first, insofar as one single cause produces its effect
> from the causality of divine providence; secondly, when from
> a concourse of many contingent causes, which can fail, one
> effect is arrived at, and God ordains each one of the causes
> to its effect in the place of that cause which fails, or, in
> order that another may not fail. . . . Thus it is in pre-
> destination. For free choice can fail of salvation: yet in him
> whom God predestines, God prepares so many other helps
> that he may not fall, or, if falling, he may rise again. . . .
> If then we consider salvation with respect to the proximate
> cause, viz., free choice, it has not certainty, but contingence;
> but with respect to the first cause, which is predestination, it
> has certainty.

De Veritate, q. 6, a. 3. resp. ad finem.

Whatever be the role of this concursus adminiculorum in the mind of St. Thomas, this much is clear: the certainty or infallibility of divine causality results from it and not, at least not immediate-ly, from the efficacity of the divine motion on the will.

To conclude this chapter, the version of St. Thomas' theory proposed by Dominic Banes insisted upon the physical elements of the divine antecedents of human choice. The divine will, deter-mining the act of free choice, was the source of the divine pre-science of choice, and the causal source too, of the object of divine prescience, the free act itself. St. Thomas had maintained that the infinite efficacity of the divine cause, which was con-stituted by God's will and intellect, accounted for all things, in-cluding free choice and the prescience of it. Freedom comes to

146

man in consequence of God's causality, which can effect freedom. And if one demands, How can God foresee what a man will freely do? St. Thomas reminds us that God, strictly, does not foresee anything. He sees everything as it is and everything is as it is caused; namely, as necessary or contingent. Molina, who did not understand St. Thomas, understood Banes still less. Banes is faithful enough to the central point in St. Thomas' theory--liberty grows out of its antecedents, divine and human--but he seems to throw the picture of the divine antecedents of choice out of focus. It is not in God's will alone that choice is determined and known, though Banes thought St. Thomas meant that. Still less is it in the human will alone that choice is determined and known, though Molina thought this to be true. Free choice, according to St. Thomas, is determined by God's will and known by his intellect; the essential status for free choice comes from the infinite ef-ficacity of the divine cause, God's will and intellect; its existential status comes from the divine will. As for Molina, he thought that Banes could not be right. How could God cause the free act before knowing it? How could man be free though predetermined? And Molina did not understand St. Thomas. There was left him only the resource of asserting that God knew the free act before he caused it and that, on the human side, the will determined the intellect.

8 MOLINIST LIBERTY IN THE CONCORDIA

Thus far we have seen Molina contend, against Luther and Calvin, that free choice is free not only from coercion but also from necessity; we have also seen him missing St. Thomas' point that an infinite cause and, analogously, an human intellectual cause are the conditions out of which free choice grows; lastly, we have seen him denying Dominic Banes' predetermining decrees.

It is time now to examine positively Molina's own concept of liberty. It is a concept which is based upon the principle that there is no intrinsically efficacious cause of free choice. That is to say, there is nothing, on the side of free choice's divine antecedents, which of its own nature has an infallible connection with choice in virtue of a physical motion determining the human will before-hand to a given act decreed beforehand by God. On the side of the human antecedents of free choice, there is no intellectual deter-mination of choice. Molina will maintain that the divine antecedents of choice are extrinsically efficacious of choice. That is to say, the divine antecedents to choice are infallibly connected with choice in virtue of a divine scientia media. This scientia media is a knowledge which God, antecedently to his absolute decrees, pos-sesses of future contingents and especially of free contingents. God knows, in other words, what a free agent would do upon any

148

hypothesis which might be posited. It is in virtue of this notion of extrinsically efficacious divine antecedents of choice that Molina connects the certainty of predestination with the infallibility of divine prescience. The nature of the means employed by God to effect choice is not the reason either why God knows with certainty man's lot or why a man comes infallibly to his predestined end. That reason is, on the one hand, divine prescience; on the other, free choice.

L. Molina, Concordia, p. 506: Secunda conclusio: Licet adultus ita praedestinatus, certo, hoc est, absque ulla Dei deceptione, vitam aeternam consequetur; certitudo tamen non est ex parte mediorum, effectusque praedestin- ationis, sed ex parte divinae praescientiae, qua Deus altitudine illimitataque perfectione sui intellectus, supra id quod natura rei habet, certo cognoscit prae- destinatum taliter pro sua libertate cooperaturum per suum arbitrium, ut eisdem mediis in vitam aeternam re ipsa debeat pervenire: cum tamen, si velit, possit re ipsa ita operari, ut neque ea media, effectusque prae- destinationis in rerum natura existant neque ipse in vitam aeternam perveniat. Itaque cum secundum se incertum sit, a libertateque proprii arbitrii creati pendeat, praedestinatum in eo ordine rerum in quo Deus eum statuit collocare, tali modo cooperaturum cum auxiliis quibus eum decrevit adjuvare, ut et effectus totus praedestinationis existat, et ille per eum in vitam aeternam perveniat: Deus altitudine sui intellectus, ante ullum actum suae voluntatis, certo novit, quid pro libertate arbitrii illius esset fut- urum, cogniturus quidem contrarium, si, ut potest, con- trarium esset re ipsa futurum: accedenteque determinatione divinae voluntatis, qua in tali ordine rerum eum collocare, taliaque auxilia illi donare statuit, remansit eo ipso praedestinatus.

As for the function of the human intellectual conditions of choice, Molina does not seem to assign to them any relevant purpose, though he does deny that they determine choice. It would seem that they are analogous to the relation of divine antecedents to choice. In general, whatever may be the antecedents of choice, their relation to choice may be described thus: granted ante- cedents A^1 for choice A^2; A^1 is such that A^2 is consequent upon A^1 in the sense that if there were an A^3 choice (instead of A^2-- there could be, in Molina's concept of liberty, an A^3 choice), then an A^3 antecedent would have preceded the A^3 choice. For it is not because of A^1 antecedents that you have an A^2 choice;

rather, <u>therefore</u> there is A^1 <u>because</u> there will be A^2.

L. Molina, Summa Haeresium Minor, in Stegmülller, op. cit.,
pp. 447, 448, 449: Quinto decimus: Cum libertas arbitrii
nostri dominiumque in nostros actus in eo sit positum,
quod in quo instanti voluntas nostra elicit aliquem actum,
possit eum non elicere aut etiam elicere contrarium, et in
quo instanti eum non elicit, possit illum elicere, sane
circa attributa aut condiciones praeexistentes aut con-
comitantes, quae in sensu composito non stant cum contrario
aut contradictorio eius quod per voluntatem creatam est
futurum, quia scil. conditiones illae aut attributa repugnan
cum eo contrario aut contradictorio, est distinguendum:
Quoniam si tales sint, quae perinde sinant voluntatem ef-
ficere re ipsa contrarium aut contradictorium, ac si illae
non essent, quoniam si per voluntatem creatam futurum esset
contrarium aut contradictorium illae non praecessissent aut
non id comitarentur quod per voluntatem creatam fit, neque
idcirco voluntas creata id efficit quia illae praecesserunt
aut concomitantur, sed e contra ideo illae praecesserunt
aut concomitantur quia id fit aut futurum erat per volun-
tatem creatam, utique eiusmodi conditiones aut attributa
nihil de libertate arbitrii tollunt, ut ex se est satis
perspicuum.
Si vero tales sint, quae voluntatem creatam non sinant
facere contrarium aut contradictorium perinde ac si illae
non fuissent, utique libertatem a voluntate creata circa
id tollunt, eamque ad id efficiendum necessitant, esto
eam non cogant sed spontaneum in eam relinquant.
Rem exemplis illustremus. Quamvis in sensu composito
haec duo non cohaereant, quod Deus praesciat Petrum in
tali instanti peccaturum et quod Petrus in eo instanti
non peccet, quia tamen tam integrum Petro manet, nihil
omnino impediente ea praescientia re ipsa in eo instanti
non peccare, ac si scientia illa non praeextitisset,
quia non ideo peccat quia Deus id praescivit, sed ideo
Deus eminentia sui intellectus id praescit, quia ita sub
illis circumstantiis pro libertate et nequitia Petri
erat futurum; si vero futurum non esset, ut potest, non
id praescivisset sed contrarium; utique attributum illud,
quod Deus praesciat, Petrum in tali instanti peccaturum
non peccet, nullam a Petro adimit libertatem ut in eo
instanti possit re ipsa non peccare, et per ipsum stat
quod non peccet.
Item quia in mediis divinae providentiae quibus ad
naturalia et ad finem supernaturalem adiuvat voluntatem
creatam nulla est certitudo quod finis sequetur, ut
dictum est, sed certitudo tota, quod is finis sequetur
per ea media aut non sequetur cooperante aut non co-

*operante ad id pro sua libertate ut oportet voluntate
creata, est ex praescientia, qua Deus praescit qui pro
sua libertate per ea media vitam in gratia finient ac
proinde sint praedestinati, et qui non, sed reprobi
sint, utique quamvis attributum hoc, quod aliquis sit
praedestinatus per haec media divinae providentiae, non
cohaereat in sensu composito cum hoc, quod is vitam
finiat in peccato ac damnetur, quia tamen tam integrum
illi manet re ipsa peccare ac finire vitam in peccato
et damnari quam si Deus non praesciret finiturum per
ea media vitam in gratia, ac proinde quam si non esset
per ea media praedestinatus sane tam liber manet ut
peccet et damnetur, ac si praedestinatus non esset.*

*Idem dicendum est de praescito et reprobo, quod ad
libertatem attinet ut bene operetur ac vitam in gratia
finiat, quoniam per ipsum sua libertate ac nequitia id
stat nihil impediente quod Deus praesciat illum finiturum
vitam in peccato atque esse reprobum.*

This is the theory subjacent to the exposition we shall now set
forth.

Two things, Molina explains, are necessary for salvation:
that God confer upon men the means which he has foreseen will
lead man to salvation and that man cooperate with these means.
The first, God's part, depends on God; the second, man's part,
upon man.

Before Augustine's time the Fathers, with an eye to man's
part in salvation, asserted that divine predestination was according to the divine prescience of the good usage of free choice.
But when Pelagius began to attribute everything to free choice
and to affirm that it alone was necessary for salvation--grace,
according to Pelagius, did not initiate salvation, though it does
make it easier--Augustine and others denied this. Grace, according to them, was conferred only according to the good pleasure of God. Whence Augustine's interpretation of the text vult
omnes homines salvos, fieri (1. Tim. 2) was that God willed the
salvation only of those who were predestined, an interpretation
which greatly perturbed the people of Marseilles, as Prosper and
Hilarion witness. Augustine's opinion was followed by St. Thomas.

The uncontroverted points were always these: man was free
in his choice; there is no salvation without grace; God forsees
the future and predestines the just; free choice is consistent with
all this. Further, the Fathers admitted that the free future act
did not depend upon divine prescience but rather the other way

about, divine prescience depended upon the free future act.

*This of course is Molina's interpretation of the Fathers,
Vid. L. Molina, Concordia, pp. 545-47. Cf. pp. 182-
88, 315-33. Augustine's doctrine is found, says Molina,
multis in locis. For Prosper and Hilarion see P. L.,
44; 947 sqq.*

But whether the beginning of salvation lay with choice or rather,
as is the case, with grace, they did not with certainty determine.

The difficulty always was, to conciliate the freedom of choice
with grace, prescience, and predestination. Some said that predestination was according to the prescience of choice; others
said that it was solely according to the good pleasure of God.
Neither school adverted to the fact that it is one thing to say that
prescience is caused by choice, it is quite another to say that
predestination is not without the prescience of choice; that is,
that predestination takes into account the prescience of choice.

*L. Molina, Concordia, p. 484: Quare neque prius vult
Deus nobis voluntate absoluta finem, quam, media, neque, prius praevidet nos habituros finem, quam prae-
videat habituros media.*

An employer, for example, hires laborers for a wage. He wills
their work and their wage in the sense that he wills their wage
only in the foreseen hypothesis of this work.

1. c.

Small wonder, then, that those who held predestination according
to prescience, and those who denied this, seemed opposed to each
other.

To reconcile this opposition, to show fully how liberty may
consort with grace, prescience, and predestination, is the purpose of the Concordia. Had the explanation therein always been
given, perhaps Pelagianism would never have arisen, nor would
Luther have denied liberty, nor would Augustine's opinion perturbed the faithful, nor finally, would disputes among Catholics
have gone on without end.

The explanation is based on the following principles. The first
principle is the divine concourse. Divine concourse is so to be
explained that it leaves unhindered the freedom of choice in whatsoever state free choice might be exercised. These states are

four in number: the state of pure nature (that is, without sin or grace); the state of innocence (that is, the state of man before original sin); the state of fallen nature (that is, the state of sin before redemption); the state of redeemed nature. In all these states divine concourse with the free act leaves untouched the freedom of the act.

L. Molina, Concordia, p. 19, 548.

Divine concourse is twofold, general and special. Special concourse is for supernatural acts. Its effect is to specify such acts--that is, make them supernatural--and it does this by enabling the will to act supernaturally. Hence the special concourse of God is operative upon the will antecedently to the will's act, and when the will freely acts, it concurs simultaneously in time and nature with the free act.

L. Molina, Concordia, p. 191: Sextum, nostra super-
naturalia opera, licet nobis etiam, tanquam per
arbitrium nostrum cooperantibus, tribuantur, a nostro-
que influxu speciem quoad actus substantiam obtineant,
in Deum tamen non solum tanquam in causam primam, com-
munemque omnium bonorum auctorem, sed etiam tanquam in
particularem eorum effectorem, a quo habent suam super-
naturalem speciem, referenda sunt. Verbi gratia, actus
nostri supernaturaliter assentiendi, revelatis et ut ad
salutem oportet, licet eatenus sint nostri, quod fiunt
cooperantibus nobis per nostrum arbitrium, et quod sine
libero nostro influxu omnino non essent, a nostroque
influxu habeant, quod sint assensus potiusquam dissensus
aut quam actus alterius potentiae, quod tamen sint super-
naturales, alteriusque speciei a se ipsis, si solis viribus
arbitrii elicerentur, habent a Deo tanquam a particulari
eorum causa per se ipsum immediate, vel per super-
naturalem habitum ab ipso infusum, tale eos efficiente.
Licet etiam contritio eatenus sit actus noster, quod sine
nostrae voluntatis libero influxu omnino non esset, et
quod ab influxu nostrae habeat quod sit dolor potius
voluntatis quam alterius speciei; attamen quod sit super-
naturalis dolor specie distinctus a mere naturali, habet
a Deo tanquam a particulari ejus actus causa; -- p. 172;
In quo latissimum est discrimen inter concursum generalem
Dei cum causis secundis ad actiones earum naturales, et
auxilium particulare, gratiamve praevenientem, qua Deus
liberum arbitrium ad opera supernaturalia credendi,
sperandi, diligendi, ac poenitendi, ut ad salutem oportet,

*evehit et coajuvat, quod pauci animaadvertunt. Etenim
auxilium particulare, quod praeveniens gratia nuncupatur,
motio quaedam est, qua liberum arbitrium excitatur et
praevenitur, potensque redditur, ut ita adjutum libero
suo influxu cooperetur ulterius ejusmodi supernaturales
actus quibus proxime aut remote ad gratiam gratum
facientem disponatur. Quare motio quaedam est in ipsam
causam, ut ea mediante in se habeat unde libere exercere
ulterius possit, si velit, ejusmodi opera qualia ad
salutem sunt necessaria, ut a disputatione octava ex
parte est explicatum, et copiosius in sequentibus dicetur;
-- p. 239-40; Dixi toties, gratiam praevenientem, qua
gratia praeveniens est, tempore vel natura antecedere
influxum liberi arbitrii: quoniam si sumatur ut posterius
tempore vel natura sortitur rationem gratiae cooperantis,
neque tempore, neque natura antecedit influxum liberi
arbitrii: quin potius perinde hi duo influxus, una cum
concursu universali, quo Deus influit etiam in eundem
actum, sunt simul, atque a se mutuo pendent, uniunturque in eandem supernaturalem actionem ab omnibus iis
tribus causis tanquam ab una integra effectam, ac influxus Dei generalis et influxus causae secundae in
rerum natura simul ponuntur, ac tolluntur, et a se mutuo
pendent, uniunturque in eandem actionem et effectum
naturalem ab utraque causa productum.*

The difficulty is with the general divine concourse. This is in
the order of efficient causality. It effects the free act whether
the act be natural or supernatural. This question is How does it
effect free acts? Molina knows that St. Thomas has taught that
God effects all actions of secondary agents "by applying their
virtues to act."

*Summa Theol., 1a q. 105, a. 5; L. Molina, Concordia,
pp. 152 sqq.*

This applicatio, we have seen, is id quod a Deo fit in re naturali
quo actualiter agat. But the question is Does the motive of God
fall first upon the free second cause (as does the special concourse for supernatural acts), or is it only a divine motion with
the free second cause upon the act of that cause? If the first
meaning is St. Thomas', Molina confesses that he does not
understand what the applicatio can be--for then God would not
immediately effect the result, but only mediately; that is, by the
medium of second causes. In this case the term of God's action
would only be the modification of the second cause.

154

L. Molina, Concordia, pp. 152-53.

Accordingly it must be said that God concurs immediately, immediatione suppositi, with second causes in their operations and effects, in such wise, namely, that, just as the second cause elicits immediately its operation and thereby produces its term or effect, so God by a sort of general concourse immediately concurs with the second cause in the same operation and through that operation or action produces its term or effect. Thus it is that the general concourse of God is not the influence of God upon the second cause, as though it, being first moved by that concourse, acts and produces its effect; but it is the influence of God immediately with the cause upon its action and effect.

An agent acts immediatione suppositi when there is no intermediary between it and its effect: e.g., fire heats the air contiguous to it immediatione suppositi. An agent acts immediatione virtutis through an intermediary; e.g., fire heats the air not contiguous to it by heating the contiguous air. Vid. L. Molina, Concordia, p. 153: Dicendum itaque est, Deum immediate immediatione suppositi concurrere cum causis secundis ad earum operationes et effectus, ita videlicet ut quemadmodum causa secunda immediate elicit suam operationem, et per eam terminum seu effectum producit; sic Deus concursu quodam generali immediate influat cum ea in eandem operationem, et per operationem seu actionem terminum illius atque effectum producat. Quo fit ut concursus Dei generalis non sit influxus Dei in causam secundam, quasi illa prius eo mota agat, et producat suum effectum, sed sit influxus immediate cum causa in illius actionem et effectum.

The general concourse of God and the action of the will are thus the integral principle of action. Each produces the whole effect as a partial cause demanding the concurrence of the other. Of course each cause (God and the creature) is integral in its own order: God as the only universal cause, creatures as the determining cause. But each cause produces the effect not in the sense that God acts upon the second cause but in the sense that both produce the same effect together.

L. Molina, Concordia, pp. 157, 158: Ex dictis intelligetur facile, si sermo sit de causa integra, ut comprehendit

omnem ad actionem necessariam, sive ea universalis sit,
sive particularis, Deum per concursum universalem cum
causis secundis efficere unam integram causam coales-
centem ex pluribus non integris comparatione cujusque
effectus, ita ut neque Deus per solum concursum uni-
versalem sine causis secundis, neque causae secundae sine
concursu universali Dei sufficiant ad effectum pro-
ducendum. At cum dicimus, neque Deum per concursum
universalem, neque causas secundas esse integras, sed
partiales causas effectuum, intelligendum id est de
partialitate causae, ut vocant, non vero de partialitate
effectus: totus quippe effectus et a Deo est, et a
causis secundis; sed neque a Deo, neque a causis secundis,
ut a tota causa, sed ut a parte causae, quae simul exigit
concursum et influxum alterius: non secus ac cum duo
trahunt navim totus motus proficiscitur ab unoquoque
trahentium, sed non tanquam a tota causa motus, siquidem
quivis eorum simul efficit cum altero omnes ac singulas
partes ejusdem motus. Si vero sermo sit de integra, sive
tota causa, non omnino, sed in aliquo gradu causae, tunc
Deus per concursum universalem est causa integra in gradu
causae maxime universalis, eo quod nulla alia cum eo con-
currat in eo gradu causae, eodemque modo variae causae
secondae possunt esse integrae ejusdem effectus,quaevis
in suo gradu, ut sol et equus comparatione alterius equi
generandi, sol quidem ut causa universalis, equus ut
causa particularis.

The parts, then, of man and God in the free supernatural act
may be decomposed thus. God is the specific cause of the supernaturality of the act through his special concourse which first of
all enables a man to act supernaturally and, if man procees freely
to act in virtue of the power thus conferred upon him, immediately together with the will effects the supernaturality of the act. God
is the efficient cause of the free act not because his general concourse effects anything in the second cause itself but because it
concurs immediately with the act of the second cause to produce
the effect. Man is the cause of the freedom of the act.

God is the specific cause of supernaturality: vid. L.
Molina, Concordia, p. 191 (p. 288, n. 2 supra); 178:
omnino est dicendum, concursum Dei particularem,
gratiamve praevenientem, semper vel tempore, vel
natura antecedere influxum liberi arbitrii ad actiones
suas supernaturales, quibus ad gratiam gratum facientem
disponitur, tanquam causa principiumque efficiens in
liberum arbitrium immissum, quo mediante Deus ulterius

una cum libero influxu ejusdem arbitrii in hujusmodi operationes supernaturales influit. At vero cum Deus per concursum universalem et causa secunda immediate influant in effectum causae secundae, tanquam duae partes unius integrae cause, quarum neutra illis praecise influxibus singularibus influit in alteram, sed utraque immediate in effectum; fit, ut neutra, illis praecise influxibus singularibus, prius altera concurrat, Deus ergo, comparatione cujusque effectus causae secundae, dicitur causa prima, tum quia causa ipsa secunda habet totum suum esse et vim operandi a Deo, atque ab actuali immediato influxu Dei pendent ea omnia, quae in ea sunt: tum etiam quia concursus Dei generalis, quo cum causis secundis ad agendum concurrit maxime universalis est, secundum rationem causae efficientis ad universos effectus sese extendens: qua ratione, si in commune spectetur, poterit dici prior natura quocunque influxu causae particularis, quatenus, ab eo ad concursum cujusque cause secundae ne convertitur existentiae consequentia, quippe recte sic liceat colligere; datur influxus hujus causae secundae: ergo datur etiam concursus generalis cause primae: non vero e contrario bene colliges; datur concursus generalis Dei: ergo datur etiam concursus hujus causae secundae. Dixi, si in commune spectetur, quoniam si concursus Dei generalis sumatur in singulari, pro concursu quo praecise cum hac causa secunda hic et nunc ad singularem aliquem effectum concurrit, concursus generalis Dei neque illo modo est prior concursu hujus causae secundae ad eundem effectum, sed a se mutuo pendent quoad existentiam, ut explicatum est. For God and man's part see pp. 209-10: *His ita constitutis cum, tangente Deo ac excitante nostrum arbitrium per auxilium gratiae praevenientis, liberum illi sit consentire, aut non consentire, atque adeo elicere vel non elicere actum credendi, sperandi, aut poenitendi, constat profecto liberum nostrum arbitrium, et gratiam illam praevenientem, esse duas partes unius integrae causae actus credendi sperandi, aut poenitendi, prout ad salutem oportet, singulosque ejusmodi actus pendere ab influxu tam liberi arbitrii, quam gratiae praevenientis; atque a libero quidem arbitrio habere ut actus illi quoad substantiam sint credere, sperare, aut poenitere: ab influxu vero gratiae praevenientis habere, ut sint supernaturales, et quales ad salutem sunt necessarii. Quare quivis illorum actuum totus est a libero arbitrio, et totus a gratia praeveniente, seu a Deo per eam tanquam per supernaturale instrumentum in eundem actum influente; at a neutro est, ut a tota et integra causa, set ut a parte integrae causae.*

Quando audis esse a Deo per gratiam praevenientem tanquam supernaturale instrumentum in eundem actum influente,

157

non intelligas ita gratiam praevenientem esse Dei instrumentum, quasi novo motu aut influxu a Deo evehatur
ad cooperandum cum libero arbitrio et producendum effectum
supernaturalem; eo modo, quo a multis Sacramenta dicuntur
evehi a Deo supernaturaliter, ut instar naturalium
causarum sint instrumenta gratiae: id quod non defuit,
qui me hoc loco intendisse fuerit arbitratus. Sed intellige
esse de numero instrumentorum ejus generis, quae, ut disputat. XXVI explantum est, sunt integra virtus causae principalis, per quam influit in effectum; eo modo, quo vis
impressa semini est integra virtus, qua animal, a quo
semen est decisum, generat; et calor est tota vis, qua ignis
producit alterum ignem; quae proinde instrumenta, ut ibidem
dictum est, non indigent novo motu, aut applicatione a
causa principali, ut agant. Quia vero gratia praeveniens
accidens est, et non substantia, esse nequit causa principalis, neque agere potest ut quod, sed ut quo, ideoque
est instrumentum: neque alterius tanquam causae principalis,
quam Dei, a quo est producta: et cum sit ordinis supernaturalis, atque adeo supernaturalis sit homini, in quo
est, jure optimo instrumentum supernaturale est a nobis
nuncupata.

Gratiam praevenientem rem esse distinctam ab actibus,
ad quos liberum arbitrium a Deo per eam excitatur, tametsi
non defuerit, qui contrarium dixerit, satis est perspicuum.
Actus namque illi a libero emanant arbitrio: gratia vero
praeveniens minime. Item gratia illa causa est efficiens
una cum libero arbitrio eorundem actuum: causa vero efficiens res est distincta a suo effectu. Praeterea gratia
illa potest cassa reddi, libero arbitrio non consentiente,
neque cooperante ad actus, ad quos hominem excitat, et a
Deo confertur: ergo res est omnino ab eis distincta.

Cum autem tam liberum arbitrium, quam gratia praeveniens
sint causae secundae actuum credendi, sperandi, et poenitendi,
ut oportet: nulla vero causa secunda, etiamsi supernaturalis
sit, efficere quicquam possit, nisi a Deo influente simul
immediate per concursum generalem in effectum adjuvetur,
idque propterea quod omnis universim effectus sicut a Deo
pendet immediate ut conservetur, ita etiam ut fiat, ut
disputatione XXV et sequentibus ostensum est, liquido sane
constat, ut liberum arbitrium una cum gratia praeveniente
producat quemcunque illorum actuum, necessarium esse, ut
Deus quoque una cum illis immediate in actum producendum
per concursum suum universalem influat. Quo fit, ut quivis
illorum trium actuum, licet sit unica actio (cui suus sit
propius assignandus terminus productus, ut q. XII art. 12
hujus primae partis ostensum est) tres nihilominus habeat
partes unius integrae causae, a qua ita emanat totus, ut
a singulis etiam partialitate, ut vocant, causae totus

*etiam emanet, diverso tamen modo. Etenim a Deo influente,
per solum concursum generalem emanat, ut a causa univerali,
a qua proinde non habet magis quod sit assensus credendi,
aut dolor de peccatis, quam vel actus oppositus, vel actus
cujusvis alterius potentiae. Ab influxa vero liberi arbitrii,
una cum notitiis et caeteris necessariis, ut quoad substantiam actus producatur, habet tanquam a causa particulari,
ut quoad substantiam actus, sit potius assensus fidei, aut
dolor de peccatis, quam aliquis alius diversus actus. A gratia
vero praeveniente, seu a Deo ut per illam, tanquam per suum
instrumentum, una cum libero arbitrio influit in eundem
actum, habet ut sit actus supernaturalis specie distinctus
ab actu pure naturali credendi, aut dolendi de peccatis,
quem liberum arbitrium suis solis viribus tunc eliceret,
si cum eo non influeret simul gratia praeveniens: quare a
concursu Dei per gratiam praevenientem habet actus ille ut
sit dispositio congruam proportionem et accommodationem
habens cum dono justificationis supernaturali.*

Clearly, Molina asserts that the principal cause of the supernatural
act is grace; the second, less principal cause is free will with grace
and the general concourse.

L. Molina, *Concordia*, pp. 28, 37, 171, 209, 502.

Freedom is thus from man's will; supernaturality is from grace.

L. Molina, *Concordia*, pp. 209, 215, 463, 471.

But there is no real distinction between what is natural and supernatural
in the act itself: the whole act is supernatural and is caused by the will
and God as by two parts of one cause.

L. Molina, *Concordia*, pp. 58, 215, 229, 461.

The will's influx presupposes the influx of grace, which enables the
will to act supernaturally, and which, if man chooses to act, concurs immediately with the act to make it supernatural.

L. Molina, *Concordia*, pp. 40, 126, 472.

But though the will is thus the cause of its freedom, and grace is
the cause of the supernaturality of the act, Molina does not deny
that God is the cause of the act or that grace is merely given to
the act and not given that a man may act. He simply distinguishes

two divine concourses and their effects: the general concourse effects, together with the will, the act; the special concourse first influences the soul's power to act supernaturally and then, concurrently with the act (if it is posited), specifies the nature of the act to be supernatural.

> *L. Molina, Concordia, p. 239: Ex hactenus dictis in-*
> *telligentur facile duo illa discrimina quae disputat.*
> *XXIX et XXX constituimus inter concursum Dei generalem*
> *cum libero arbitrio ad actus naturales, et auxilium*
> *gratiae praevenientis, ea ex parte qua gratia praeveniens*
> *est, ad actus liberi arbitrii supernaturales, quibus ad*
> *gratiam se disponit. Primum erat, quod concursus Dei*
> *generalis ad actus naturales non est concursus Dei in*
> *liberum arbitrium ut causa est illorum actuum, quasi*
> *prius suscipiat in se eum motum, eoque applicetur et*
> *potens reddatur ad influendum in actum; sed est influxus*
> *immediatus una cum libero arbitrio in actum: at vero*
> *auxilium gratiae praevenientis, ea ex parte qua gratia*
> *praeveniens est, est influxus Dei in liberum arbitrium,*
> *quo illud movet et excitat, potensque reddit, ut eo*
> *pacto motum, tanquam habens jam in seipso principium ef-*
> *ficiens actuum supernaturalium, simul influendo ulterius*
> *eos producat. Secundum discrimen, quod ex hoc primo oritur,*
> *erat, quod influxus Dei cum libero arbitrio per concursum*
> *generalem ac actus naturales, nec tempore nec natura*
> *antecedit influxum liberi arbitrii in eosdem actus: sed*
> *a se mutuo pendent, simulque omnino sunt in rerum natura,*
> *et in eandem numero actionem et effectum uniuntur, gratia*
> *vero praeveniens, qua praeveniens gratia est, tempore vel*
> *natura antecedere solet influxum liberi arbitrii ad actum*
> *supernaturalem, potestque frustrari, si arbitrium ipsum*
> *pro sua innata libertate non velit cum ea elicere actum,*
> *per quem ad justificationem disponatur. Cf. p. 153, n.,*
> *supra, and L. Molina, Concordia, pp. 152-88.*

The essential point in the above explanation is this: the divine concourse, necessary for all action, is simultaneous with that action. God produces acts and their effects with and at the same time as second causes. He does not effect acts and their results by first affecting second causes; second causes are not inter-mediaries between God and the acts or effects which they produce. God and second causes act immediately together as partial causes, each dependently on the other, of the total effect.

With such a concept of divine concourse which determines the supernaturality of an act but leaves untouched the liberty of the act, it may be truly said that it is dependent upon man's choice whether he is converted or not converted--not indeed that he could be converted without grace--in the sense that it is grace together with free choice which effects conversion.

L. Molina, Concordia, pp. 238-39: Hinc patet merito affirandum esse, in sensu composito fieri non posse ut adsit influxus gratiae cooperantis, seu (quod idem est) auxilium cooperantis gratiae, quatenus est cooperans conversionem, quin peccator per suum arbitrium convertatur nihilominus tamen in sensu diviso, atque simpliciter in eo ipso instanti, in quo peccator convertitur, esse in facultate arbitrii ipsius non converti, atque adeo ita libere adhibere consensum, influxum, et cooperationem ad credendum, sperandum, et poenitendum, ut possit tunc eam continere, et non converti, quin et dissentire. Ratio horum est quoniam, licet gratia praeveniens, qua praeveniens est, antecedat consensum nostri arbitrii et cooperationem ipsius ad actus credendi, sperandi, et poenitendi quibus ad Deum convertimur; influxus tamen et cooperatio ejusdem gratiae cum nostro arbitrio ad eosdem actus, a quo gratia praeveniens rationem sortitur gratiae cooperantis, non antecedit liberum nostrum consensum et cooperationem ad nostram conversionem, sed concomitatur et ab ea pendet: non secus atque concursus et influxus habituum virtutum ad nostras operationes pendet a cooperatione ipsarum potentiarum, ut supra fuit explicatum: id quod in causa est, ut habitibus utamur ad nostras operationes quando pro arbitrio nostro volumus operari, eisque non utamur quando ab operatione pro eodem arbitrio cessare volumus. Quare, sicut in sensu composito implicat contradictionem eos habitus, qui in nostris potentiis resident, operationem habere, quin et potentiae cooperentur, et nihilominus in sensu diviso, ac simpliciter, potentiae, quae libero arbitrio subsunt, libere tunc operantur, possuntque non operari; quia non prius est habitus cum illis cooperari, quam ipsae cum illis libere cooperentur: ita in re proposita, licet contradictionem involvat, esse influxum illum gratiae praevenientis cum nostro arbitrio a quo gratia illa sortitur rationem gratiae cooperantis conversionem nostram, quin arbitrium ipsum eandem cooperetur, ac convertatur, quia tamen influxus ille gratiae cooperantis non antecedit consensum, determinationem, et cooperationem arbitrii nostri ad eandem conversionem, quin potius ab ea pendet ut sit in rerum natura, nullam omnino necessitatem, nisi tantum consequentiae, imponit arbitrio nostro, neque ab illo facultatem aufert non cooperandi, si velit, in eo ipso instanti, in quo conversionem ipsam cooperatur. Quo fit ut necessitas illa in sensu composito non proficiscatur ex efficacia qua auxilium gratiae cooperantis moveat ad conversionem arbitrium nostrum, ita ut in instanti, in quo convertitur, integrum illi non sit converti aut ita ut existente aequali influxu gratiae cooperantis, non possit unus pro sua libertate majori conatu, intensiorique actu converti quam alius. Cf. pp. 209, 223, 458, 462, 595, 58, 158, 461.

The difference between this notion of divine concourse and the notion of Dominic Banes--and this is the main difference between the two men--is noted by Molina in his Summa Haeresium Maior. Molina believes that second causes modify, determine, the general divine concourse in the sense that they are part causes of their acts. Banes answers: Nos autem talem modificationem respectu primae causae in d. Thoma non invenimus sed potius oppositum.

> *D. Banes, Schol. Comment. in I partem, ed. Douai, 1614, p. 286 a E, in Stegmüller, op. cit., p. 415. For Molina's text vid Stegmüller. 1. c.*

The oppositum which Banes thinks to find in St. Thomas is this: "the divine will modifies everything, since it is the most universal cause of everything's becoming, being, and manner of being." Banes' reasons are 1) otherwise, the divine will would not determine itself but would be determined by second causes; 2) such a position (as Molina's) would argue an imperfection in God; 3) free human choice is not determined by the means which it uses to execute its designs--for example, the choice of the means used by an artist-- a fortiori God is not so determined; 4) otherwise God would depend upon creatures.

> *D. Banes, op. cit., p. 244 a B, in Stegmüller, op. cit., pp 407, 408. For St. Thomas' texts vid. p. 63, n., supra.*

Molina strongly objects. Such a doctrine puts liberty in God, but not in man. This is Luther's position. Further, such a doctrine makes God the cause of sin. As for Banes' arguments, Molina answers them by his notion of simultaneous concourse: without such concourse creatures cannot act, but in the case of free creatures [talis est] ille influxus . . . ut iuxta eandem innatom ipsarum [causarum sc., liberarum] libertatem suo peculiari influxu determinare eum possent . . . ut mallent.

In Stegmüller, op. cit., pp. 409-11, ad calc.

Molina then repeats the doctrine of the <u>Concordia</u>, and proceeds to identify Banes and Luther in their opposition to it.

1. c., pp. 412, 413, 414. Vid. L. Molina, <u>Concordia</u>, p. 156. For Luther vid. p. 10, n., supra.

Obviously, the bone of contention between Molina and Banes here is, apart from the philosophical issue, St. Thomas Aquinas. St. Thomas, as we have seen, teaches that God moves the will by a naturally determined movement, <u>velle</u> <u>bonum</u>, which can be directed to various objects, <u>velle</u> <u>bona</u>. That the will have chosen this or that <u>bonum</u> is, in relation to the divine causality of choice, the effect of the naturally determinate divine movement to will the good.

Vid., pp. 58-62, supra.

Banes holds that this means that God predetermines the free act.

Vid. p. 120, n., supra.

Molina holds that this means that second causes determine the divine causality.

L. Molina, <u>Summa Haeresium Maior</u>, in Stegmüller; op. cit., p. 411; see p. 162, supra.

Neither seems to follow St. Thomas here. St. Thomas simply says that God causes the free act by a naturally determined movement which a man can, by his reason, direct to various objects.

Vid. pp. 91-95, supra.

That a man's actual choice is determined by God, St. Thomas holds, but he maintains that it is determined in the way just described. He never says that choice is predetermined. Still less of course is St. Thomas a patron of simultaneous concourse.

If it be objected that St. Thomas' position leaves the question of predetermining versus simultaneous concourse undecided, the answer seems to be that that is true. Still, such a position may be itself a decision of the issue. In short, it does not seem

163

necessary to start from this disjunction: concourse is either predetermining or simultaneous. Such a dilemma raises a pseudo-
question, a question which is consequential upon the doctrine of
Calvin and Luther. Neither Banes nor Molina should have accepted,
much less attempted to answer, the disjunction. To do so lands
one into the contradiction of saying either that God predetermines
what is free--and this means that God causes the free act before
he knows it and that man is thus predetermined to choose freely,
as we have seen Banes maintain--or else that man's choice determines God--and this means that God knows the free act before he
causes it and that man's free choice is thus ultimately independent
of any condition, as we have seen Molina maintain. St. Thomas
seems to leave it at this: God causes the free act by a naturally
determined movement (velle bonum) which man by reason can
direct to various objects. Is, then, man the cause of his choice?
Certainly. He limits by his reason, and this is free choice, the
velle bonum. Is God the cause of free choice? Certainly. It is
because of the divinely caused velle bonum that a man can freely
choose at all. But how can God cause and see the free act? He is
an omnipotent cause.

Summa Theol., *1a, q. 22, a. 4.*

The second principle upon which Molina bases his reconciliation
of grace and freedom is this: the efficacity of grace does not lie
wholly in the nature of grace itself but in the futurible free choice
of man and in God's knowledge of that choice. That is, grace is
efficacious from its nature, of course, but also from the fact
that God has foreseen that a man would freely consent to it.

*L. Molina, Concordia, p. 548: Secundum est, legitima,
seu potius orthodoxa, de modo doni perseverantiae
explicatio. Etenim ostendimus, nullum quidem adultum
perseverare posse diu in gratia sine speciali auxilio
Dei, ob idque perseverantiam in gratia esse Dei donum:
at nulli Deum denegare auxilium quod ad perseverandum
sit satis. Praeterea cum auxilio, quo cum unus usque
ad finem vitae perseverat, posse, si velit, non perseverare: et cum auxilio, quod Deus confert, praestove
est conferre ei qui non perseverat, posse perseverare,
per eumque stare quod non perseveret. Quo fit ut ad
donum perseverantiae duo sint necessaria. Unum ex parte
Dei, videlicet ut ea auxilia conferre statuerit, cum
quibus praevidebat adultum pro sua libertate persever-
aturum. Alterum ex parte arbitrii adulti tanquam con-*

164

ditio sine qua voluntas conferendi talia auxilia non
habuisset rationem voluntatis conferendi donum per-
severantiae, nempe ut adultus pro sua libertate ita sit
cum eis cooperaturus ut perseveret, quod in postestate
ipsius est collocatum. Quare non ita intelligendum
est donum perseverantiae esse a Deo, quasi per illud
potestatem auferat ad non perseverandum, aut quasi per
Deum stet, quominus is perseveret, qui in peccatum labitur.
Haec omnia manifesta sunt ex dictis praecipue quaest, XIV
art. 13 disputat XIV et a disputatione XVII. Atque ex his
duobus principiis satis dilucide, ne fallimur, artic. 13
citato libertatem arbitrii nostri cum divine gratia con-
ciliavimus. Cf. L. Molina, Concordia, p. 51.

The second principle of Molina leads immediately to his third,
the scientia media. His notion is this: if God foresees free acts
solely because he has willed them, it follows that God predetermines those acts, and this, he maintains (compare with his first
principle, the divine concourse), is Luther's and Banes's position.
If, on the other hand, God foresees free acts before he wills them,
it follows that God knows only what a man could freely do, not what
a man will do. (The supposition of course is that a man chooses
only what God wills, and because God wills.) To avoid the Scylla
of predetermination and the Charybdis of divine ignorance (at
bottom Molina thinks it is a question of Lutheranism or Calvinism versus Pelagianism), Molina posits a divine knowledge midway (Media) between the divine knowledge of what will be (scientia
libera) and the divine knowledge of what can be (scientia naturalis).
This median knowledge is the divine knowledge of what would
freely be if a man were confronted with choice.

L. Molina, Concordia, p. 549: Tertium est: Praescientia
illa media inter scientiam Dei liberam et mere natural-
em, qua, ut eodem art. disp. L et tribus sequentibus
ostensum est, ante actum liberum suae voluntatis cognovit
Deus, quid in unoquoque rerum ordine per arbitrium
creatum esset futurum, ex hypothesi quod hos homines
aut angelos in hoc vel illo ordine rerum collocare stat-
ueret, qua tamen cogniturus erat contrarium, si contrarium,
ut potest, pro libertate arbitrii creati esset futurum.
Atque ex hoc principio ibidem ostendimus libertatem
creati arbitrii cum divina praescientia cohaerere.
Cf. pp. 317, 318: Triplicem scientiam oportet dis-
tinguamus in Deo, nisi periculose in concilianda
libertate arbitrii nostri et contingentia rerum cum
divina praescientia hallucinari velimus. Unam mere natur-

*alem, quae proinde nulla ratione potuit esse aliter in
Deo, per quam omnia ea cognovit ad quae divina potentia
sive immediate sive interventu causarum secundarum
sese extendit, tum quoad naturas singulorum, et complexiones eorum necessarias, tum etiam quoad contingentes,
non quidem quod futurae essent, vel non essent determinate, sed quod indifferenter esse et non esse possent,
quod eis necessario competit, atque adeo sub scientiam
Dei naturalem etiam cadit. Aliam mere liberam, qua Deus
post liberum actum suae voluntatis absque hypothesi et
conditione aliqua cognovit absolute et determinate ex
complexionibus omnibus contingentibus, quaenam re ipsa
essent futurae, quae non item. Tertiam denique mediam
scientiam, qua ex altissima et inscrutabili comprehensione cujusque liberi arbitrii in sua essentia intuitus
est, quid pro sua innata libertate, si in hoc, vel illo,
vel etiam infinitis rerum ordinibus collocaretur,
acturum esset, cum tamen posset, si vellet, facere
reipsa oppositum, ut ex dictis disput. XLVII et XLVIII
manifestum est.*

    *Sciscitabitur forte aliquis, an hujus modi scienti
media appellanda sit libera, an naturalis. Ad quod in
primis respondendum est eam nulla ratione esse dicendam
liberam, tum quia antecedit omnem liberum actum voluntatis divinae, tum etiam quia in postestate Dei non fuit
scire per eam scientiam aliud quam re ipsa sciverit. Deinde
dicendum neque etiam in eo sensu esse naturalem, quasi
ita innata sit Deo, ut non potuerit scire oppositum ejus
quod per eam cognoscit. Si namque liberum arbitrium
creatum acturum esset oppositum, ut revera potest, idipsum scivisset per eandem scientiam, non autem quod reipsa
scit. Quare non est magis innatum Deo scire per eam
scientiam hanc partem contradictionis ab arbitrio creato
pendentem, quam oppositam. Dicendum ergo est partim habere
conditionem scientiae naturalis, quatenus praevenit actum
liberum voluntatis divinae, neque in potestate Dei fuit
aliud scire, partim habere conditionem scientiae liberae,
quatenus quod sit unius potius partis quam alterius, habet
ex eo quod liberum arbitrium, ex hypothesi quod crearetur
in uno aut altero ordine rerum, esset potius facturum unum
quam aliud, cum utrumvis indifferenter posset facere. Atque
hoc sane postulat libertas arbitrii creati, quae, posita
etiam praescientia divina, non minus est de fide, quam
eadem praescientia et praedestinatio, ut disputatione XXIII
late ostensum est. Idem apertissime sonant testimonia
sanctorum quae mox referemus. Consonat etiam communis
Theologorum sententia quam disputatione praecedente ex
parte retulimus, et de qua paulo post dicemus. Ne vero
primo suo aspectu te haec doctrina perturbet, memento*

ista omnia quae sequentur, apertissime inter se convenire et
cohaerere: Nihil esse in potestate creaturae, quod etiam
non sit in potestate Dei; Deum sua omnipotentia inflectere
posse nostrum liberum arbitrium quocunque ipse voluerit,
praeterquam in peccatum, id enim contradictionem implicat,
ut disputatione XXXI demonstratum est; Deum, quicquid
faciet interventu causae secondae, posse efficere se solo,
nisi in effectu involvatur, ut sit a causa secunda; Deum
permittere posse peccata, non vero praecipere, aut ad ea
incitare vel inclinare; item quod res libero arbitrio
praedita, si in certo ordine rerum et circumstantiarum
collocetur, in unam aut alteram partem se flectat, non
provenire ex praescientia Dei, Quin potius ideo Deum id
praescire, quia ipsa res libero arbitrio praedicta
libere id ipsum agere debet, neque provenire ex eo quod Deus
velit id ab ea fieri, sed ex eo quod ipsa libere id velit
facere. Inde vero apertissime sequitur, scientiam, qua
Deus, antequam statuat eam creare, praevidet quid sit
factura, ex hypothesi quod in eo rerum ordine collocetur,
pendere ex eo quod ipsa pro sua libertate hoc vel illud
sit factura et non e contrario. Scientia vero qua Deus
absque ulla hypothesi absolute scit quid per liberum
arbitrium creatum sit reipsa futurum, semper est in Deo
libera, pendetque a determinatione libera suae voluntatis,
qua tale liberum arbitrium in tali vel tali ordine rerum
creare statuit.

It was said above that Molina's contradiction seems to lie in
the notion that God knows a free act before he causes it.

Vid. supra, p. 138.

Whereas Molina says here that if God knows a free act before he
causes it, there is no Providence, which he is concerned to
maintain. The contradiction between my assertion and Molina's
is only apparent. God causes the actual free act, since he posits
the circumstances under which he had foreseen, scientia media,
what a man would freely choose. But God does not cause the
futurible free act, and it is of the knowledge of this act that it
was said that God knows the free act before he causes it.

To continue with Molina, by reason of this scientia media
Molina feels able to save the gratuity of grace, his fourth principle, for it is solely according to God's good pleasure that
man is saved. The reason is that God freely elects and effects
the hypotheses (grace) under which he has foreseen (scientia
media) the salvation of man. Since, then, the hypothesis was

167

that a man have chosen freely, liberty is saved too.

*L. Molina, Concordia, pp. 549, 550: Quartum est, quod
Deus hunc potius ordinem rerum, quam alium voluerit
creare, et in eo haec potius auxilia, quam alia, conferre, cum quibus praevidebat hos, et non illos, pro
libertate sui arbitrii perventuros in vitam aeternam,
nullam fuisse causam aut rationem ex parte adultorum
praedestinatorum et reproborum. Atque ex hoc capite
hactenus diximus praedestinationem non habere causam
aut rationem ex parte usus liberi arbitrii praedes-
tinatiorum et reproborum, sed in solam liberam Dei
voluntatem esse reducendam. Quod vero voluntas creandi
eum ordinem rerum, et in eo conferendi haec et non
alia auxilia, rationem praedestinationis comparatione
horum adultorum, et non illorum, fuerit sortita, pendens
fuit ex eo, quod unus potius usus, quam alius, pro
libertate arbitrii eorum esset futurus, atque adeo ex
quod Deus futurum eum praeviderit, quia pro eorum
libertate erat futurus. Atque ex hoc capite diximus
dari rationem praedestinationis adultorum ex parte usus
liberi arbitrii praevisi. Ex eodem etiam capite ostendimus libertatem arbitrii eorum ad operandum prout
oportet ad vitam aeternam assequendam, aut contrario
modo, perinde consentire cum praedestinatione per ea
ipsa media per quae ex parte Dei ab aeternitiate praedestinati sunt, ac si in Deo non esset praedestinatio,
sed tantum providentia per eadem media, tamque incertum
Deo esset an per ipsorum arbitrium ita essent cooper-
aturi ut in vitam aeternam pervenirent, quam incertum
id secundum se est. Denique ostendimus non aliam esse
difficultatem in concilianda libertate arbitrii nostri
cum divina praedestinatione, quam in eadem ipsa cum
divina praescientia concilianda reperiatur.*

With these four principles Molina professes to conciliate the
two schools: the one which holds that predestination is according
to prescience; the one which holds that predestination is according to God's will. The conciliation is this: predestination is
not according to a divine prescience caused by free choice; on
the other hand, predestination is not without the prescience of
free choice. Predestination is according to the divine prescience
(scientia media) of futurible choice. Yet, since God freely
effects the hypotheses (grace) in which he had foreseen what
a man would freely do, predestination is solely according to
the will of God.

*L. Molina, <u>Concordia</u>, p. 550: Juxta haec, distinximus
duos illos sensus, in quorum altero negandum erat cum
Augustino praedestinationem fuisse secundum praescientiam
usus arbitrii cujusque praevisi. In altero vero id ipsum
sine scrupulo cum aliis Patribus omnini concedendum erat.
Modo addimus duo. Primum est, Scripturas sanctas ita
exponendas esse, ut neque juxta primum sensum affirmemus
praedestinationem fuisse secundum praescientiam usus
liberi arbitrii meritorumque cuiusque adulti; neque
iuxta secundum id negemus. Secundum est, Patres quodammodo eatenus ad concordiam posse reduci, si, qui negant
praedestinationem fuisse secundum praescientiam meritorum
ab boni usus liberi arbitrii futuri accipiantur in priori
sensu, quatenus eorum dicta id patientur; in quibus est
Augustinus, et ejus sectatores. Qui vero fuisse affirmant
secundum merita et bonum usum praevisum, exponantur in
sensu posteriori, quatenus eorum dicta id ferent, de
quorum numero sunt, Origenes, Athanasius, Chrysostomus,
Ambrosius, Theodoretus, Theophylactus, omnes in cap.
nonum Epistolae ad Rom. Hieronymus in illud ad Galat. I.
Cum placuit ei qui segregavit ex utero matris meae, Ep. ad
Hedibiam in expositione quaest. decimae. Faustus (non
Manichaeus, sed in Gallia episcopus) libro primo de Gratia
et libero arbitrio cap. iv, et lib. II c. vi tom. V
bibliothecae Patrum, et plerique alii, Neque vero dubito
quin ab August, et caeteris Patribus unanimi consensu
comprobata fuisset haec nostra de praedestinatione
sententia, ratioque conciliandi libertatem arbitrii cum
divina gratia, praescientia, et praedestinatione,
si eis proposita fuisset. Cf. p. 546.*

The same doctrine which has been drawn mainly from the <u>Con-
cordia</u>, is found throughout Molina's writings. For the sake of com-
pleteness I shall give two other expositions of it, one from Molina's
<u>De Scientia Dei</u> and one from his <u>Epitome De Praedestinatione</u>.

In Stegmüller, op. cit., pp. 202 sqq., and pp. 306 sqq.

The point to notice in these two versions, as in the preceding, is
the notion of free choice implied or expressed, as occasion offers,
by Molina: on the side of its divine antecedents, free choice is in
its futurible state independent of divine causality; on the side of
its human antecedents, free choice is an act of the will undetermined by the intellect. The reason that such a notion of free
choice is subjacent to Molinism is as follows: God does not know,

169

according to Molina, what a man will actually choose, unless there have preceded the divine knowledge of what a man would do in any given hypothesis--<u>scientia</u> <u>media</u>. Further, God does not effect free choice by a determination of it which causally antecedes the will's own determination; rather, he effects the free act concurrently with the will--simultaneous concourse. Last, just as the divine antecedents suppose the free act, in its futurible state, so its human antecedents suppose the free act in the sense that <u>therefore</u> there are these antecedents <u>because</u> there will be this choice.

Cf. L. Molina, <u>Summa Haeresium Maior</u>, in Stegmüller op. cit., pp. 447, 448.

Now, in the assertion of <u>scientia</u> <u>media</u> and in the denial of efficacious predetermining decrees, we have the essence of Molinism. And the two assertions demand the complete antecedent indetermination of choice.

9 MOLINIST LIBERTY IN THE UTRUM SCIENTIA DEI SIT CAUSA RERUM

Commenting on the first part of the Summa Theol., utrum scientia Dei sit causa rerum,

Summa Theol., 1a, q. 14, a. 8.

Molina advances the thesis that the knowledge of God can be viewed in two ways: as the knowledge by which God knows what he can do and as the knowledge by which he knows what he will do. The first sort of divine knowledge is natural and unfree, and antecedes the second. The second sort is free knowledge and is consequent upon the determination of God's will. God's knowledge of the future, then, depends upon his voluntary determination of what will be.

L. Molina, De Scientia Dei, in Stegmüller, op. cit., pp. 202, 203: Quia enim Deus libere voluit mundum creare . . . scivit mundum fore . . . et non e contra, quia scivit (res) futuras, ideo voluit ut essent, quin potius si noluisset ut essent, non scivisset eas futuras. Cf. L. Molina, Concordia, pp. 1, 2.

Whence, only God's natural knowledge is the cause of things. God's free knowledge is not their cause. For God's natural knowledge is the plan of his operation, anteceding the determination of his will and determined by his will in ordine ad opus; whereas, God's free knowledge does not direct his will or antecede it. It is mere vision. Augustine's dictum (creaturas . . . non quia sunt, ideo novit Deus; sed ideo sunt, quia novit)

De Trin. 1. 5, c. 13, P.L.; 42: 1076.

must therefore be understood of God's natural knowledge. It is not because God knows what he can do that he knows what he will do; rather, because God knows what he will do, therefore, does he know what will be. And Origen's dictum, non propterea aliquid erit, quia id scit Deus futurum, sed quia futurum est, ideo scitur a Deo, antequm fiat

Comm. ad Rom. 8, 30, 1. 7, n. 8, and 1. 1, n. 3. P. G., 14: 1124 and 845 notes.

must be understood as true in regard to its first part. For, as was said, God's knowledge of what will be is not the cause of things. As to its second part, if the meaning be that because the future comes from the determination of God's will--with the concurrence of the human will (if such be the kind of future event contemplated by God)--therefore is the future known by God, then this is true. In this sense creatures are not the cause of divine knowledge; rather, the determination of the divine will is the cause of God's knowledge. The a priori reason of the divine knowledge that some-thing contingent will be (for example, Peter's sitting down at a given hour) is God's will, penetratis omnino naturis . . . etiam libero arbitrio, quoad quam partem libere sit determinaturum.

L. Molina, De Scientia Dei, in Stegmüller, op. cit., pp. 203, 204. Cf. L. Molina, Concordia, p. 2.

The whole point of Molina's contention is that God's knowledge of what will be is not, as such, the cause of things; it is his knowledge of what can be that is their cause.

Moving on to the thirteenth article of the same question (14), Molina then transcribes from St. Thomas some of the difficulties against the contention that God knows contingent futures. The difficulties are these. First, God's knowledge is necessary, and since from a necessary cause there follows necessarily an effect, this makes all things known by God necessary. Second, posito antecedente, ponitur consequens. But the antecedent, God knows the future, must be posited; so too, then, must the consequent be posited. Thus, no consequent can be contingent. Third, what we know must be; a fortiori what God knows must be. But no contingent must be. Whence, no future contingent is known by God. Molina adds to these some difficulties of his own. Fourth, no contingent future can fail to occur; otherwise God would be deceived. Therefore, nothing known to God is contingent, for what is contingent can be or not be. Fifth, contingents are no less necessary, if God truly knows them, than the propositions enuntiating them are true. So too, then, must be the things expressed by the propositions. Whence if God truly knows contingents, it follows that they occur necessarily. Sixth, divine prescience of the future destroys liberty, for if God knows that Socrates will sin, Socrates will sin. And Socrates cannot sublate the antecedent (for that matter, neither can God); whence Socrates must sin.

L. Molina, De Scientia Dei, in Stegmüller, op. cit. pp. pp. 204, 205. Cf. L. Molina, Concordia, pp. 315, 316.

Molina's problem is this: how can divine prescience stand together with human freedom? Two errors, he says, must be avoided: the denial of prescience, the denial of liberty. The latter was Luther's way out.

L. Molina, De Scientia Dei, in Stegmüller, op. cit., pp. 205-07. Cf. L. Molina, Concordia, pp. 314, 316, and Luther, Assertio, ed. Weimar, vol. 7, p. 142.

To answer this problem it must first be determined what liberty means. Liberty is opposed to coercion and necessity or to servitude. The question is about the first kind; namely, the liberty opposed to coercion and necessity. In this sense liberty can further mean two things: liberty as opposed to coercion in the sense that what occurs spontaneously (that is, is not coerced, is free); and liberty as opposed to necessity (for example, the liberty of an agent which when all the conditions for acting are present can act or not act, act thus or contrariwise). This, then, is the sense of liberty as understood by Molina. A free agent is distinguished from a natural agent in that a natural agent must act (whereas, a free agent need not) when the conditions for acting are posited.

L. Molina, De Scientia Dei, in Stegmüller, op. cit., pp. 207, 208. Cf. L. Molina, Concordia, pp. 10, 11.

The proof of the existence of such liberty Molina draws mainly from experience. We know that we have it in our power to stand, to sit, to walk here or there, to consent or not to consent, and so forth. Scotus he quotes approvingly, probe sat Scotus, to the effect that those who deny liberty should be punished until they admit that their tormentors can desist. Further, without liberty there is no imputability or sin.

L. Molina, De Scientia Dei, in Stegmüller, op. cit., pp. 208, 209. Scotus' text is in Op. Ox. 1. 39, a. 3, no. 1, 1117 d. Quarrachi, ed., p. 1215.

Conceiving liberty in that way, Molina next discusses St. Thomas' contention, and Scotus' denial, that future contingents are known by God as present to his eternity.

L. Molina, De Scientia Dei, in Stegmüller, op. cit., pp. 216–18. Cf. L. Molina, Concordia, p. 295; St. Thomas, Summa Theol., 1a q. 14, a. 13; Scotus, Op. Ox., 1. 1. D. 39, q. 1 a. 2, 1112–13, Quarrachi, ed., pp. 1210, 1211.

St. Thomas' explanation we have already seen. He bases the possibility of previsible future contingents upon the omnipotence of God; their actual existence he bases upon the liberty of God.

> *Summa Theol., 1a q. 22, a. 4, ad 3um et resp.: Necessarium et contingens proprie consequuntur ens, in quantum huiusmodi. Unde modus contingentiae et necessitatis cadit sub provisione Dei, qui est universalis provisor totius entis . . . et ideo [quia ad divinam providentiam pertinet omnes gradus entium producere] quibusdam effectibus praeparavit causas necessarias, ut necessario evenirent; quibusdam vero causas contingentes, ut evenirent contingenter, secundum conditionem proximarum causarum.*

Scotus put the source of contingence in the liberty of God; that is, he put it in the divine will freely concurring with second causes.

L. Molina, De Scientia Dei, in Stegmüller, op. cit., p. 232. Cf. L. Molina, Concordia, p. 203. Molina's reference to Scotus is 1. d. 2. q. 2, # ostenso esse and d. 39,

contra ista. These may be found in Op. Ox., n. 244,
Quarrachi, ed., p. 201, and in n. 1115, Quarrachi, ed.,
p. 1213. Cf. Op. Ox., 1. 39. 3. n. 1118, p. 1215: Nulla
causatio alicuius causae potest salvare contingentiam,
nisi Prima causa ponatur immediate contingenter causare,
et hoc ponendo in Prima causa perfectam causalitatem,
sicut Catholici ponunt.

Whence, for Thomas God sees future contingents as present; for
Scotus, God sees future contingents in the determination of his
own free will. Molina is discontented with both these solutions.

L. Molina, De Scientia Dei, in Stegmüller, op. cit., p.
226: opinio . . . d. Thomae hoc loco quatenus asserit
futura contingentia neque a Deo . . . cognosci certo in
suis atque ex suis causis, sed cognosci certo quatenus
in sua aeternitate sunt extra suas causas in suo esse
existentiae, numquam nihi placuit. Cf. L. Molina, Concordia, p. 221. For Molina's opinion of Scotus' doctrine
see Stegmüller, op. cit., p. 223: Hinc intelliges non
recta sensisse Scotum in 1. d. 2. q. 2. # ostenso esse
[in Op. Ox., n. 244, Quarrachi, p. 201] et d. 39 #
contra ista [n. 1115, Quarrachi, p. 1213]--dum dixit,
radicem contingentiae in effectibus emanantibus a causis
secundis esse contingentiam, hoc est libertatem, in
divina voluntate, qua libere concurrit cum causis secundis.
Cf. L. Molina, Concordia, p. 203.

Against St. Thomas he advances the arguments we have already
seen from the Concordia.

Vid. supra pp. 136 sqq. The parallel references to these
arguments in Molina's De Scientia Dei are pp. 226-29 in
Stegmüller, op. cit.

Against Scotus' opinion--namely, that the source of contingence is
God's liberty; that is in the divine will by which God freely concurs
with second causes (and therewith is also indicated Scotus' medium
of divine prescience, the divine will)--Molina argues that this
destroys liberty. For the divine concourse, though it is within
God's power, is not within the power of man.

Scotus' position upon the relation of divine knowledge to
free choice is this: if we suppose that God knows the free
future events apart from his will, then either the free
future event is contingent--and so, God's knowledge of it

175

It must be said, then, that the divine concourse with second
causes is not the divine motion in causem but the divine motion
una cum causa. Thus, God of himself and without the mediation
of the second cause (Deus immediate, immediatione suppositi)
attains the effect una cum causa secunda. The whole effect is
from God but not as though he were the total cause of the effect;
he is only partialiter the cause. So too, the whole effect is from
the second cause but not as though it were the total cause; it is
only partialiter the cause. The same may be said of the action
which produces the effect: it is wholly from God or the second
cause respectively, non totaliter totalitate causae, sed partialiter. God's action is called the universal concourse; the
creature's action is called the particular concourse. Nor is it
because of God's universal concourse that the action produced is
of a given kind. The kind of action performed is from the particular concourse. For the universal concourse is ex se indifferent to many effects. It is the particular concourse a quo determinatur (influxus Dei generalis) and from which sequitur talis
vel talis effectus, et talis vel talis actio.

*L. Molina, De Scientia Dei, in Stegmüller, op. cit., p.
234: dicendum est, concursum Dei universalem non esse
influxum et motum Dei in causam, ut agat (quando enim
ignis calefacit non movetur sed movet), sed esse influxum Dei in effectum una cum causa secunda. Ita quod
Deus immediate immediatione suppositi attingit effectum
per concursum universalem una cum causa secunda; et totus
effectus est a Deo non totaliter totalitate causae sed
partialiter; et totus est a causa secunda non totaliter
totalitate causae sed partialiter. Tota item actio, qua
producitur effectus, est a Deo, non totaliter totalitate
causae sed partialiter, et tota est a causa secunda non
totaliter sed partialiter. Et eadem actio, ut a Deo,
dicitur concursus Dei universalis; ut a causa vero
secunda, dicitur concursus particularis causae secundae.*

Neque habet talis actio, ut est a Deo, quod sit talis,
puta calefactio aut volitio, sed ut est a causa secunda,
puta ab igne aut a voluntate. Si enim cum Deo influente
per concursum universalem concurreret aqua et non ignis,
actio esset frigefactio et non calefactio; et si con-
curreret voluntas pro sua libertate ad nolitionem et non
ad volitionem, actio esset nolito et non volitio. In-
fluxus enim universalis Dei indifferens est ex se ad
plures effectus; et prout fuerit influxus causae particular-
is, a quo determinatur, sequitur talis vel talis effectus
et talis vel talis actio. Cf. L. Molina, De Concursu
Generali, in Stegmüller, op. cit., pp. 194 sqq. and L.
Molina, Concordia, pp. 154-204.

Thus, even if the general divine concourse were necessary and
not free--Molina is here arguing against Scotus--nevertheless,
since the general concourse pendeat a concursu causae secundae
ab illoque determinatur ad speciem actus et effectus, existente
libertate in causa secunda, contingence would still be saved.

L. Molina, De Scientia Dei, in Stegmüller, op. cit.,
pp. 234, 235.

As for Scotus' contention that God knows future contingents in
the free determination of his will,

Op. Ox. 1. D. 39, n. 1099, Quarrachi, pp. 1205 sqq.

it is not a sufficient explanation of the manner of the divine knowledge. The explantion of Scotus would be satisfactory if all future
contingents depended for their existence immediately upon God
or, if only mediately dependent on God, they were necessary in
their causes. But free choice is not necessary in its cause. If
God sees future free choice in the determination of his own will,
apart from the determination of the human will, "How, " Molina
asks, "can liberty of choice be preserved?" To say that it is
enough for liberty if choice can be otherwise, but not on the supposition of God's knowledge and determination of choice, does
not solve the difficulty. Whence, when theologians say that upon
the supposition that God knows Socrates will sin Socrates in sensu
diviso is able not to sin but is not able in sensu composito, this
may mean two things. It may mean either that God's prescience
destroys Socrates' liberty--and this is false--or it may mean that
if Socrates does not sin, as may be the fact, God would never

have had such prescience--and this is true.

> *L. Molina, De Scientia Dei, in Stegmüller, op. cit., pp.*
> *236-38. Cf. L. Molina, Concordia, p. 298. Here again, in*
> *the sensus divisus and compositus distinction, we find*
> *Banes' and Molina's answer--though each in a different*
> *sense--to the pseudo-problem raised by Luther. Vid.*
> *supra, p. 94.*

These difficulties Molina adduces not so much in order to
reject Scotus as to make clear the following solution. God knows
what a free agent would choose in any circumstance of choice,
manente de facto libero arbitrio.

> *L. Molina, De Scientia Dei, in Stegmüller, op. cit. pp.*
> *238, 239: Deum ex comprehensione et omnimoda penetratione*
> *per suam scientiam naturalem omnium causarum in sua es-*
> *sentia, etiam liberarum, ad quam partem pro sua libertate*
> *cum his aut illis circumstantiis se essent determinaturae,*
> *ex suppositione tamen seu sub conditione: si creentur*
> *hoc aut illo modo, cum his aut illis circumstantiis etc.,*
> *una cum determinatione libera suae voluntatis, qua statuit*
> *creare mundum eo modo quo creavit et cum circumstantiis*
> *quae de facto cernuntur praecognovisse certo et infallib-*
> *iliter omnia futura contingentia, manente de facto libero*
> *arbitrio in causis agentibus per intellectum et voluntatem.*
> *Cf. Molina, Concordia, pp. 302, 317.*

To understand this it must be realized that before God determines to do anything, he first knows by his natural knowledge
what he can do. Further, he knows what future free acts would be,
not absolutely in their esse futurum, but conditionally; namely,
upon the condition that he create the circumstances under which
such acts will freely be: for example, God knew the penance of
Tyre and Sidon.

> *L. Molina, De Scientia Dei, in Stegmüller, op. cit., pp.*
> *239, 240: Ad huius rei intelligentiam sciendum est, Deum*
> *in sua aeternitate ante determinationem liberam suae*
> *voluntatis ad aliquid creandum aut producendum ex in-*
> *tuitu suae voluntatis ad aliquid congnovisse per scientiam*
> *naturalem omnia quae poterat facere. . . . Sciendum est*
> *praeterea, in eadem sua aeternitate ante determinationem*
> *suae voluntatis eadem scientia naturali ex omnimoda*
> *comprehensione et penetratione rerum atque causarum vidisse,*
> *quid esset futurum, si hunc ordinem aut illum eligeret pro-*

178

ducere. . . . Hactenus ergo Deus optimus nulli adimens
libertatem arbitrii sua scientia naturali congnoscit
in sua essentia atque potentia omnia contingentia futura,
non in esse futuri absolute sed sub conditione, si per
determinationem liberam suae voluntatis statuit creare
hunc aut illum ordinem rerum, cognoscitque non solum
ea, quae de facto sunt, fuerunt aut erunt, sed etiam
infinita alia, quae essent si alium ordinem statueret
aut si in hoc ordine statueret alias circumstantias;
scit enim futuram fuisse paenitentiam Tyriorum et
Sidoniorum in cinere et cilicio ex suppositione si
statuisset, ut in Tyro et Sidone fierent virtutes et
miracula, quae Corozaim et Bethsaidae facta sunt.

When, therefore, God determines to create, he knows absolutely
what will freely be. And this determination leaves liberty intact.
For man's free choice in the actual order of being, whichever
way that choice takes, would have been known by God in its
futurible state.

1. c. p. 240: Accedente ergo libera determinatione suae
voluntatis qua ab aeterno statuit et elegit creare
ordinem eorum quae de facto creavit cum circumstantiis
quae de facto sunt, ab aeterno libere scivit, omnia con-
tingentia futura in esse futuri absolute, nulli adimens
libertatem arbitrii, sed ipsum relinquens potentem ut
de facto possit facere oppositum. Si tamen ipse de facto
esset pro sua libertate facturus oppositum, ut potest,
Deus id praescivisset, et non id quod de facto modo scit;
unde praescientia aut electio voluntatis divinae nulli
necessitatem imponit aut adimit libertatem. Cf. L. Molina,
Concordia, p. 317.

The difficulty against this scientia media is this: how can God
know the determination of choice before it is determined? Molina
sees the difficulty.

Cf. p. 141, supra.

His answer is that God must know this determination of the will,
since his knowledge is infinite, but how we do not know. Molina
feels confident, nevertheless, that he is right in maintaining a
scientia media. His reason is that there is no other way of reconciling free choice with the efficacity of its antecedents. Yet,
according to theology, we must admit that choice is free and its

antecedents efficacious. Besides, Molina assures himself that he has established his point by argument.

Cf. pp. 136-40, supra.

The fact is that Molina's arguments prove only that God knows futurible free choice; they do not at all prove that God knows futurible choice in a medium distinct from divine causality. They do not, I say, prove this except on the supposition that Molina's dilemma is valid. The dilemma: if God knows the future only because he knows what can be, there is no providence; if he knows it only because he knows what will be, there is no liberty. The answer to this disjunction is to distinguish the second member: divine prescience of the future destroys contingence only if God does not cause, and therefore does not know, contingence; other-wise it does not. If it be urged that God cannot know a free act which he causes, this shows only that one underestimates the virtue of the cause. It is an infinite cause.

L. Molina, De Scientia Dei, in Stegmüller, op. cit., pp. 240, 241: Sententia haec nostra ex impugnationibus caeterarum et maxime ex argumentis factis contra opinionem d. Thomae satis est confirmata; tum etiam ex eo, quod ea scientia videtur salvari libertas arbitrii cum praescientia et determinatione libera voluntatis divinae, quam libertatem apertissimis rationibus et testimoniis Scripturae supra ostendimus confitendam; in hacque sola sententia videtur quiescere intellectus.

Solumque est quod ei obiciatur, quinam fieri possit, ut in causa libera, quae retinens eandem prorsus naturam et existentibus eisdem circumstantiis potest se libere in utramvis partem determinare, cognoscatur determinatio in alteram partem, antequam sit.

Ad quod respondeo, id provenire ex eminentia et perfectione scientiae divinae, cui plura tribuenda sunt quam in hac vita concipere valeamus, maxime si perfectione talis scientiae digna sint et consona aliis veritatibus fidei, qualis est in proposito consonantia liberi arbitrii cum praescientia divina. Cum ergo autori naturae, a quo omnia, etiam natura ipsa liberi arbitrii, tamquam a fonte emanarunt, id tribuatur, consonetque maxime scripturis sacris et veritatibus fidei, dignumque sit perfectione et eminentia scientiae divinae, nihil mirum in tali assertione iudicari debet, tametsi modus, quo Deus in tali causa cognoscat praedictam determinationem, forte in hac vita non valet explicari.

Cf. L. Molina, *Concordia,* pp. *311, 312: asserimus Deum
ex altitudine et perfectione sui intellectus atque suae
essentiae, tanquam objecti primarii, certissime cognoscere in se ipso, et in causis secundis quid pro
libertate earum contingenter sit futurum, esset, ut re
vera potest, Deus ex aeternitate id certissime scivisset, et non id quod actu scit. Quare, servato integro
jure libertatis arbitrii creati, illaesaque omnino per-
sistente contingentia rerum, non secus ac si in Deo
nulla esset praescientia, Deus certissime cognoscit
futura contingentia, non quidem certitudine quae proveniat ex objecto, quod in se est contingens, potestque
aliter re ipsa evenire, sed certitudine quae proficiscitur ex altitudine atque infinita illimitataque
perfectione cognoscentis, qui certo ex se ipso cognoscit
objectum, quod secundum se est incertum et fallax. Quo
fit ut rerum contingentia, atque libertas arbitrii in
futurum optime consentiant cum certa et non solum omnino
immutabili Dei tam scientia, quam voluntate, sed etiam
ita fixa ac stabili, ut jam modo contradictionem im-
plicet Deum ex aeternitate contrarium voluisse aut
cognovisse eventurum.*

Molina has his answers ready now to the difficulties which he
has transcribed from St. Thomas.

See pp. 172-73, supra.

Solution of the first difficulty: If the statement, the knowledge of
God is the cause of things, means that God's knowledge of the
future is the cause of things, this must be denied; for God's
knowledge of the future is subsequent to his will that there be a
future, and the causal knowledge of God dictates his action and
antecedes his will. Such causal knowledge, then, cannot be of
the future. If, however, the statement refers to the knowledge of
God which antecedes his will, then the major premise, necessary effects follow from necessary causes, must be distinguished.
Necessary effects do follow from necessary causes, if the causes
in question are the total, sufficient, sole, and unimpeded causes
of those effects. But such a cause the divine knowledge which
antecedes the divine will is not, for that knowledge needs the
free concourse of God's will, by reason of which concourse effects are either necessary or contingent.

To the second difficulty Molina answers as follows. The absolutely necessary can be understood in two ways: first, as the
necessary which arises from the nature and cause of the terms

which absolute necessity affects; for example, Man is an animal.
So too, these propositions are necessary: A swan is white. There
will be an eclipse on such and such a day. Man is an animal is
necessary from the nature of its terms; A swan is white is necessary from the causes which naturally cannot be impeded.

Second, the necessary can be considered as arising from a
condition which, being posited, implies the necessity of the con-
sequence--for example, Adam existed is today absolutely true;
yet Adam could not have existed. Whence, to the difficulty posito
antecedente ponendum consequens it should be answered that the
consequent must be posited if the antecedent is absolutely necessary in the first sense; but the consequent need not be posited if
the antecedent is true only in the second sense. For the second
sort of necessary antecedent is simply contingent; nor need its
positing entrain the necessity of the consequent but only the necessity of the consequence. That is, granted God's knowledge of
what will be, that will be which God knows will be. Yet, what will
be is not certainly known by God from the proximate cause of what
will be (for thus, in its cause, a free event can not be). Rather, it
is known from the perfection of the divine intellect, which can tell
from itself that which in itself (that is, in the second cause) is uncertain; namely, free future choice.

Molina's point seems to be this. He distinguishes two senses
of the proposition If God knows the future, the future will be.
First sense: the consequent (the future will be) is absolutely necessary from the necessity of its nature; this he denies. Second sense:
the consequent is necessary from the posited condition of God's
knowledge; this he grants. But God's knowledge leaves liberty
intact, libere enim Deus scivit hoc esse futurum, et scivisset
oppositum, si homo de facto per liberum arbitrium esset facturus
oppositum.

*L. Molina, De Scientia Dei, in Stegmüller, op. cit., p.
250.*

The principle back of Molina's answer is thus the scientia media
and its object, futurible free choice. The reason that there is no
necessity of the consequent, but only necessity of the consequence,
in Molina's proposition is the block of futurible being which is,
ex supposito, uncaused except by itself. To put it in another way:
Molina's antecedent God knows the future, could have been different, for scivisset [Deus] oppositum, si homo de facto per
liberum arbitrium esset facturus oppositum. St. Thomas' answer

182

to the difficulty is si dicam: si Deus scivit aliquid, illus erit; consequens intelligendum est prout est in sua praesentialitiate.

Summa Theol., 1a q. 14, a. 13, ad 2um.

But Molina did not think highly of this presentiality notion. The fact is that St. Thomas maintains freedom in choice because God is its cause. Molina maintains it because it has no cause except itself. As to the third difficulty--namely, what God knows, must be--Molina distinguishes it in the same way. The consequent must be, necessitate consequentiae, he admits. The consequent must be, necessitate consequentis, he denies. He denies, too, the proof; namely, if what we know must be, a fortiori what God knows must be. Our knowledge depends on objects. God's knowledge does not so depend. His reason for so answering is the same: scientia media and its object, futurible choice. St. Thomas' answer is, in principle, the same as was his answer to the second difficulty:

ea quae temporaliter in actum reducuntur, a nobis successive cognoscuntur in tempore, sed a Deo in aeternitate, quae est supra tempus. . . . et ideo illus quod acitur a nobis, oportet esse necessarium etiam secundum quod est in se, quia ea quae in se sunt contingentia futura a nobis sciri non possunt; sed ea quae sunt scita a Deo oportet esse necessaria secundum modum quo subsunt divinae scientiae, ut dictum est, non autem absolute, secundum, quod in propriis causis considerantur.

Summa Theol., 1a q. 14, a. 13, ad 3um.

The fourth antecedent--no future event known to God can fail to occur--Molina denies. Its proof--otherwise God would be deceived--he maintains is inconsequential. For divine knowledge is such that God can infallibly know whatever can or cannot be.

The major of the fifth difficulty is denied, and for the reason assigned in answer to the third objection: the certitude of our knowledge is measured by the certainty of the object, but the certitude of God's knowledge is from the nature of the knower.

So, too, is denied the antecedent of the sixth difficulty: prescience destroys liberty. He admits the proof of this antecedent --God knows Socrates will sin, therefore he will sin--up to the point at which it is asserted that Socrates cannot sublate the antecedent. This Socrates can do; for if Socrates does not sin, as may quite well be the case, there would not have been that antecedent.

L. Molina, De Scientia Dei, in Stegmüller, op. cit., pp. 248-51. Cf. L. Molina, Concordia, pp. 328, 330, 331, 332.

To repeat, the principle back of all Molina's solutions is the scientia media. God knows the future with certainty; yet human choice is free. To conciliate the two truths Molina sees only this way: before God knew what would be, he knew what would be upon the condition that he would will the circumstances of human choice. Since, then, the circumstances of choice depend on God (who creates or does not create them), God certainly knows the future. Yet his knowledge leaves intact human freedom; for man's actual choice has simply moved into the real order of things from its futurible state where it was seen by God as free choice. Simultaneous divine concourse is consequent upon scientia media; for future choice is determined only so far forth as was the same choice determined in its futurible state, and there it was at least undetermined by, if not determining, the divine concourse.

L. Molina, Summa Haeresium Maior, in Stegmüller, op. cit., p. 411: Ad eandem quoque sapientiam et potentiam spectabat, ut talis esset ille influxus [sc. generalis] et tam indifferens in se ad assensum ac dissensum, ut iuxta eandem innatam ipsarum [causarum secondarum] libertatem suo peculiari influxu determinare eum possent ad assensum vel dissensum ut mallent.

Before moving on to Molina's shortest and clearest exposition of his theory, in his Epitome de Praedestinatione, it may be well to dwell upon the author whom he has just been quoting, Duns Scotus. The comparison of Scotus with Molina may bring still more into focus the Molinist concept of liberty. The comparison may be made by using as a point of reference the theory of St. Thomas Aquinas. We may consider in order the theories of divine and human causality.

St. Thomas and Duns Scotus seem to differ only in the emphasis which each places upon the elements of the divine causality of free human choice. For St. Thomas the divine previsibility of contingent future events is founded upon the omnipotent causality of God; the prevision of such events is had, because God's free choice has made them present to his eternity.

Cont. Gent., *3, 94: etsi divina Providentia sit per se
causa huius effectus futuri, est etiam praesentis et
prateriti, magis autem ab aeterno. Non tamen sequitur
. . . quod effectus sit de necessitate futurus; est enim
divina Providentia per se causa quod hic effectus contingenter proveniat, et hoc cassari non potest. Ex quo
etiam patet quod haec conditionalis est vera: Si Deus
providet hoc futurum, hoc erit . . . Sed sic erit sicut
Deus providit illud esse futurum; providit autem illud
esse futurum contingenter; sequitur ergo infallibiliter,
quod erit contingenter, non necessario. Cf. Summa Theol.,
1a q. 22, a. 4: Respondeo dicendum, quod providentia quibusdam rebus necessitatem imponit, non autem omnibus . . .
Ad providentiam enim pertinet ordinare res in finem. . . .
et ideo quibusdam effectibus praeparavit causas necessarias, ut necessario evenirent; quibusdam vero causas
contingentes, ut evenirent contingenter, secundum conditionem proximarum causarum. . . . Ad tertium dicendum
quod indissolubilitas illa et immutabilitas quam Boetius
tangit [De Consolat., IV pr. 6: fatum ab immobilibus
providentiae proficiscens exordiis, actus fortunasque
hominum indissolubili causarum connexione adstringit]
pertinet ad certitudinem providentiae quae non deficit
a suo effectu, neque a modo eveniendi, quem providit;
non autem pertinet ad necessitatem effectum. Et considerandum est quod necessarium et contingens proprie
consequuntur ens, in quantum huiusmodi. Unde modus contingentiae et necessitatis cadit sub provisione Dei,
qui est universalis provisor totius entis . . .*

For Scotus the divine previsibility and prevision of contingent
futures have their source in the divine knowledge of the divine will.

Cf. p. 14, n. 2; p. 16, n. 2; p. 17, n. 2.

If Scotus seems to make a point of saying that unless divine
liberty be the source of human liberty there will be no contingence, since God if not a free cause, is a necessary cause;
and so too, therefore, will be his effects. If Scotus seems, I
say, to make a point here, it must be remembered that, after
all, divine omnipotence in St. Thomas is free omnipotence.

*E. Gilson, Esprit de la philosophie mediévale, II Vrin,
p. 267. Cf. the references there cited: Summa Theol.,
1a q. 22, a. 4., resp. et ad 3um; Op. Ox., 1. 39, 1.
3, 14, Quarracchi, n. 1118, p. 1215; 8 and 9, nn. 1112-
13, pp. 1210-12.*

Scotus seems to make the divine will alone carry the burden of contingence, though he allows the divine intellect too its place in the scheme of divine causality.

De rerum princ., q. 4, a. 1, Sect. III ad fin., Vives, vol. 4, p. 307 b: Quum voluntas Dei non feratur per se nisi ad bonum adequatum quod est sua bonitas, non fertur ad volendum necessario nisi illa quae suae bonitati essentialiter sunt annexa . . . omnis autem creatura ad bonitatem Dei accidentalem habet ordinem. If Scotus is asked, Why, then does God create? his answer is (Op. Ox., 1. 2, d. 1, q. 2, ad 4um, Quarracchi, p. 31): Indisciplinati est quaerere omnium demonstationem. . . principiorum enim demonstrationis non est demonstratio . . . et ideo ista voluntas qua vult hoc et producit pro nunc, est immediata et prima causa, cuius non est aliqua alia causa quaerenda . . . tantum quia voluit hoc esse, ideo bonum fuit illud esse, et quaerere huius propositionis . . . immediate causam, est quaerere causam . . . cuius non est ratio quaerenda. But God's intellect has in Scotus something to do with his will (De rerum princ., q. 4, a. 2, s. 3, Vives, vol. 4, p. 310 b); intellectu cognoscente rem producendam, non propterea res producitur, nisi imperet voluntas et ad opus potentia applicetur . . . Unde . . . scientia vel intellectus quasi ordinans; voluntas autem ut movens. Cf. De rerum princ., q. 2, a. 2, Vives, vol. 4, p. 282 b; and E. Gilson, La Liberte chez Descartes et les théologiens, pp. 144, 145.

St. Thomas allows that God's will has no cause,

Cont. Gent., 1. 87; Summa Theol., q. 19, a. 5; De Veritate q. 6, a. 2.

but aliquibus rebus secundum modum suae naturae, competit quod sint contingentes, non necessariae, igitur vult aliquas res esse, contingentes.

Cont. Gent., 1. 85, 1.

In other words, the existence of things has no cause but God's will, but what it is that exists has its foundation in the competentia rerum, which is the bonum universi.

Cont. Gent., 1. 86.

Thus is excluded the error of some who say that everything comes from God according to his simple will, in such wise that no reason need be given for anything except that God wills it. This is also contrary to Scripture, according to which God makes everything according to the order of his wisdom . . .

> *Cont. Gent.*, 1. 87. Cf. *Summa Theol.*, 1. q. 19, a. 5;
> *De Veritate*, q. 6, a. 2.

In short, that there be a free act is for St. Thomas because of God's will, that an act be free because of his intelligence. God's will makes free acts to exist; that the existing act be free depends upon the divine will joined to the divine intelligence.

> *Summa Theol.*, 1a q. 19, a. 5, resp: Vult ergo (Deus)
> hoc esse propter hoc, sed non propter hoc vult. . . .
> voluntas Dei rationabilis est, non quod aliquid sit Deo
> causa volendi, sed in quantum vult unum esse propter
> aliud.

Scotus seems so to emphasize the role of the divine will that the divine intellect--though Scotus assigns to it its part--seems to recede into the background of divine causality.

> *The reason for the difference in viewpoint upon divine
> causality between St. Thomas and Scotus seems trace-
> able ultimately to their different theories of essence
> and existence. Essence is distinct from existence in
> St. Thomas' view. They are the same in Scotus: If the
> same, then since existence comes from the will, so too
> does essence. And this in the divine as well as the human
> order. Hence, God's intellect is not the cause of his
> free choice; nor is man's intellect the cause of his
> free choice. Choice is solely in either instance, from
> the will. This is St. Thomas' view: If different, then
> since essence comes from the intellect and existence
> from the will, it follows that God wills what he knows
> (the necessary necessarily, the contingent freely), and
> man wills what he knows. Hence, God's intellect is partly
> the cause of his choice, and so is man's. Complete re-
> ferences are not given, because this is not the writer's
> subject, though it might be expected of him to state
> what he thinks. Cf. Op. Ox., 1. 2, e. 1, q. 3, n. 33,
> Quarrachi, ed., p. 29.*

187

Now if omnipotence and liberty had been left together, perhaps the solution of the difficulty which Scotus raises would not, under Molina's manipulation, have issued into simultaneous concourse and scientia media. Anyhow, such was the issue of the difficulty. If Molina looks to Scotistic divine liberty, apart from divine omnipotence, as the cause of free human choice, he sees there predetermination, which he tries to escape by simultaneous concourse.

L. Molina, De Scientia Dei, in Stegmüller, op. cit., pp. 232, 233, 234, 235: Hinc intelliges non recte sensisse Scotum in 1, d. 2, q. 2, paragr. ostenso esse et d. 39 paragr. contra ista atque aliis locis suae doctrinae, dum dixit, radicem contingentiae in effectibus emanantibus a causis secundis esse contingentiam, hoc est libertatem, in divina voluntate, qua libere concurrit cum causis secundis. Credit enim quod si in Deo non esset libertas, sed Deus ageret ex necessitate naturae, esto non influeret maiori concursu quam de facto influat, nullus esset effectus contingens. Unde in 2. d. 1 q. 3 paulo ante paragr tenentes autem, inquit, philosophos asserentes Deum agere ex necessitate naturae et nihilominus esse effectus contingentes in hoc universo latenter asseruisse contradictori Et adverte Scotum non tantum voluisse quod si Deus concedatur omnipotens, hoc est potens facere quidquid non implicat contradictionem ut conceditur a Christianis, et simul asseratur agere ex necessitate naturae, sequuntur duo contradictoria; id enim verissimum est; sed hoc et ultra voluisse quod, esto posset solum influere cum causis secundis ut de facto influit, tamquam causa prima, si concursus ille esset naturalis et non liber, nullus esset effectus contingens hoc universo etiam in voluntate humana.

Et probat id primo: quia causa movens in quantum mota, si necessario movetur, necessario movet. Sed omnis causa secunda (etiam voluntas humana) est movens in quantum mota a prima; ergo si necessario movetur a prima, necessario movet et producit effectum. Si ergo ponatur causam primam non libere sed ex necessitate naturae concurrere cum causis secundis, fit, ut nullus effectus eveniat contingenter. Minor probatur: quia causa secunda nihil producit nisi in virtute primae.

Secundo: Quia prima causa prius naturaliter respicit effectum quam secunda; ergo si necessario et non libere causat, omnis effectus in illo priori habet habitudinem necessariam ad illam; ergo nullus effectus fit contingenter. Patet haec ultima consequentia, quia fieri nequit, ut idem effectus habeat habitudinem necessarii et contingentis, neque respectu eiusdem causae neque respectu diversarum.

Tertio: Omnis effectus qui producitur mediantibus causis secundis potest produci idem numero a solo Deo. Sed tunc totam contingentiam habebit a solo Deo; ergo et modo, esto concurrant causae secundae, contingentiam habet a Deo.

Scotus hac sua sententia videtur asserere, concursum Dei universalem cum causis secundis ad suos effectus esse influxum et motum in causam, ut ulterius causa influat in effectum, necessitareque causam ad productionem effectus.

Quo dato non video, quomodo salvari possit libertas arbitrii in nobis. Si enim a concursu Dei universali ad volendum necessitatur voluntas ad eliciendum volitionem, concursusque ille est in potestate Dei influentis, non vero in potestate voluntatis volentis, non video, quomodo in nostra voluntate salvetur libertas arbitrii. Quare opinio Scoti hac in parte neque vera neque tuta videtur. Iuxta ea ergo, quae de concursu universali Dei dicta et ostensa sunt q. 8. art. 1 disp. ultima, dicendum est, concursum Dei universalem non esse influxum et motum Dei in causam, ut agat (quando enim ignis calefacit non movetur sed movet), sed esse influxum Dei in effectum una cum causa secunda. Ita quod Deus immediate immediatione suppositi attingit effectum per concursum universalem una cum causa secunda; et totus effectus est a Deo non totaliter totalitate causae sed partialiter; et totus est a causa secunda non totaliter totalitate causae sed partialiter. Tota item actio, qua producitur effectus est a Deo, non totaliter totalitate causae sed partialiter, et tota est a causa secunda non totaliter sed partialiter. Et eadem actio, ut a Deo, dicitur concursus Dei universalis; ut a causa vero secunda, dicitur concursus particularis causae secundae. Neque habet talis actio, ut est a Deo, quod sit talis, puta calefactio aut volitio, sed ut est a causa secunda puta ab igne aut a voluntate. Si enim cum Deo influente per concursum universalem concurreret aqua et non ignis, actio esset frigefactio et non calefactio; et si concurreret voluntas pro sua libertate ad nolitionem et non ad volitionem, actio esset nolitio et non volitio. Influxus enim universalis Dei indifferens est ex se ad plures effectus; et prout fuerit influxus causae particularis, a quo determinatur, sequitur talis vel talis effectus et talis vel talis actio.

Praeterea: Ut causa secunda sine concursu universali Dei non potest producere effectum, ita concursus praecisus universalis Dei non potest producere effectum sine concursu causae secundae, licet Deus se solo concurrens maiori concursu possit producere sine cause secunda quid-

*quid mediante causa secunda producit. Ut etiam actio causae
secundae esse nequit sine actione et concursu Dei, ita
actio et concursus universalis Dei esse nequit sine concursu
causae secundae. Quare ut in fornace Babylonica cessante
concursu universali Dei cessavit calefactio ignis, ita
cessante influxu voluntatis libero ad volendum cessat concursus universalis Dei. Esto ergo concursus universalis
Dei naturalis esset et non liber, cum pendeat a concursu causae secundae ab eoque determinetur ad speciem actus
et effectus, existente libertate in causa secunda, ut de
facto est in voluntate nostra, salvaretur contingentia
rerum. Ac proinde philosophi asserentes, Deum concursu
quo de facto concurrit agere ex necessitate naturae et
non libere, et simul esse contingentiam in rebus, non
asseruerunt contradictoria, quia contingentia provenire
posset, ut de facto provenit, ex libertate nostra, quam
in se ipsis experiebantur. Ex necessitate enim solius
causae universalis non sequitur necessitas effectus,
quia cum pendeat etiam a causa particulari, ab illa, si
fuerit libera, poterit esse contingens; quemadmodum in
syllogismis maiore existente necessaria poterit conclusio
esse contingens propter minorem contingentem, quia sola
maior non est sufficiens causa ad inferendum conclusionem,
sed illatio pendet etiam ex minore.*

If he looks to divine omnipotence, he does not see how God can
effect, and therefore know, free choice--not, that is, unless
the divine knowledge of a divinely uncaused block of being
(namely, futurible choice) have anteceded God's actual knowledge,
and therefore causality, of human choice.

*L. Molina, De Scientia Dei, in Stegmüller, op. cit., p.
226: Licet proposito, d. Thomae in sensu a Caietano,
Capredo et Ferrariensi explicato ita facile defendatur,
opinio tamen d. Thomae hoc loco quatenus asserit futura
contingentia neque a Deo optimo maximo cognosci certo
in suis atque ex suis causis, sed cognosci certo quatenus in sua aeternitate sunt extra suas causas in suo
esse existentiae, numquam nihi placuit: neque video
quantum conferat propositio illa in sensu explicato
ad hanc sententiam statuendam. examinatis
     p. 238: His ergo opinionibus examinatis dicendum est,
Deum ex comprehensione et omnimoda penetratione per suam
scientiam naturalem omnium causarum in sua essentia,
etiam liberarum, ad quam partem pro sua libertate cum
his aut illis circumstantiis se essent determinaturae,
ex suppositione tamen seu sub conditione: si creentur*

hoc aut illo modo cum his aut illis circumstantiis etc.,
una cum determinatione libera suae voluntatis, qua
statuit creare mundum eo modo quo creavit et cum
circumstantiis quae de facto cernantur, praecognovisse
certo et infallibiliter omnia futura contingentia, manente
de facto libero arbitrio in causis agentibus per intel-
lectum et voluntatem.

At bottom Molina does not see how the status of free human
choice is one of dependence upon God. The answer in Scotus
was that free human choice is caused by divine liberty. In St.
Thomas the answer was that free human choice is caused exist-
entially by divine liberty and essentially by divine omnipotence
(which includes divine knowledge) which can effect all being, the
necessary, the accidental, the free. Now it would seem that
Scotus merely emphasizes divine liberty; whereas, St. Thomas
synthesizes omnipotence and liberty; and Molina, on the other
hand, tries to analyze. So it is that Scotus' emphasis issues,
under Molina's manipulation, into simultaneous concourse and
scientia media. The result of these two, simultaneous concourse
and scientia media, is that Molina's free human choice is antecedently quite undetermined. The peculiarity of this result is that in
one respect at least it coincides with Scotus' theory of liberty. In
Scotus the human will is not determined by the human intellect. But
the reason for this in Scotus is not the same as the reason in Molina.
In Molina the reason for the absence of the intellectual determination of choice is really his failure to perceive that free choice is
caused. Scotus knew that choice was caused, but he put the cause
of it in the divine will--not, with the same emphasis as St. Thomas,
in the divine intellect. Molina, who rejects any antecedent cause
of choice, rejects both the divine and the human intellectual determination of choice.

L. Molina, De Scientia Dei, in Stegmüller, op. cit., p.
234: Influxus enim universalis Dei indifferens est ex
se ad plures effectus; et prout fuerit influxus causae
particularis, a quo determinatur, sequitur talis vel
talis effectus et talis vel talis actio. For Molina's
notion of the function of intellect in choice cf. his
definition of liberty, p. 1, n., supra, and pp. 107-
13.

But, as was said, he did not do so for the same reason. Molina's
theory is the outgrowth of scientia media and its consequence,
simultaneous concourse. Scotus' theory results from a certain

concept of the nature of man.

In the ninth book of Aristotle's metaphysics occurs this passage:

Bk. Theta, 2 or 1046 b sqq. Ross's ed., Oxford, 1928.

> Since some such originative sources are present [i.e.,
> potencies corresponding to privations: e.g., not to have
> a certain quality, not to have it but to be able to have it,
> etc.] in soulless things, and others in things possessed of
> soul, and in soul, and in the rational part of the soul, clearly
> some potencies will be nonrational and some will be ac-
> companied by a rational formula . . . And each of those
> which are accompanied by a rational formula is alike cap-
> able of contrary effects, but one non-rational power produces
> one effect; e.g., the hot is capable only of heating, but the
> medical art can produce both disease and health.

St. Thomas comments on this passage as follows: Natural
things operate by forms inherent in them. For contrary forms
cannot be in the same thing. Whence, the same natural thing
cannot do contrary things. Now, knowledge is a kind of potency
for acting, inasmuch as someone has a plan of what he wishes
to do, and this is the principle of motion in the soul. Since this
is so, natural things do only one thing: healthful things give
health; hot things heat; and so forth. But one who acts by knowledge effects two opposites because there is the same plan for
both in the soul. Whence, just as natural action, because proceding from the one form whose similitude is left in the effect,
effects only one thing, so the soul's action, because proceding
from one principle of two opposites, effects both opposites.
Rational powers, therefore, effect contraries; irrational powers
effect only one thing. And this because unum principium oppositorum continetur in ratione scientali. Reason specifies man,
because it is ad terminos contrarios, and the principle which is
ad terminos contrarios is the root of all human activity. Sense is
always ad unum.

*In Arist. Stagir. lib. comment. 9, lect. 2, #4, Vives.
See also Summa Theol., 1a q. 76, a 1.*

The commentary seems reasonable. But not to Scotus. According to Scotus the Aristotelian distinction of rational powers

(namely, _quod est ad terminos contrarios_) applies equally well, if not better, to the will. An active potency can have contrary terms inasmuch as it can realize an act or its contrary, inasmuch as it can act or not act. Now, what active potency is rational? Aristotle seems to think it is the intellect, capable of assimilating intention-ally, contrary objects. But an active potency of this sort does not differ at all from an irrational one; the intellect's indifference to contrary terms is no different from, for example, the sun's in-difference to its opposite effects, liquefaction, solidification. Aristotle should not seek the difference of rational and irrational powers in the difference of the objects of these powers but in their way of attaining these objects. And looking at their way of attain-ing their objects, we find two potencies: those which in themselves are so determined to act that they cannot but act, _salvo impedi-mento_; those which are so undetermined to act that they can act or not act, do this or that. Whence, potencies are natural (determined) or voluntary (undetermined), and these are the ultimate divisions of physical causality. Further, indetermination can be passive when it needs for its actualization the determinative causality of something else. Such is the indetermination of the intellect in relation to the object it knows. Then there is an active indeter-mination, which is the capacity of self determination to act or not to act, to act thus or so. The last is the will's indetermination alone. Clearly, the natural powers of Scotus cover more than the irrational powers of Aristotle; they cover Aristotle's rational powers as well. The reason is that Scotus means by his natural powers, passively undetermined powers. Now, if rational and irrational powers coincide, in that both are determined, it is clear that we must seek the specific difference of man in his will, which is actively undeter-mined. Natural rational powers are determined. The intellect in the presence of its object cannot but know. And further, in the presence of two possible courses of action it would never, without the will, determine itself; whereas, the voluntary rational power in the presence of the good can choose it or not, choose it or an-other good. Thus, far from being a specific difference of man, the natural power of reason is just as irrational (in Scotus' sense) as a stick or stone. The natural power of reason and the natural power of anything are determined. The specific difference of man, therefore, is his will.

D. Scotus, Meta. text., 9, S. 1, c. 2, sed contra, Vives, vol. 6. p. 317; Quaes. super li metaphy.Arist., 9, q. 15, Vives, vol. 7, pp. 606-17. Cf. Carreras y Artau, J., Ensayo sobre el voluntarismo de J. D. Scot, Gerona, 1923.

In Aristotle's meaning of the word rational (quod est ad terminos contrarios), the intellect, Scotus thinks, is rather irrational, quia cadit sub natura.

D. Scotus, Quaes. in Met. Arist., 9, q. 15, ad fin., Vives, vol. 7, p. 610 b.

Of course the intellect, too, can be called rational but only insofar as it receives from the will the initial impulse necessary to remove its indetermination. It is really the will which is the source of human activity: Si voluntas moveretur ab intellectu naturaliter moto, voluntas naturaliter moveretur, et sic homo esset unum bonum brutum.

D. Scotus, Quodlib. 21, Vives, vol. 26, p. 340 b.

The will, then, is the distinguishing trait of man. The intellect is like other natural powers in that it and all natural powers are determined.

According to St. Thomas, as we have seen, there are three kinds of appetite: natural, sense, and rational. The first is without knowledge, the second is with sense knowledge, the third is with rational knowledge. The last sort of appetite, since it is the appetite of a good presented by the intellect and since the good so presented, being particular, does not exhaust all the possibilities of the good, is alone free. The indetermination, then, of the intellect before goods which do not exhaust the good is the cause of liberty.

De Veritate, q. 23, a. 1; Summa Theol., 1a q. 78 et sqq.

But, Scotus urges, what about the physical causality of will acts? This sort of causality has no radix in the intellect conceiving particular goods. Far from it. That sort of intellectual indetermination (the presentation of particular goods) is rather the matter upon which will be exercised free choice. Now this exercise, or the active determination of one of the conceived possibilities, is not an intellectual act; it is an election, and the will alone can elect. Communicated to the intellect, this election removes the indifference of the intellect. In the order of action, the physical causality of the will is original, while that of the intellect is borrowed from the will. Strictly, will and intellect are opposed as active and passive cause.

D. Scotus, Quaes. in lib. Met. Arist., 9, q. 14, Vives, vol. 7, p. 602.

The spontaneity of the will is the very essence of its causality, and there is no sense in seeking a reason for this trait of the will in some other power.

Compare the same explanation of the divine will, supra, pp. 186 sqq.

The will is built to act that way; liberty is its very essence, not a derivative of its intellectual character.

1, c. 9, q. 15, Vives, vol. 7, p. 611.

Hence, Scotus calls the will an appetitus liber, not as did St. Thomas, an appetitus intellectivus. It is not any intellectual character which distinguishes voluntary appetite from other human powers, least of all from sense and intellect; it is the liberty of such an appetite. This liberty is the real radix of free human acts.

D. Scotus, Op. Ox., 2, D. 35, q. unic., n. 16, Quarracchi, ed., pp. 685-703, and ibid., D. 34-37, a. 4, pp. 823 sqq. For appetitus liber see Quaes. in lib. Met. Arist., 9, q. 14, Vives, vol. 7, p. 595.

Thus, the efficient causality of the intellect in choice is only metaphoric. The intellect's job is done when it has presented to the will the good to be or not to be chosen. And the two factors constituting the act of the intellect are itself and its object; whereas, the only ultimately efficient factor in the act of the will is the will itself. The object moves it only as an end. Once more it appears that the intellect is determined, the will undetermined; and this, once more, is the reason for seeking the specific difference of man in his will rather than in his intellect.

D. Scotus, Op. Ox., 1. D. 3, q. 9, a. 2 and Quaes. in lib. Met. Arist., 9, q. 14, Vives, vol. 7, p. 603.

To resume: for Scotus what is necessary cannot be free. Now, all natures, because they are determined and because they are principles of determination, are necessary; whereas, the will is undetermined and the principle of indetermination. But reason falls into the class of natural things. Free choice, therefore, cannot be ascribed to rational judgments proposing alternatives. Rather, it is to the spontaneity of the will that the removal of all these alternatives except the one chosen is due.

> *Cf. E. Gilson, L'esprit de la philosophie mediévale, II, Vrin. pp. 104-05 and the references there given: Op. Ox., 2. 25, Quarracchi, ed., pp. 701-04; Quaes. in lib. Met. Arist. 9, q. 15, Vives, vol. 7, pp. 606-17.*

The essential point in this explanation, as in the explanation of the liberty of God, is that no intellectual reason for acting can be the total cause for acting. This, not merely because the will is needed as a part cause of action, but because the essential indetermination of the will determines the alternative's being chosen. Several undetermined judgments do not, for Scotus, constitute free choice.

> *E. Gilson, op. cit., p. 107, and see D. Scotus, Quaes. in lib. Met. Arist., 9. q. 15, Vives, pp. 606-17.*

The reason, once more, is that given its object, the intellect exit in actum, like a penny in the slot. But the law of the will is the law of liberty, of the voluntary, of indetermination; given its object, the will chooses or not, chooses it or another, and it does this by an active power of which it alone is the source. The notion of St. Thomas is this: the root of liberty lies in reason. Reason criticizes the possible options, and affirms, by an affirmation which responds to desire, one to be better than the others. Thanks to this rational critique, man is free. And what is the will's part? It has been stated. The will's part is to will to act or not act, to act thus or so. Free choice is a sort of free judgment (sort of, because it is essentially an act of the will which wills, not of the reason which judges); it is, too, an act of the will but an act which is the conclusion of a practical syllogism.

> *De Veritate, q. 24, a. 1, 20um: electio . . . quoddam judicium de angendis vel judicium consequatur; Cf. Summa Theol., 1a 2ae q. 13, a. 1, ad 2um; and E. Gilson, op. cit., pp. 107-09.*

Free choice is a judgment which comes from the will, insofar as the will's election is a sort of judgment, a judgment too which affects the will insofar as one can judge one's very choice.

De Veritate, q. 24, a. 1; Cf. *Summa Theol.,* 1a q. 83,
a. 3, ad 2um.

To put it in another way, election (the free act) is the convergent
result from two sources: reason, which presents a particular
good in the guise of a particular truth; and will, which accepts a
particular good in the guise of a particular good.

De Malo, 6, art. unic., in corp.

In still another way: the will influences the judgment (by removing
its indetermination) not merely <u>quoad</u> <u>exercitium</u> <u>tantum</u> <u>actus</u>
(this <u>tantum</u> is, I believe, Scotus' position) but <u>quoad</u> <u>specifi-</u>
<u>cationem</u> <u>judicii</u> as well, inasmuch as this truth (the "white" or
"black" of action) is also a particular good; and the judgment influences the will not merely <u>quoad</u> <u>specificationem</u> <u>tantum</u> <u>actus</u>
(again, this <u>tantum</u> is Scotus' position) but <u>quoad</u> <u>exercitium</u> <u>actus</u>
as well, inasmuch as this element (to act or not to act) is a parti-
cular kind of truth.

*John of St. Thomas, De Anima, 12, 2, circa init., puts
this in a nutshell: indifferentia consistit in potestate
voluntatis non solum super actum suum ad quem movet, sed
etiam super judicium a quo movetur.*

If, therefore, one asks, To which is due the kind of action one
will perform, will or intellect? the answer is that it is to the intellect. If one asks, To which is due the determination to act,
or not to act, will or intellect? the answer is that it is to the
will. But this is just what Scotus says! Not exactly. In the above
answer, the kind of action is also a kind of good, and the determination to act or not act is a kind of truth. Thus, the will is the
cause of the attraction it undergoes because it depends on the will
to bring the intellect to judge that such and such a good is of a
sort to move it (the will); the will is the cause of the direction it
receives, in that it moves the intellect to give it (the will) its
direction. In a word, there is in election a mutual priority of
cause in different orders of causality: what I choose is from the
intellect specifying and from the will making the intellect so to
specify; that I choose is from the will acting, and from the intellect specifying the "to-act-or-not-to-act" as a kind of truth.

As regards divine causality, then, Molina opposes St. Thomas
in that he cannot admit without reservations that God can ante-

cedently cause a free act and leave that act free. St. Thomas had
said that God knows, because he causes, the free act; and if he
cannot cause it, how can be be omnipotent? Molina's reservations
are these: granting that God causes the free act, he does so in the
sense that there antecedes the actual divine knowledge and causality
of the future act the futurible free choice and God's knowledge of
it--scientia media. Molina's theory thus professes to escape the
divine determination of choice by positing a block of being, futurible choice, which is known and caused by God only because
God can know what is in itself uncertain, and can transpose that
futurible choice from its futurible state (where it was divinely
undetermined) into its future state, where God's governance of
it parallels its governance of itself--simultaneous concourse.

L. Molina, De Scientia Dei, in Stegmüller, op. cit., p.
249: stante scientia [divina] ut est, non possit non esse
[aliquod contingens] in sensu composito una cum ipsa
scientia, sed certo . . . sit eventurum . . . certitudine
--ex parte. scientis, qui certo--penetrat quod est in se
incertum, nimirum, ad quam partem se libere sit determinaturum liberum arbitrium. And cf. op. cit., p. 234,
3-30.

Molina did not understand that St. Thomas' point was precisely
that the divine causality effects choice. He did not see that free
choice, whether future or futurible, depends on God: future choice
for its actual existence; futurible, for its possibility; and the possibility of free choice, which includes its previsibility, together
with its actuality depends upon the omnipotent causality of God.
Besides, Molina had run across Banes' version of St. Thomas:
God wills, before he knows, free choice. Molina opposes Scotus
because, though Scotistic divine liberty might account for the
contingence of events not emanating from free choice, it does
not account for the contingence of choice. His reason is that God's
choice accounts for his liberty but not for the liberty of man.

L. Molina, De Scientia Dei, in Stegmüller, op. cit.,
pp. 236, 237, 238: Scotus in 1. d. 39 inquit, Deum
in determinatione libera suae voluntatis cognoscere certo
et infallibiliter futura contingentia. Quod ita explicat:
quemadmodum, inquit, Deus scientia naturali videt in sua
essentia omnia simplicia et omnes complexiones necessarias, ita videt omnes complexiones contingentes non in
esse futuri sed in esse complexionum possibilium, videns
unamquamque de se indifferentem, ut sit aut non sit. Hoc

enim totum ex naturis extremorum cognitis in sua essentia cognosci potest evidenter. Accedente vero libera determinatione suae voluntatis, qua eligit alteram partem contradictionis pro aliquo instante, scit determinate et infallibiliter illam fore, quia in determinatione libera suae voluntatis, quam videt esse immutabilem et inimpedibilem, certo et infallibiliter videt determinationem talis partis ad esse.

Sententia haec non explicat etiam sufficienter modum quo futura contingentia praenoscuntur a Deo. Ad cuius evidentiam sciendum est, inter futura contingentia quaedam esse, quae producuntur immediate a solo Deo, ut est existentia mundi pro tali vel tali tempore; quaedam vero esse, quae producuntur mediantibus causis secundis. Et inter haec quaedam esse, quae producuntur mediantibus causis secundis agentibus omnino ex necessitate naturae; quaedam vero esse, quae producuntur mediantibus causis secundis agentibus libere aut cum vestigio quodam libertatis, ut visum est. Si ergo futura omnia contingentia essent primi aut secundi generis, non esset difficultas in sententia Scoti. Cum enim existentia mundi aliorumque, quae a solo Deo immediate producuntur, ex sola determinatione voluntatis divinae pendeat, in ea certo et infallibiliter futura omnia contingentia primi generis cognosci possunt. Cum etiam positis in hoc universo solis causis agentibus ex necessitate naturae ex eis certo et infallibiliter evenirent effectus, ut in superioribus est explicatum, in eadem determinatione voluntatis divinae, qua Deus statueret producere se solo immediate causas, cognoscerentur ulterius omnes effectus, qui inde ex necessitate naturae infallibiliter essent eventuri.

Difficultas ergo est circa futura contingentia tertii generis, ut circa deambulationem aut furtum futurum Socratis cras. Si enim ad hunc sensum dicatur, Deum in libera electione suae voluntatis cognoscere Socratem deambulaturum aut furaturum cras, quod videns se posse creare mundum in ea dispositione in qua eum creavit, et collocare cras Socratem cum dispositionibus et circumstantiis, cum quibus de facto erit et cum quibus possible est eum velle ambulare et non velle ambulare, Deo libere eligente ut ambulet, Socrates ambulabit, et Deo libere eligente ut non ambulet, Socrates non ambulabit manentibus eisdem circumstantiis, ita quod esse deambulaturum aut non deambulaturum, furaturum aut non furaturum pendeat ex electione, qua Deus eligat eum cum eisdem circumstantiis ambulare aut non ambulare, permittere furari aut non permittere furari, non video quomodo salvetur libertas arbitrii in Socrate, et quomodo a benignissimo Deo dicetur positus in manu consilii sui, ut ad quod voluerit porrigat manum. Si namque, non praevisa

*determinatione liberi arbitrii Socratis pro sua libertate
ad alteram partem contradictionis, in suppositione tamen
quod creetur in tali vel tali parte temporis et cum talibus
vel talibus circumstantiis, Deus pro sua voluntate statuit
quod vult circa liberum arbitrium Socratis, et illud infallibiliter evenit, quomodo quaeso salvatur in eo libertas
arbitrii? Dicere namque, ad libertatem arbitrii sufficere,
quod ex se possit oppositum, non tamen stante praescientia
aut electione voluntatis divinae circa alteram partem contradictionis, non solvit difficultatem. Cum namque praescie
et electio voluntatis divinae de facto sint, Deo libere
eligente et sciente quod pro sua voluntate vult, si stante
praescientia et electione Socrates non potest oppositum, pî
de facto non habet libertatem arbitrii, sed haberet si non
esset praescientia et praeelectio divina relinquereturque
suae libertati.*

In respect to the human causes of free choice we have already
seen Molina opposing St. Thomas upon the theory of the intellectual
determination of choice.

See supra., pp. 107 sqq.

Now, there was in Scotus' theory of liberty no intellectual determination of choice. Scotus' theory of liberty thus fell in with
Molina's own, not of course in respect to that part of Scotus'
theory which concerned the divine cause of human liberty but in
respect to that part which concerned the human antecedents of
the free act. These intellectual antecedents did not determine free
choice either for Scotus or Molina.

The historical connection between Molina and Scotus--thus far
the philosophical connection has been our main interest--seems
to be through Dominic Banes. Banes has written, "Whensoever the
act of the will arises from the aforesaid root of the judgment, it
will always be free." This, Molina thinks, is favorable to heresy.
For it is little or nothing short of the opinion which denies the
liberty opposed to necessity and holds that the will is determined
ad unum. (The fact is, Banes' opinion is nothing of the sort. Banes
contended simply that the intellectual determination of choice arising
from an indifferent judgment, concerning the means to an end, is
free choice.)

*D. Banes, Schol. Comment. in I partem, ed. cit., p. 255
aD, in Stegmüller, op. cit., p. 492. See p. 124, n.,
supra.*

200

But it is the reason that Molina thinks Banes wrong that interests us. After noting that, according to Bellarmine, the heretics never denied that men had the perfect use of reason when they acted freely,

> R. Bellarmine, De. Grat. et lib. arbit., 1. 4., c. 14.

and that the heretics thus preserved iudicium illud de medio indifferenti in which alone Banes put liberty, Molina argues thus: either the council of Trent had no reason to condemn the heretics or else Banes should be condemned too.

> L. Molina, Censura Contra D. Bannes, in Stegmüller, op. cit., pp. 492, 492. As is clear, Molina is missing Banes' point. There is no question of the perfect or imperfect use of reason in Banes' theory of liberty--or in St. Thomas'. The question is Is, or is not, intellection the radix libertatis?

Then he goes on to state that Banes' doctrine is against the common opinion of the Fathers, the Scholastics, and Scotus: qui omnes actum liberum nequaquam censent qui a voluntate non oritur--quod vel ipse Bannes--fatetur . . . Sic in commentariis in 1. p. q. 41, a. 2, dub. 2, dicto 3, in probatione contra Scotum.

> L. Molina, 1. c., p. 497. Banes' text is cited by Stegmuller from Banes' Schol. Comment. in I partem, ed. Rom. 1584, col. 625 F.

10 MOLINIST LIBERTY FROM THE EPITOME DE PRAEDESTINATIONE

A third exposition of Molina's theory is found in his Epitome de Praedestinatione.

In Stegmüller, op. cit., pp. 336 sqq.

On the supposition that spontaneity alone is not sufficient for the freedom of choice, for beasts too act spontaneously; and on the supposition that freedom necessarily implies that the will can when it wills also not will or will the opposite; and on the supposition, lastly, that man is predestined--this--is the way Molina conciliates a spontaneity which is free from necessity and God's efficacious part in the plan of salvation. He places in God, before the free act of the divine will, a divine prescience by which God foresees what each free choice would be in whatsoever hypothetical circumstances God might wish to place a free agent.

Op. cit., p. 336: Y aunque de ordinario ay inconueniente en uerse fragmentos solos de obras, y mucho mas en dezirse en summa lo que prouado y deduzido de principios parece otra cosa, supponiendo que ad arbitrii libertatem no basta sponte operari ut Lutherani voluerunt, id namque

bestiis etiam conuenit, mas ser necessario nihil im-
pedientibus circumstantiis omnibus concurrentibus,
esse in facultate voluntatis, quando aliquid libere
uult, illud non uelle aut etiam nolle, vel uelle con-
trarium, prout fuerit libertas vel ad solum exercitium
vel etiam ad speciem actus. Lo que digo en breues
palabras es lo siguiente:

Como en la materia de praescientia largamente proue,
pongo en Dios ante actum liberum suae voluntatis praes-
cientiam, qua ex eminentissimo modo, quo altitudine il-
limatataque perfectione sui intellectus in sua essentia
singula comprehendit quae sua omnipotentia esse possunt,
praevidit quid per unumquodque liberum arbitrium esset
futurum, ex hypothesi quod hos vel illos homines aut
angelos ex infinitis quos potest creare collocare vellet in
hoc vel in illo ordine rerum, cum his vel illis auxiliis,
etc.

Molina puts in his last supposition farther on in his
present work: vid. p. 344: Ex dictis quoque intelligetur
facillima ratio conciliandi libertatem arbitrii nostri cum
divina praedestinatione. Etenim ex dictis constat, liber-
tatem adulti praedestinati consentire cum eo actu divinae
voluntatis, quo pro suo tantum beneplacito statuit Deus ea
media ex sua parte eidem conferre, quibus reipsa in vitam
aeternam perveniet. Ostensum namque est nihil eo actu ac
mediis impedientibus posse reipsa, si velit, deflectere
in aeternam miseriam, non secus ac si actus ille non com-
pleret rationem praedestinationis, sed providentiae dum-
taxat, ex illoque solo capite certum non esse, perventurum
illum in vitam aeternam, sed solum ex parte praescientiae,
quam praedestinatio ex parte divini intellectus includit.

Since this divine prescience antecedes the free act of the divine
will, it is not free. Nor does the certainty of this prescience come
from its object, which in itself is uncertain, but from the perfection
of the divine intellect. Thus, it is not because God knows, say,
Peter's future sin that Peter will sin; rather, Peter will sin, and
God knows it because Peter will sin consequently upon the futurible
hypothesis, later posited by God, under which God had seen him
freely sinning--and God would have known the contrary if, as was
possible, there was no sin.

Op. cit., pp. 336, 337: Haec scientia cum, nostro intel-
ligendi modo cum fundamento in re, antecedat liberum actum
voluntatis divinae, libera non est in Deo. Cum item sit de
re quae per arbitrium creatum libere est futura, est illa
quidem certissima, sed certitudine proveniente ex illi-

203

mitata perfectione divini intellectus, qui eminentissima comprehensione arbitrii creati certissime cognoscit quod in se est incertum; non vero certitudine proveniente ex objecto, quod et esse et non esse indifferenter potest, eo ipso quod in facultate est arbitrii creati. Quare scientia illa est de re in se et ex natura sua incerta, certissime tamen cognita ex perfectione cognoscentis. Utrumque docuit regius Propheta [Ps. 50. 8] verbis illis: Incerta et occulta sapientiae tuae manifestasti mihi. Dum enim futura contingentia sibi revelata incerta et occulta appellavit, naturam eorum expressit. Dum vero sapientia divina cognita ea dixit, certitudinem ex eminentia cognoscentis aperte docuit.

Illud etiam loco citato cum communi Patrum sententia ostendimus: non quia Deus ex illa hypothesi scivit hoc vet illud per liberum arbitrium creatum futurum, ut Petrum peccaturum etc., ideo id futurum; id scivisse; sciturusque fuisset contrarium, si, ut poterat, contrarium esset futurum.

Whence the sort of divine knowledge which is at the root of Molina's system is called <u>scientia media</u>. The reason is that, anteceding the act of the divine will, it is not free knowledge. Yet, because God could have known the contrary (upon the hypothesis that Peter did not sin), it is nevertheless not wholly a divine natural knowledge, which cannot be otherwise in God than as it is--for example, his knowledge of necessary objects.

Op. cit., p. 337: Atque hac de causa scientiam hanc loco citato appellavimus mediam inter liberam et mere naturalem. Quia enim scientia illa antecedit actum divinae voluntatis, libera non est; quia vero scire potuit Deus contrarium, scivissetque reipsa, si ut poterat, contrarium ex ea hypothesi esset futurum, deficit a ratione scientiae omnino naturalis, quae nulla ratione habere aliter potuit in Deo, qualis est ea quam Deus de rebus necessariis habet.

<u>Scientia media</u> is thus midway between divine necessary and divine free knowledge.

There are, then, three sorts of knowledge in God: first, a natural knowledge, which is had of all necessary and contingent reality;

The contingent reality here meant does not emanate from free choice; it is the accidental.

second, a scientia media, by which God knows what free agents
would do under whatsoever hypothesis he might care to effect
(for example, God knew that Tyre and Sidon would have done
penance had the miracles been worked in those cities which
Corozain and Bethsaida witnessed); third, a knowledge which is
consequent upon God's free decision to effect the circumstances
under which he has already foreseen, scientia media, the free
acts of free agents.

*Op. cit., p. 337: Hinc perspicuitatis gratia triplicem
scientiam nostro intelligendi modo distinguimus in Deo.
Unam mere naturalem, qua Deus suam essentiam, naturas
omnium rerum, complexiones omnes necessarias necnon contingentes (quod esse tamen possint et quod possint non
esse, quo pacto necessariae sunt) cognovit.*

*Alteram, mediam illam inter mere naturalem et liberam,
qua ex hypothesi, quod sua libera voluntate condere vellet
hunc vel illum ordinem rerum et collocare in eis has vel
illas creaturas libero arbitrio praeditas cum his vel illis
auxiliis etc., cognovit omnia universim futura contingentia,
non quidem quod simpliciter et absolute essent futura, sed
ex hypothesi, si hunc vel illum ordinem rerum cum his vel
illis circumstantiis et vel illis auxiliis condere vellet.
Atque hac scientia, ut cognovit Deus infinita alia futura
contingentia, quae per arbitrium creatum futura erant in
infinitis aliis ordinibus rerum, si hos condere voluisset,
sic etiam cognovit Tyrios et Sidonios facturos fuisse
paenitentiam, ex hypothesi quod in eis factae fuissent
virtutes quae Corozain et Bethsaidae sunt factae.*

*Tertiam, qua post determinationem liberam suae volun-
tatis, per quam condere statuit eum ordinem rerum, circumstantiarum et auxiliorum, quae facere decrevit, in ea
ipsa libera determinatione, praevisis illis aliis duabus
scientiis, absolute cognovit futura omnia contingentia
quae re ipsa sunt futura. Cf. L. Molina, Concordia, pp. 317,
318 54 a.*

The intellectual part of Providence--that is, God's knowledge
of the suitable means for leading all creatures to their ends,
and in particular free agents--is obviously linked with his scientia
media. So, too, is linked with scientia media the intellectual aspect of predestination; that is, God's knowledge of the actual means
by which those who are to be saved will be saved. For though the
complete notions of Providence and predestination contain a divine
voluntary element, which is the actual divine decision to elect the
means by which he has foreseen, scientia media, that all creatures

are to come to their end (Providence) or only rational creatures
(predestination), nevertheless the intellectual element of scientia
media has preceded the voluntary element in the two notions of
Providence and predestination.

*Op. cit., p. 338: Cum scientia illa media inter liberam
et mere naturalem coniuncta est cognitio seu ratio
mediorum accommodatorum, tum creaturarum omnium ad suos
fines, in qua est posita ratio providentiae circa creaturas
omnes quoad id, quod providentia dicit ex parte intellectus
tum in particulari ratio mediorum creaturarum mente praedi-
tarum ad sempiternam beatitudinem, in qua similiter est
posita ratio providentiae circa creaturas intellectuales
ad beatitudinem supernaturalem; tum denique ratio mediorum
quibus hae vel illae in particulari reipsa beatitudinem
assequentur, in qua posita est ratio praedestinationis
quoad id, quod praedestinatio dicit ex parte intellectus.
Etenim cum tam scientia naturalis quam media illa inter
liberam et mere naturalem antecedant in Deo actum liberum
suae voluntatis, per easque Deus non solum cognoscat natura.
omnium rerum, fines omnes ad quos sua omnipotentia possunt
ordinari, et media omnia ad eos accommodata, sed etiam quid
futurum sit per liberum arbitrium creatum, ex hypothesi
quod collocatur in hoc vel in illo ordine rerum, cum his
vel illis auxiliis, donis ac mediis, quae misericorditer
velit illi concedere; sane ante actum liberum suae voluntat
habuit Deus rationem mediorum accommodatorum, tum creaturar
omnium ad suos fines, tum in particulari creaturarum intel-
lectualium ad sempiternam beatitudinem si per ipsas non
staret consequendam, tum denique quibus hae vel illae in
particulari reipsa eum assequerentur, ex hypothesi quod hic
vel ille rerum ordo circumstantiarum et auxiliorum con-
deretur.*

*Quo fit, ut sicut ars divini intellectus, qua Deus
modum novit fabricandi res omnes quae sua omnipotentia esse
poterant, antecessit determinationem liberam suae voluntati
qua has vel illas res decrevit facere, sic ratio mediorum
omnium, quibus providere poterat rebus omnibus ad fines
tam naturales quam supernaturales, et quibus praedestinare
poterat quoscumque vellet, antecesserit determinationem
liberam voluntatis, per quam rationes formales providentiae
et praedestinationis sunt completae. Est namque providentia.
ratio seu conceptio ordinis rerum in suos fines in mente
divina existens, cum proposito eam per se vel etiam interventu causarum secundarum executioni mandandi. Et praedestinatio: ratio in Deo ordinis seu mediorum, quibus praevidit has vel illas creaturas mente praeditas vitam aeterna
assecuturas, cum proposito eundem ordinem executioni mandandi. Cf. L. Molina, Concordia, p. 549.*

206

There is, therefore, no cause, reason, or necessary condition
in any free act of any free agent, or in the total series of such acts,
which explains why God has chosen these whom he has predestined.
Predestination is to be referred wholly to the free and merciful
will of God. The reason, once more, is that though God has foreseen what a free agent would freely do in any hypothesis of choice,
it is nevertheless God who has effected the hypothesis.

*Op. cit., pp. 338, 339: Hinc dicimus: Cum praedestinationis
ratio (sicut et providentiae cuius est quasi pars subjecta),
licet praecipue in actu intellectus sit posita, per actum
tamen voluntatis divinae compleatur quo Deus ea media adulto
praedestinando conferre statuit, quibus praevidebat eum
sua libertate perventurum in vitam aeternam; cum item ea
omnia, quae praedestinatio ex parte divini intellectus includit, liberum omnem actum divinae voluntatis antecedent,
ac proinde libera non sint in Deo, consequens profecto est,
ut quaestio: an praedestinationis adulti detur causa, ratio
aut conditio, cur a Deo sit praedestinatus, in eo versetur:
an actus voluntatis divinae, quo ea media tali adulto conferre voluit, detur ex parte arbitrii illius causa, ratio
aut conditio ob quam vel illi vel potius illi quam alteri
sint volita, an vere nihil tale detur, sed omnino id totum
in liberam ac misericordem Dei voluntatem, qua pro solo
suo beneplacito id ita voluit, sit referendum.
Nosque dicimus: Neque quod Deus elegerit hunc potius
ordinem rerum, quem creare statuit, quam alium, neque quod
in Christo hos potius in vitam aeternam elegerit quam
alios, neque item quod per Christum ea media eis voluerit
confere, quibus praevidebat eos pro sua libertate perventuros in vitam aeternam, dari causam aliquam, rationem,
aut conditionem etiam sine qua non, ex parte usus liberi
arbitrii eorum praevisi, ob quam illos praedestinaverit,
volueritve illis ea media quibus praevidit perventuros in
vitam aeternam, aut cur potius haec ipsa eis voluerit quam
aliis; sed totum referendum esse solum in liberam ac
misericordem Dei voluntatem, quae pro solo suo beneplacito
id ita voluit.
Unde dicimus: praescientiam usus liberi arbitrii
praedestinatorum, futuraeve talis liberae cooperationis
eorum cum donis et auxiliis Dei, ut ad vitam aeternam in
hoc ordine rerum, quem Deus creare statuit, pervenirent,
non fuisse causam, rationem aut conditionem, quare vel
praedestinatione in genere hi essent praedestinati, aut hi
potius quam alii, vel quare ea ipsa numero praedestinatione, qua re ipsa praedestinati sunt, fuerint praedestinati, quasi Deus voluerit ex parte sua conferre illis ea
ipsa media, quae conferre illis statuit per eaque eos prae-*

207

*destinare, quia praevidit illos ita pro sua libertate co-
operaturos, ut ea via ad vitam aeternam pervenirent, aut
quasi id fuerit conditio qua existente aut qua praevisa id
Deus erat facturus, et sine qua id non erat voliturus;
sed pro sua tantum libera voluntate ea media illis conferre voluisse per quae eos praedestinavit; id quod fusius,
et forte efficacius quam alii, ex Scripturis sanctis et
variis capitibus, quae longum esset referre, demonstramus.*

*Etenim Deus, licet nulli adulto deneget auxilia neces-
saria ad salutem, non tamen pro ratione usus liberi
arbitrii praevisi sed pro sua tantum libera voluntate
distribuit sua dona, quibus vult, quando vult, quantum
vult et eo modo quo vult; pro eademque sola sua libera
voluntate ex sua aeternitate statuit, eo pacto illa
distribuere quo in tempore eo distribuit. Cf. L. Molina,
Concordia, pp. 549, 550.*

Hence, it is no contradiction to say that a man's predestination
depends upon his free choice in such wise that he can, if he wishes,
fail to cooperate with the grace of God, and to say at the same time
that a man's predestination depends upon God. The reason: God
has chosen the hypotheses in which he has foreseen, scientia
media, that his elect would freely come to salvation.

*Op. cit., pp. 340-42: Con todo esto, sumpto quovis adulto
isto modo ex aeternitate praedestinato dezimos, a nada
de lo dicho repugnar neque salva fide catholica posse
negari, rem quae est effectus praedestinationis sine quo
iste ad vitam aeternam non perveniet, pendere, ut sit in
rerum natura, ab usu liberi arbitrii talis adulti tamquam
a parte eiusdem effectus, a qua habitus supernaturales
pendent, et sine qua simpliciter effectus praedestinationis
non erit neque adultus ille ad vitam aeternam perveniet.
Verbi gratia, si is infidelis sit, qui ad fidem sit
vocandus quique fidelis factus saepe labetur in lethalia
peccata et resurget tandemque vitam in gratia finiet et
ad gloriam perveniet, pendere ab omnibus actibus liberi
arbitrii, quibus auxiliis gratiae praeventus libere con-
sentiet seque prima vice ad fidem, spem, caritatem et
gratiam disponet, et quibus postea in progressu vitae a
peccatis libere resurget, post recuperatam gratiam opera
meriteria incrementi illius et gloriae exercebit et
tentationibus ad vitae usque terminum resistet. Eiusmodi
vero actus duas causas habere liberas, a quarum quavis
tamquam a parte unius integrae eorum causae ita pendent,
ut altera earum libere, ut potest, non influente futuri
omnino non sint in rerum natura.*

Prior et praecipua est Deus, qui per sua dona con-

cursum et auxilia cooperatur totum illum bonum usum et
singulas illus partes. Posterior vero ac minus praecipua.
ipsum arbitrium, quod libero suo influxu eundem supernaturalem suum usum et singulas illius partes ita cooperatur,
ut reipsa possit, si velit, non cooperari. In concilio namque Tridentino sess. 6 c 5 definitur, peccatorem justifi-
care libere assentiendo et cooperando Deo praevenienti et
excitanti per gratiam praevenientem et coadiuvatem, ita ut
tangente Deo cor hominis per Spiritus Sancti illuminationem neque homo ipse nihil omnino agat inspirationem
illam recipiens, quippe qui illam et abicere potest. Et
can. 4 subiungitur: Si quis dixerit, liberum hominis
arbitrium a Deo motum et excitatum nihil cooperari assentiendo Deo excitanti atque vocanti, quo ad obtinendam
instificationis gratiam se disponat ac praeparet, neque
posse dissentire si velit, anathema sit. Idemque est de
ceteris actibus, quibus tentationibus resistit bonaque
operatur meritoria augmenti gratiae et gloriae. Licet
enim ea omnia dona Dei sint, idcirca tamen simul sunt
merita hominis eadem cooperantis, rationemque virtutis
habent, et propter illa laude est dignus, quia in facultate
ipsius est ea non elicere divinaeque gratiae et adiutorio
non cooperari in eo ipso temporis momento quo illa elicit.
   Qyo fit, ut quicumque eiusmodi supernaturalis usus
liberi arbitrii totus sit a Deo, totalitate ut vocant
effectus, non causae; et totus licet minus praecipue sit
ab arbitrio creato, tametsi a Deo habeat, ut sit ordinis
supernaturalis effectusque praedestinationis, non vero
ab arbitrio creato. Fit etiam, ut sicut si Deus in illum
non influeret supernaturaliter, omnino non esset, sic
etiam si arbitrium ipsum, ut potest, non cooperaretur,
penitus non esset. Atque hinc est, quod nihil omnino
impediente aeterna praedestinatione, qua praevidens Deus
per quae media pro nostra libertate perventuri eramus in
vitam aeternam, ex sola sua misericordia, et non quia
praevidit nos ita cooperaturos ut ad eam perveniremus,
constituit, ea nobis donare, integrum nobis sit, non ita
cooperari, impedire praedestinationis effectum et damnari,
non secus ac si in Deo non esset talis praescientia.
Neque in Deo voluntas eo modo ex sua parte nobis opitulandi haberet rationem praedestinationis, sed providentiae
dumtaxat ad vitam aeternam, ut habet voluntas opitulandi
aliis eo modo, quo, si vellent, pervenirent in vitam
aeternam. Deus tamen praevidit illos pro sua libertate et
nequitia non ita cooperaturos, ut ad illam pervenirent,
culpaque ipsorum damnandos.
   Est namque ante oculos habendum quod, sicut in destinatione sagittae ad scopum aliud est sagitta quae destinatur,
aliud vis quae illi a sagittario imprimitur, qua in scopum

209

*ab eo destinari dicitur, sic in destinatione, qua adultus
a Deo in aeternam beatitudinem destinatur, aliud est quod
destinatur, aliud media quibus a Deo destinatur. Cum autem
adultus ita a Deo per suum arbitrium in vitam aeternam
destinetur, ut propria libertate atque adeo propriis
meritis, quae simul dona sint ipsius, in vitam aeternam
sic perveniat, ut, si velit, possit ab ea deflectere,
quatenus ea ratione laude praemio et honore sit dignus,
sane ex parte destinati tenet se adultus ipse suaque
innata libertas, per quam dominus est suorum operum
positusque est in manu consilii sui, ut libero suo influxu ad quod voluerit porrigat manum (Eccli, 15, 17),
vel ita cooperando cum Deo auxiliisque ac donis ipsius,
ut vitam aeternam assequatur, vel ita influendo, ut
cassa illa reddat, a sempiternaque felicitate in extremam miseriam per letalia peccata deflectat. Quin et
eiusmodi innata libertas in ratione adulti qua adultus
est includitur.*

*Ex parte vero destinationis seu praedestinationis
divinae tenent se ea omnia, quibus (adulto libere, ut
dictum est, cooperante) adiuvatur in vitamque aeternam
perducitur, quae omnia, ut a Deo, effectus sunt praedestinationis. Cum vero nulla omnino, non solum res
sed neque ratio formalis, sit in adulto praedestinato,
per quam discernatur a non praedestinato et per quam in
vitam aeternam perducatur, quae non sit a Deo magis
praecipue quam ab ipso praedestinato libere cooperante,
etiam si id sit vel minimus liberi arbitrii actus minimave
ratio formalis illius, liberque influxus et cooperatio,
quam dicimus se tenere ex parte adulti praedestinati, non
aliud sit quam ipsimet actus liberi arbitrii, rationesve
formales eorum, quae simul et praecipue sunt a Deo, sed
spectatae praecise, ut sunt ab arbitrio creato tamquam a
parte causae earum liberae, dicuntur influxus liberi
arbitrii, spectatae vero, ut sunt a Deo tamquam a parte
altera magis praecipua eiusdem integrae earum causae,
dicuntur et sunt influxus et effectus Dei; non secus ac
eadem calefactio spectata ut est a Deo est influxus dei, et
spectata ut ab igne est influxus ignis, cum tamen in ea
unica sit tantum ratio formalis actionis; consequens profecto est, ut nihil sit in praedestinato, quo in vitam
aeternam tendat, neque etiam bonus ipse usus liberi
arbitrii, quod non sit a Deo, atque adeo quod non sit
praedestinationis effectus. Habet tamen quod sit effectus
praedestinationis, ut a Deo emanat; pendetque ut sit in
rerum natura, a libera cooperatione arbitrii praedestinati,
ut ostensum est; Deo id ita sapientissime disponente sua-
viterque praedestinante accommodate ad praedestinati
naturam. Cf. L. Molina, Concordia, p. 549 ad calc. For*

the canon of the Council of Trent see Denzinger-
Bannwart, Enchiridion Symbolorum, 815; cf. n. 814.

It follows that the efficacity of predestination does not lie
wholly in the means to salvation; that is, grace. (The Reformers
had put it there, to the denial of the immunity of choice from necessity; Banes had put it there, to the assertion of such immunity,
precisely because God thus effected the freedom of choice.) A
man can, as was shown, freely reject grace. The efficacity of
predestination lies also in the taproot of scientia media; from it
spring the free acts by which the elect will infallibly be saved.

> *Op. cit., p. 343: Ex dictis intelligetur facile, cer-*
> *titudinem seu infallibilitatem, quod eiusmodi adultus*
> *perveniet in vitam aeternam, non esse in mediis, quae*
> *Deus ex sua parte illi conferre statuit quibusque illum*
> *praedestinavit. Ut enim ostensum est, adultus innata sua*
> *libertate liberoque suo influxu potest ea cassa reddere,*
> *a sempiternaque felicitate in extremam miseriam per*
> *letalia peccata deflectere, non secus ac si praedestinatus*
> *non esset; voluntasque divina eo modo ex sua parte illi*
> *opitulandi rationem solum providentiae, non vero prae-*
> *destinationis compleret. Sed infallibilitatem totam esse*
> *tamquam in radice quidem in praescientia illa media, qua*
> *Deus praevidit, ex hypothesi quod ex parte sua conferre*
> *illi vellet ea media, ita illum cooperaturum ut ad vitam*
> *aeternam perveniret, cum tamen neque mediis neque praes-*
> *cientia illa id impedientibus re ipsa posset, si vellet,*
> *contrario modo operari. Cf. L. Molina, Concordia, pp. 51,*
> *548, 565.*

Molina is now ready to draw his conclusions. Liberty and predestination are conciliated, because there has preceded God's
choice of his elect the knowledge, scientia media, by which he
foresaw them freely coming to heaven, and because God chooses
the hypotheses in which he foresaw that the elect would freely be
saved.

> *Op. cit., p. 344: Ex dictis quoque intelligetur facillima*
> *ratio concilliandi libertatem arbitrii nostri cum divina*
> *praedestinatione. Etenim ex dictis constat, libertatem*
> *adulti praedestinati consentire cum eo actu divinae*
> *voluntatis, quo pro suo tantum beneplacito statuit*
> *Deus ea media ex sua parte eidem conferre, quibus reipsa*
> *in vitam aeternam perveniet. Ostensum namque est nihil*
> *eo actu ac mediis impedientibus posse reipsa, si velit,*

deflectere in aeternam miseriam, non secus ac si actus
ille non compleret rationem praedestinationis, sed pro-
videntiae dumtaxat, ex illoque solo capite certum non
esse, perventurum illum in vitam aeternam, sed solum
ex parte praescientiae, quam praedestinatio ex parte
divini intellectus includit.

    Cum hac vero praescientia ea ratione libertas eius-
dem praedestinati consentit, quoniam cum non ideo sit
suo arbitrio cooperaturus, eo pacto ut ad vitam aeternam
perveniat, quia Deus id praescivit, sed e contrario id-
circo Deus illimitata sui intellectus perfectione supra
id, quod natura obiecti habet, id praesciat, quia pro
arbitrii libertate erat futurum, praescivissetque con-
trarium, si ut reipsa potest pro eadem arbitrii libertate
esset futurum, sane nihil omnino impediente illa praes-
cientia ex sola eminentia et perfectione cognoscentis
perfecta tam integrum ac liberum praedestinato manet non
operari eo pacto, ut ad vitam aeternam perveniat, de-
flectereque in extremam miseriam, ac si praedestinatus
non esset, eaque praescientia in Deo non praeextitisset.
Cf. L. Molina, Concordia, pp. 549, 550.

In sensu diviso a praedestinatione, one predestined can not be
saved; in sensu composito cum praedestinatione, one predestined
must be saved. For the condition sine qua non of the existence of
scientia media in God is the future free acts of men, and since
this condition also affects God's free knowledge (that is, his
knowledge which is consequent upon his choice of the hypotheses
under which he has foreseen the future free acts of men), human
freedom is a condition, not that one be predestined (only God can
determine that) but that if one be predestined, one is free withal.

    Op. cit., p. 345: Quo fit, ut in sensu diviso simpliciter
et absolute possit praedestinatus non salvari, nihil
omnino impedientibus praedestinatione et praescientia
ex aeternitate praeexistentibus, nihil etiam impediente
implicare iam modo contradictionem ut non praeextiterint;
in sensu tamen composito ea ratione non posse non salvari,
quia haec duo cohaerere non possunt, ut ille praedes-
tinatus sit Deusque praeviderit mediis, quae ex sola sua
misericordia statuit illi conferre, perventurum illum
pro sua libertate in vitam aeternam, et quod ad eam
non perveniat. Si tamen, ut potest, perventurus non
esset, procul dubio neque Deus ex aeternitate prae-
scivisset illum perventurum ea via in vitam aeternam,
neque voluntas conferendi ex sua parte ea media compleret
rationem praedestinationis sed providentiae dumtaxat
circa illum in beatitudinem.

212

Illud item ex dictis facile constat, conditionem, sine qua non praeextitisset in Deo media illa praescientia non libera, quam toties diximum esse de ratione praedestinationis cuiusque adulti, esse quod adultus ipse ita pro sua libertate esset cooperaturus cum mediis per quae est praedestinatus, ut ad vitam aeternam perveniat. Ostensum namque est, non ideo illum ita esse cooperaturum, quia Deus id praescivit, sed e contrario idcirco Deum id praescivisse, quia ita pro arbitrii illius libertate erat futurum, praescivissetque contrarium si, ut reipsa poterat, esset futurum. Quare dubitare nemo potest, id conditionem fuisse, sine qua in Deo non fuisset praescientia illa.

Cum vero ostensum sit, reliqua quae praedestinatio talis adulti tam ex parte divini intellectus quam ex parte divinae voluntatis includit, a praescientia illa pendere, non quidem ut sint in Deo, sed ut rationem praedestinationis, non vero solius providentiae circa talem adultum, habeant, consequens profecto est, ut adultum illum ita pro sua libertate cooperaturum esse cum eisdem mediis, ut ad vitam aeternam perveniat, conditio sit, sine qua illa rationem praedestinationis non habuissent in Deo, sed solum providentiae circa illum in beatitudinem. Cf. L. Molina, Concordia, p. 549.

The same, mutatis mutandis, may be said of reprobation.

Op. cit., pp. 345, 346.

A last resume of Molina's tortuous thought may be pardoned. On the supposition that liberty is not mere spontaneity, as the Reformers had asserted, and on the supposition that liberty also demands freedom from necessity, Molina sets out to conciliate his liberty with the prescience, providence, election, and reprobation of God. Free choice and God's part are infallibly connected. How explain this connection and preserve both liberty and the necessary, divine element? Now Luther, Calvin, and others had preserved the connection by sacrificing the immunity of choice from necessity. The only way Molina saw to preserve both liberty and God's efficacity, together with the infallible connection between the two, was as follows. To leave, say, Peter's act free, the necessary connection between the antecedents of Peter's act (God's prescience, providence, and so forth) and the act itself cannot lie wholly in the nature of the antecedents themselves. On the other hand, in order to preserve the infallibility of the connection between Peter's act and its antecedents, it will not do to say that with those antecedents Peter could act freely. In the first case--that is, if the infallible connection between Peter's act and its divine antecedents lay wholly in the nature of the antecedents themselves--Peter's act would not be free. In the second case--that is, if the said connection were such that Peter simply could act freely in consequence of the antecedents--there would be no infallibility in the connection between antecedents and consequent. What merely can be, Peter's act, may quite well not be because Peter may freely not act. To preserve therefore both the liberty of Peter's act and the infallibility of the connection it has with its antecedents, it must be that midway between God's knowledge of what Peter can do (which knowledge is not yet certain knowledge, because it is not of what Peter will do) and God's knowledge of what Peter will do (which knowledge, if based solely upon antecedents which exclude Peter's choice, would destroy Peter's liberty), it must be, Molina says, that midway between these two sorts of divine knowledge (God's necessary, and God's free knowledge) there lies God's knowledge of what Peter freely would do were Peter confronted with choice. With this scientia media Molina has a ready answer to the Reformers. Man is predestined. Of course. Then how can his choice be free from necessity? Because God knows, scientia media, before he predestined Peter, what Peter freely would do under the circumstances of Peter's choice. Man is free. Of course. Then how can he be predestined? Because God, in the inscrutable depths of his will, has chosen to effect the circumstances under which he foresaw, scientia media, what Peter would freely do.

Thus the theory of Molinist liberty is motivated by a desire to keep free choice clear of necessity. That Catholic theology demanded such immunity of choice from necessity is unquestionable. Molina knew this. He took this as his starting point.

Op. cit., p. 353: non ideo arbitrium nostrum in unam aut alteram partem pro sua libertate flectendum, quia Deus id praescivit, sed a contrario Deum id praescivisse, quia ita pro arbitrii libertate erat futurum, et affirmat communis Patrum scholasticorumque sententia, de quorum numero sunt Altissiodorensis et reliqui, quorum modum conciliandi arbitrium nostrum cum praescientia et praedestinatione paulo ante retulimus, ut in materia de praescientia ostendimus. Et nisi ita dicatur, profecto licet spontanei ratio in nostro arbitrio inconcussa maneat, libertas tamen ad culpam et meritum necessaria dominumque in nostros actus, ratione cuius Augustinus dixit, qui fecit te sine te,

non salvabit te sine te, non possunt salva consistere.
For Augustine's words see <u>sermo</u> 106, C. 11, n. 13.,
P.L., 38: 923.

But he did not see how choice could be free from necessity unless
it were, in a sense, causally independent of its antecedents. Choice
was independent of its divine antecedents because of the block of
futurible choice. In virtue of this block of being, future choice
will not be because God knows it but rather the other way about:
God knows future choice because it will be consequently upon the
hypothesis that it would be if God chose the hypothesis, and God
knows that.

> *Op. cit., p. 351: Ad argumentum vero neganda est con-*
> *secutio. Cum enim Deus ita provideat ad beatitudinem*
> *adultis omnibus, tam praedestinatis quam reprobis, ut in*
> *manu consilii eorum eos relinquat, liberum illus faciens*
> *vel ad vitam aeternam pervenire vel ad extremam miseriam*
> *deflectere; quod ex nostra sententia sequitur, immo quod*
> *aperte asserimus, est: Data quacumque eiusmodi providentia*
> *per certa quaedam media quae Deus ex sua parte statuat dare*
> *adulto, sive ea adiunctam habeat rationem praedestinationis,*
> *quia praevidet Deus illum pro sua libertate perventurum*
> *per ea media in beatitudinem, sive coniuncta cum ea sit*
> *reprobatio, quia praevidet pro eadem libertate non per-*
> *venturum illum in vitam aeternam sed finiturum vitam in*
> *peccatis propter quae damnetur, semper in facultate*
> *arbitrii talis adulti positum esse facere contrarium.*
> *Quod si, ut potest, esset futurum, quemadmodum Deus id*
> *ex aeternitate praevidisset futurum et non id quod prae-*
> *vidit, sic ratio illa providentiae haberet adiunctam con-*
> *trariam praedestinationis aut reprobationis rationem.*
> *Antequam tamen Deus illam statueret, integrum illi fuisset*
> *non eundem ordinem rerum eandemve rationem providendi*
> *tali adulto eligere, sed unam ex infinitis aliis, in qui-*
> *bus praevidebat pro eadem arbitrii illius libertate con-*
> *trarium esse futurum. Quare non est in potestate hominis*
> *adulti efficere, ut ex aeternitate fuerit a Deo prae-*
> *destinatus, sed ex sola libera voluntate Dei dependet,*
> *tametsi, in quocumque ordine rerum collocetur, in potestate*
> *ipsius sit facere contrarium eius quod reipsa est facturus.*

Choice was independent of its human antecedents because the human intellect does not determine choice. Not therefore will there
be choice because of its intellectual antecedents; rather, therefore are there these antecedents because there will be this choice.

215

The writer is without the slightest desire to be facetious in a matter whose importance is apparent. But simply because it so seems to him, the clearest, because homeliest, way he knows how to put the matter is thus: the relation of Molina's ante-cedents to choice seems to be like the relation of the man to his wife, with whom he always agreed; he always let her have her way. If the comparison be inept, let it go. But the truth under-lying it seems clear: Molina's free choice is antecedently quite undetermined. If so, there is no philosophical reason for denying, or asserting, that choice is immune from necessity. A theologian will assert that it is, or is not, according to his theology. Luther asserted that choice was not immune from necessity. Molina asserted that it was. In the field of philosophy there is, if choice be antecedently undetermined, no issue to the question, Is choice necessitated or unnecessitated? One may, of course, say: it is not necessitated because such is the fact. But a statement of fact is not yet philosophy. If, then, to be a theologian means to let theology preside over one's thought, Molina was a theologian. If to be a good theologian means to let good theology preside over one's thought, Molina was a good theologian, or not, dependent upon the estimates one makes of his theology. But if there be a question of letting theology fecundate one's thought until the whole, or at least some of it, becomes leavened, Molina was far from this. He was not up to giving reasons. He asserted what were, in his theology, facts. But he cut from beneath his feet the only philosophical grounds upon which necessity in choice might be excluded: freedom of choice grows out of its antecedents.

It may be that in the man himself some reason for his attitude can be found. The next chapter will deal with the moral sources of Molinist liberty.

For theological reasons Molina hung on the absence of necessity in choice. He might have adduced, though he did not, reasons
for his position which were drawn from philosophy. His reason
for not doing so, it would seem, was simply that he did not understand what a philosophy of liberty was. Obviously, he thought that
his indetermination of the will in choice was a philosophy. But
unless freedom in choice grows out of its antecedents, there is no
reason for asserting that choice must be free. And only the field
of reason, the "must," the necessary, is philosophical, not the
field of fact. Still, a man may be right without knowing why. And
if Molina's theology be considered correct, he was right by his
faith, without knowing, by his reason, why. If, then, Molina's
theology be admitted as true, he landed, so to say, right side up,
and he lit on his feet because of that theology and despite his
philosophy. He met his adversaries without fully estimating his
resources. However, unlike his gospel predecessor, he did not
sue for peace. For with his faith he deemed himself triply armed.
And in a sense he was. The faith in Molina's thought was like the
leaven in the meal, but his thought was not wholly leavened.

It might have been expected. Molina's character made him
cling to essentials; his was a sort of hew-to-the-line-and-let-the-

217

chips-fall-where-they-may attitude. The trait would be at once his triumph and his failing. His triumph because it is something to stick to the main point, to turn up on the right side, to sound a correct note. His failing because it is something also to be comprehensive, to assimilate, to synthesize, to understand.

But Molina did not have it in him to be perfectly balanced. He was one of the world's worst writers, yet he wrote one of the world's best sellers.

> *Bellarmine's opinion of Molina's style will not be gain-said (in X-M. Le Bachelet, S.J., Auotarium Bellarminum, Beauchesne, 1913, p. 110b): cum tamen ipse tam prolixe, confuse, obscure loquatur ut vix intelligi possit quid sibi velit. The opinion of the Portuguese Jesuit Censors of Molina's work is the same (in L. Molina, Ad Censuram Societatis Responsio, in Stegmuller, op. cit., p. 372): conclusiones et parentheses nimis prolixae videntur, in probando et refellendo crebrae et verbosae repetitiones. Methodus ipsa distractis et dissipatis constat membris, ut vix ad unum corpus pertinere aut certum exitum habere videatur. Ordo . . . obscurior . . . Yet the Concordia went to five editions within six years of its publication. The seventh is the Paris edition, 1876, cited throughout this work. Cf. J. Brodrick, S.J., Blessed R. Bellarmine, vol. 2, Burns Oates, 1928, p. 28.*

He was a man virtuous to a degree recognized even by his brother religious, and--like men living together on a raft--brother religious make no mistake about such matters. Yet he could write of his theory: "I do not doubt that Augustine and the other Fathers would have unanimously approved this opinion of ours . . . had it been proposed to them."

> *On Molina's character vid. Stegmüller, op. cit., pp. 772, 782: Molinas Charakterbild: Die Tradition des Jesuitenordens nennt als Haupteigenschaften Molinas seine Regeltreue, seinen Gebetseifer, seine Liebe zur Armut, seine Bescheidenheit, seine Demut und Lenk-barkeit. . . . Seine Kolleghefte habe er auf alte Zettel und schlechtes Papier geschrieben. Als er von Cuenca nach Madrid ubersiedelte, habe er seine Papiere in einem alten Sack mitgenommen, und habe also gar nicht viel Aufhebens von seinen Werken gemacht. . . . Zu Beginn des Gnadenstreites habe er nach Rom gewollt, um sich zu verteidigen, aber er habe sich dann im Gehorsam der übschlagigen Weisung seiner Oberen gefügt. Er sei sehr leicht lenkbar gewesen und habe gern fremden Rat angenom-*

*men. On Molina's opinion of himself see L. Molina, Con-
cordia, p. 550, and Summa Haeresium Maior, in Stegmüller,
op. cit., pp. 339, 437. Bellarmine and the Portuguese
Censors, 1. c., thought that Molina boasted.*

Never was a book scanned so often and so minutely by Rome; yet
the <u>Concordia</u> still holds its ground. No man ever fought harder
against the condemnation of his book. Yet even that, Molina would
have borne obediently. Secretive in guarding his counsel, he was
quite open with his superiors; convinced that his was the only
solution to the problem he set out to solve, he told his friends
at the house of his death that they could do what they wished with
his manuscripts over there in the sack. If, then, just as to the
accusation that Molina was an abominable writer it might be
answered that his book still sells; if, as to the accusation that
he was proud, it might be answered that his brother religious
thought him a good man; if, though opinionated, he was ready to
yield to the judgment of Rome; if, though passionately attached
to his work, he was ready to consign it and his manuscripts <u>au
diable</u> when he came to die; if all this may be said of the man,
may not Molina's theory be a bit like him, a theory of which one
might say, <u>est aliquid ibi</u>, <u>sed nequaquam in isto sunt omnia</u>?
One may desiderate in a man or his thought a well rounded com-
prehensiveness without loose ends, but if, with the exception of
the perfect men, there are loose ends in all of us, it is well
that the mainstays at least be taut and trim. And one feels that
in Molina they were. His faith preserved an element in liberty
demanded of him by his theology, even though his reason did not
succeed in rendering a philosophic account of his faith.

Given such a man, put him into the proper milieu, and you
have the reason, in part, why he reacted as he did. Luis de
Molina was a member of the Society of Jesus, an order whose
founder, St. Ignatius of Loyola (n. 1491, ob. 1556), was a
contemporary of Martin Luther (n. 1483, ob. 1546). The coin-
cidence of these dates becomes significant when we recall that
it was Ignatius of Loyola with his Company of Jesus who was to
offer the greatest single force of opposition to the movement of
the Reformation.

The diametric, and dramatic, opposition of the Lutheran and
Jesuit <u>Weltanschauungen</u> is clearly indicated in their founders'
respective epopees of humanity. According to Luther, there are
carnal men whom Satan leads fatally to damnation; there are the
just who, thanks to the operation of the Holy Spirit, come neces-

sarily to salvation. Between these two stands, like a horse, the human will. If God mounts it, it goes where he wills, and this is the meaning of the psalm: "I am as a beast before thee." If Satan mounts it, it goes where he wills. It is not within the will's power to run to or to seek one of these riders; it is the riders who strive to get at and control the will.

Luthers Werke, Weimar ed., vol. 18, p. 635.

In fact, not even Satan can oppose God: it is God who moves all with necessity; it is he who does everything, even with Satan and the impious.

Loc. cit., p. 709.

According to St. Ignatius there are two standards: one Christ's, the other Lucifer's. Lucifer disperses his minions throughout the world to trap men and lead them to sin. Christ sends his servants and friends throughout the world to lead men through the steps of poverty, contempt, humility, to the heights of all virtue.

The Text of the Spiritual Exercises of St. Ignatius, Burns Oates and Washbourne, 1923, pp. 45 sqq.

Clearly, the two men have entirely different notions about the value of human effort. Luther believes that we cannot do anything about the fix we are in. Ignatius thinks that despite original sin we can nevertheless do something about it. "The fault lies, not in our stars, but in ourselves, that we are underlings" might be well have been an Ignatian motto.

But it was a motto whose doctrinal foundation was to be established with prudence. A Jesuit was to speak warily, if at all, of predestination, of liberty, of grace.

> Although it is very true that no one can be saved without being predestined, and without having faith and grace, we must be very careful in our manner of speaking and treating of all this subject. We ought not habitually to speak much of Predestination; but if sometimes mention be made of it in any way, we must so speak that the common people may not fall into error, as happens sometimes when they say: "It is already fixed whether I am to be saved or damned, and there cannot be any

other result whether I do good or ill"; and, becoming slothful
in consequence, they neglect works conducive to their salvation,
and to the spiritual profit of their souls. In the same way it is
to be noticed that we must take heed lest by speaking much with
great earnestness on Faith, without any distinction or explanation,
occasion be given to the people to become slothful and sluggish
in good works . . . In like manner we ought not to speak or to
insist on the doctrine of Grace so strongly, as to give rise to
that poisonous teaching that takes away free-will. Therefore, we
may treat of Faith and Grace, as far as we may with the help of
God, for the greater praise of his Divine Majesty; but not in
such a way, especially in these dangerous times of ours, that
works or free-will receive any detriment, or come to be
accounted for nothing.

*Op. cit., "Rules for thinking with the Church," rules 14,
15, 16, 17. Italics mine.*

Molina knew these directions and their spirit.

*L. Molina, Epitome de Praedestinatione, in Stegmüller,
op. cit., p. 354.*

But though he was thus possessed of the prudent guidance of his
chief, it was perhaps unfortunate that he felt called upon to speak
at all. He was not philosophically equipped to shoulder the task
of combatting Luther and Calvin. His philosophy differed only by
the difference of a yea and nay from the doctrines he set out to
combat. Given such a man, given his task, it becomes morally
intelligible that he reacted as he did. He went off "half-cocked"
to meet a problem which, philosophically, can be solved only
by a knowledge per causas. Molina had no knowledge per causas
of liberty.

The essence of Molinism is the assertion of scientia media
and the denial of efficacious, predetermining decrees. God does
not effect the free act by a determination of it which causally
antecedes the will's own determination; rather, he effects the
free act concurrently with the will--simultaneous concourse.
Nor does God know what a man will actually choose, unless there
have anteceded such knowledge the knowledge of what a man would
choose in any given hypothesis--scientia media. The principle
commanding these two points is the previsibility by God of human
free choice before it is actually willed; that is, caused by God.

221

Upon this principle is erected Molina's notion of liberty: the absence of necessity, in free choice, arising from any determination which is not from the will; or, positively, liberty in Molina lies solely in the self-determination of the will. Neither divine nor human antecedents of choice determine choice. Not the divine antecedents, which are God's knowledge and will. For, previous to God's knowledge or what a man will choose (which knowledge is consequent upon God's will that a man choose thus or so) there is the divine knowledge of what a man would freely do in any hypothesis of choice; and since what a man would do is not caused by God's knowledge of such futurible choice, there is thus a block of being, the futurible choice, which escapes the causality of divine knowledge. As for the divine will, it effects actual free choice only because it elects and effects the circumstances under which it has been foreseen, scientia media, what a man would freely choose. Here, too, the same block of being, the futurible choice, escapes the causality of the divine will. And if futurible choice moves into the sphere of future choice nevertheless, taking its place thus among those things which will be, choice is still undetermined by its divine antecedents; for, though what will be--namely, a given free choice-- is known and willed by God (and what will be will be because known and willed by God) still the same block of futurible being moves now only amidst the circumstances, the hypotheses, of choice, and under those hypotheses it was foreseen, scientia media, to have been free choice. Future choice, which is caused by God who effects the hypothesis, comes from futurible choice, which has no efficient cause not itself.

If free choice is thus undetermined by its divine antecedents a fortiori, it is undetermined by its human antecedents. The human antecedents are the intellectual conditions of choice; namely, the judgment. This, according to Molina, does not determine choice; it is simply a prerequisite in order that that choice be rational. Free choice, then, on this head too is undetermined. The result of all this is that the will alone is the cause of its own determination, and this is Molina's notion of liberty.

The difference between this notion and that of Luther is a theologic difference. Luther is convinced that because human nature is corrupted by original sin, there is left in it only the power of self-determination (spontaneity) under the efficacious and necessitating causality of God. The two elements of Lutheran choice, spontaneity and necessity, are philosophically quite compatible. It may well be that we must choose what we do choose

and withal be inclined thereto, or vice versa, that we be inclined
to choose what we must choose. There is no contradiction in that
we must like what, de facto, we do like. Such is, as Molina admits, the nature of animal choice. If, then, there be a difference
between Molina's notion of liberty and Luther's, it is a theologic,
not a philosophic difference. A theologic difference: for in fact
Molina's theology does teach that choice though spontaneous is
not necessitated. But not a philosophic difference: for first Molina
adduces no philosophic reason for his spontaneity's not being
necessitated.

All his reasons are theological reasons. He does indeed invoke
psychology, but all that psychology can show is that we are either
the source of our elections or the mode of free acts; it cannot
show that our choices are undetermined or explain the essence
of free acts. Psychology can assure us that when we choose it is
we who choose--that is, it can assure us of the spontaneity of
choice but not of its antecedent immunity from necessity; it can
evince doubtless the mode but not the nature of liberty. Nor,
second, can Molina adduce a philosophic difference between himself and Luther. Unless a proposition have a middle term to
prove it or unless it be itself self-evident, it is not necessarily
true, and only a necessarily true proposition is philosophic. Now
Molina's proposition, choice is spontaneous and unnecessitated,
is not self-evident; and although it may or may not be a fact that
choice is such, still it is not immediately evident that it is a fact.
As for a middle term which might prove his point, Molina has
cut off this possibility by denying the intrinsic causality of the
antecedents of choice. God does not cause freedom, nor does
freedom grow from the intrinsic causality of its intellectual antecedents. If, then, choice be free, the only reason, apart from
philosophy, by which we can know this is some fact which attests
it. Now the fact which does this for Molina is revelation; and in
his system, despite his appeal to psychology, it is the only fact
which can do it. Molina's theology, in short, kept him from thinking as Luther thought, but his philosophy--or rather his psychology
(and his philosophy, because, in this instance, it was a psychology)--
gave him no footing, no grounds, for denying necessity in choice.
He knew quite well from his theology that choice is unnecessitated,
but he did not know why. He saw quite well that Luther departed
from the Catholic position, but he was not philosophically equipped
to combat Luther. He would have been better advised to oppose
only his theology to Luther's theology. There was plenty of reason
in his theology to show why Luther was wrong in Luther's inter-

223

pretation of that theology. But theology does not give reasons. Once given its premises, which are not philosophical, theology will indeed pursue a philosophical method. But the premises of theology purport to be facts. It is no proof, therefore, of un-necessitated spontaneity in choice simply to say that such is the case.

The difference between Molina and St. Thomas is not theologic but philosophic. Both are agreed that choice is unnecessitated and spontaneous. But St. Thomas gives his reason: The divine ante-cedents of choice effect, because they are infinitely efficacious, the freedom of choice; the human antecedents of choice are such that freedom must necessarily grow out of them. Choice is a judgment which the will has caused to be exercised; it is a willed judging, or a judged willing; the will is the spontaneous source of its elections; the intellect is the determining, but not necessi-tating (because its judgment is indifferent) reason for the election. One may deny that St. Thomas' reasons are valid. At any rate they are reasons. Molina's reasons for the absence of necessity are assertions. In theology these assertions are true enough, but in philosophy they are not true because they are asserted.

So too, the difference between Molina and Banes is a philosophic difference. But here, unlike the difference with St. Thomas, their philosophic difference seems in part to be like that of two men who are both wrong. Banes' principle is right: choice is free-- first because God causes it, second because it grows out of in-tellectual antecedents which necessarily imply liberty. But Banes demands that God will the free act before he knows it and con-sequently that free choice be physically predetermined. This emphasis upon God's will and upon its physical correlate, pre-determination, makes it impossible to conceive that necessity be absent from choice. St. Thomas had said that God knows the free act because he causes it, that divine causality is constituted by the divine will and intellect, that consequently previsibility and prevision of free choice come from the omnipotent divine causality which makes present to eternity all being, the necessary, the accidental, the free. The difficulties which are unsolved by Banes are not left without answer in St. Thomas. How is free choice previsible? By reason of the omnipotent causality of God. How is it foreseen? Strictly, since a cause is presently related to its effect because it is seen. On the other hand, Molina would have God know free choice before, in the sense already explained, he causes it. And this subtracts being from its dependence upon God. Both Molina and Banes seem to go off the track: Banes because with him God causes free choice before he knows it, Molina because God knows free choice before he causes it. St. Thomas had said that God knows free acts because he causes them. Against this only he can object who denies divine omnipotence or the existence of free natures.

To conclude: in the interest of a liberty which was exempt from coercion and necessity, Luis de Molina accorded to Luther and Calvin the proposition that choice cannot be free if it be efficaciously determined by God. The relation, then, between choice and its divine antecedents must be, he thought, such that the infallible connection between the two lies in scientia media and in its correlate, simultaneous concourse. God knows what a man will freely do because he knows what a man would freely do, and God effects the future free choice by effecting the circumstances (grace or natural concourse) under which choice was seen to have been free. This implies a theory of liberty in which voluntary determination is caused only by itself: it is not efficaciously determined by God, since God wills only what, ex supposito, has been foreseen to be free; it is not determined by its human intellectual antecedents because these are such as they are only because there will be such and such a choice. Freedom in choice is thus asserted, not proved. Luther held the contrary: choice is not coerced, but it is necessitated. He has no theological and less philosophical reason for his assertion than had Molina. Both men made assertions. But back of their assertions lay their principles. Luther's principle was the corruption of human nature. Molina's principle was the previsibility of free choice by scientia media. And both arrived at a concept of liberty in which the writer can see no philosophical difference: a spontaneity which is necessitated, a spontaneity immune from necessity. For if free choice be only spontaneous, there is no more philosophical reason for asserting the absence of necessity in it than for denying it. Perhaps the reason that these two adversaries, who would be astonished at their identification, land in the same philosophical camp is this: there is little philosophic difference in the principle that nature is corrupt and therefore unfree and the principle that the acts of a free nature are, in a sense, uncaused by God. In the first case there is no free nature; in the second case it is there, but there is no reason why it should be. In either case God does not cause freedom. And to say that God does not cause freedom or that there is no freedom is to say pretty much the same thing.

225

SELECT BIBLIOGRAPHY

Acta Apostolica Sedis. Vol. VI, 1914.

Aquinas, St. Thomas. Opera Omnia. 34 volumes. Paris: Vives, 1871-1880.

Astrain, Antonio, S.J. Historia de la Compañía de Jesús en la asistencia de España. Madrid: Razon y Fe, 1909, 1913, 1916.

Augustine of Hippo, St. Opera Omnia. P. L. Vols. 32-45.

Banes, Dominico, O.P. Scholastica Commentaria in Primam Partem Summae Theologicae Sancti Thomae Aquinatis. Madrid: Editorial F. E. D. A., 1873.

Bellarmine, St. Robert. Opera Omnia. 12 volumes. Edited by J. Fevre. Paris: Vives, 1873.

Bernard of Clairvaux, St. De Gratia et Libero Arbitrio. P. L. Vol. 182.

Billot, Louis, S. J. De gratia Christi et libero hominis arbitrio. Rome: Gregorianum, 1908.

Billuart, Charles René, O.P. Summa Sancti Thomae. 4 volumes. Rome: Crispinus Pucceinelli, 1834.

Boethius, Anicius Manlius Severinus. De Consolatione Philosophiae. London: Burns, Oates and Washburne, 1925.

Broderick, James, S.J. Blessed Robert Bellarmine. 2 volumes. London: Burns, Oates and Washburne, 1928.

Calvin, Jean. Opera Omnia. 9 volumes. Amsterdam, 1671.

Carreras y Artau, J. Ensayo sobre el voluntarismo de Juan Duns Scotus. Gerona, 1923.

Castro, Alfonso de. Adversus omnes haeresses. Cologne, 1539.

Cochlaeus, Johannes. De actis et scriptis Martini Luther ("Corpus Catholicorum," Vol. II). Munster: Aschendorff, n. d.

D'Ales, A., S.J. Dictionnaire apologétique de la Foi catholique. 4 volumes. Paris: G. Beauchesne, 1927.

Denzinger, Heinrich, and Clement Bannwart. Enchiridion Symbolorum. Freiburg: Herder and Company, 1932.

Dummermuth, A. M., O.P. St. Thomas et doctrina praemotionis physicae, seu responsio ad R.P. Schneemann, S.J., aliosque doctrinae scholae Thomisticae impugnatores. Paris, 1886.

----- Defensio doctrinae S. Thomae Aquinatis de praemotione physica seu responsio da R.P.V. Frins, S.J. Louvain: Uyspruyst, 1895.

Feldner, G., O.P. Die Lehre des heiliges Thomas von Aquin über die Willensfreiheit des vernunftigen Wesens. Graz, 1890.

Fonseca, Pedro, S.J. Institutionum Dialecticarum. 8 volumes. Cologne: Apud Maternum Cholinum, 1567.

----- Commentarium in 11 Metaphysicorum Aristotelis Stagiritae. 4 volumes. Rome: Apud Franciscum Zanettum et Bartholomaeum Tosium, socios, 1577, 1580, 1589. Cologne: Impensis Lazari Zetznesi, 1615.

Franzelin, Jean Baptiste, S.J. De Deo uno secundam naturam. Rome: Typis de Sacrae Congregationis de Propaganda Fide, 1876.

Frins, Victor, S.J. Sancti Thomae Aquinatis, O.P., doctrina de cooperatione Dei cum omnia natura creata, praesertim libera, Responsio ad R.P.F.A.M. Dummermuth, O.P. Paris, 1892.

Garrigou La Grange, Réginald, O.P. Dieu, son éxistence, sa nature. Paris: G. Beauchesne, 1892.

Gayraud, Hippolitus, O.P. Thomisme et Molinisme. Paris, 1890.

----- St. Thomas et le prédéterminisme. Paris: Lethielleux, 1895.

Gilson, Etienne. La Liberté chez Descartes et la théologie. Paris: Alcan, 1913.

----- Avicenne et le point de départ de Duns Scot. (Archives d'histoire doctrinale et littéraire du Moyen Age) Paris: J. Vrin, 1927.

----- L'Esprit de la philosophie médiévale. Second edition. Revised. Paris: J. Vrin, 1944.

----- Le Moyen Age et le naturalisme antique. (Archives d'histoire doctrinale et littéraire du Moyen Age) Paris: J. Vrin, 1933.

Gonet, F. J. B., O.P. Clypeus Theologiae Thomisticae. 6 volumes. Paris: Vives, 1875.

Grisar, Hartmann, S.J. Martin Luther. Translated from the German by E. M. Lamond. Edited by Luigi Cappadelta. 6 volumes. Saint Louis: B. Herder Book Company, 1913-1917.

John of St. Thomas, O.P. Cursus Philosophicus Thomisticus. 3 volumes. Edited by Beato Reiser. Turin: Marietti, 1930-1937.

Kaulen, Francis, and Joseph Cardinal Hergenrother. Kirchen-lexicon. 12 volumes. Freiburg: Herder and Company, 1882.

Le Bachelet, Xavier Marie, S.J. Auctarium Bellarminum. Paris: G. Beauchesne, 1913.

----- Prédestination et grâce efficace. 2 volumes. Louvain: Museum Lessianum, 1931.

Lottin, O. La Théorie du libre arbitre depuis Saint Anselme jusqu' a Saint Thomas d'Aquin. Louvain: Abbaye du Mont-Cesar, 1929.

Luther, Martin. Werke, Kritische Gesammtausgabe. 56 volumes. Weimar, 1883.

Maritain, Jacques. The Three Reformers. London: Methuen and Company, 1926.

Minges, P. Ist Duns Scotus indeterminist? Munster, 1905.

Molina, Luis de, S.J. Concordia liberi arbitrii cum gratiae donis, divina praescientia, providentia, praedestinatione, et reprobatione. Paris: Lethielleux, 1876.

Pastor, Ludwig von. The History of the Popes from the Close of the Middle Ages. 40 volumes. Edited by R. F. Kerr. Saint Louis: B. Herder Book Company, 1854.

Petau, Denis, S.J. Dogmata theologica. 8 volumes. Paris: Vives, 1866.

----- De Pelagianorum et semi-pelagianorum dogmatum historia. Paris: Cramoisy, 1643.

Regnon, Thomas de, S.J. Banes et Molina, histoire, doctrines, critique, metaphysique. Paris, 1883.
----- Bannesianisme et Molinisme. Paris, 1890.
Rousselot, Pierre, S.J. L'Intellectualisme de S. Thomas. Paris: G. Beauchesne, 1924.

San, Louis de, S.J. De Deo Uno. Paris, 1894.
Schneemann, Gerard, S.J. Controversarium de divinae gratiae liberique arbitrii concordia initia et progressus. Freiburg: Herder and Company, 1881.
Scoraille, R. de, S.J. François Suarez. 2 volumes. Paris, 1912.
Scotus, John Duns. Opera Omnia. 26 volumes. Paris: Vives, 1891-1895.
Sertillanges, A. D., O.P. Saint Thomas d'Aquin. 2 volumes. Paris, 1910.
----- Les Grandes Thèses de la philosophie thomiste. Paris: Bloud, 1929.
Stegmuller, F. Neue Molinaschriften. (Beitrage zur Geschichte der Philosophie und Theologie des Mittelalters, Band XXXII). Munster: Aschendorff, 1935.
Stufler, John, S.J. Divi Thomae Aquinatis doctrina de Deo operante in omni operatione naturae creatae praesertim liberi arbitrii. Innsbruck, 1923.
Suarez, Francis, S.J. Opera Omnia. 30 volumes. Paris: Vives, 1858.

Toletus, Francis, S.J. In Summam theologiae S. Thomae Aquinatis enarratio. 4 volumes. Rome: Marietti, 1869-1870.

Vacant, Alfred. Dictionnaire de théologie catholique. 15 volumes. Paris: Librairie Letonzey et Ane, 1901.

Willman, M. Die Ethik des Aristoteles. Regensburg, 1920.
----- Aristoteles und die Willensfreiheit. Fulda, 1921.